To Carol & Charles,

With affection, every good wish, and deep appreciation for all that you do for the Jewish community!

Rabbi Dan

Copyright © 2012 by Daniel S Alexander
All rights reserved.

ISBN: 978-1-4675-5773-3

"Rider in the Desert" woodcut by Jacob Pins used with permission from Gesellschaft, Kunstverein Hoexter e. V.
Unpublished material by Alan Morinis in "The Virtue of Truth" printed with permission from the author.
Anecdote by Rabbi Harold Kushner about painting of Ten Commandments in
"The Final Exam" used with permission from Rabbi Kushner.
Reuven Bulka story in "For Kindness and the Love of Kindness" and Edward Feinstein story in
"For Kindness and the Love of Kindness" reprinted with permission from Behrman House, Inc.

SEEKING THE WAY

JEWISH REFLECTIONS ON MATTERS OF *THE HEAD, THE HEART, AND THE HAND*

Shimon the Righteous was among the last of the Great Assembly. He used to say: "The world rests on three things, on Torah, on worship, and on deeds of kindness."

Pirke Avot 1:2

CONTENTS

THE HEAD I: *Matters of Theology*

- *14* Belief and Doubt
- *22* Giving Life to the Dead
- *29* I Believe with Perfect Faith
- *38* Standing before God
- *43* Universalism from within Particularism
- *48* In the Image
- *52* When Life Is Unfair
- *57* Regarding the Law
- *61* From the Diary of Abraham
- *65* Father Jacob and Uncle Ho
- *68* Ezekiel's Dry Bones
- *72* The Final Exam

THE HEAD II: *The Binding of Isaac*

- *80* The Failure of Abraham
- *85* Two Paradigms of Faith
- *90* The Test of the Text
- *95* From the Other End of the Knife
- *100* The Two Walked On Together
- *104* To Hold and Let Go

THE HEART I: *Standing in the Doorway*

- *110* Standing in the Doorway
- *116* Altars of the Heart
- *119* Lessons from the Nolichucky
- *126* The Meaning of "I Am Jewish"
- *133* On Jewish Time
- *138* Searching for Wholeness

145 The Torah of Being Where We Are
151 On Being Called to the Rabbinate
156 The Image of the Resting Cloud
160 Falling Gracefully

THE HEART II: *Moral Virtues*

166 The Virtue of Truth
173 For Kindness and the Love of Kindness
180 Leadership and the Quality of Patience
186 Regarding the Spies through the Lens of Humility
190 Engaging the Day with Zeal
197 A Moral Virtue for a New Year

THE HAND: *Deeds of Kindness and Justice*

206 What Is Blessing?
215 Rite versus Right
221 For the Sin of Environmental Abuse
227 Give Me Your Hand
235 The Way We Speak
240 On Homosexuality
247 Tzedakah
252 Inward, Upward, and Outward
259 Israel and Hope
266 On the Ethics of Jewish Eating
272 The Challenge of Yigal Amir

ACKNOWLEDGMENTS

BIBLIOGRAPHY OF SECONDARY SOURCES

AUTHOR'S PREFACE

A man lost his way in a great forest. After a while another lost his way and chanced on the first. Without knowing what had happened to him, he asked the way out of the woods. "I don't know," said the first. "But, I can point out the ways that lead further into the thicket, and after that let us try to find the way together." (Rabbi Hayyim of Zans, in Martin Buber, *Tales of the Hasidim: Later Masters*, p. 213)

As I write these words, I have now completed thirty-three years of rabbinic service in one community. My wife, Dela, and I arrived in the university town of Charlottesville, Virginia, immediately following my rabbinic ordination in 1979 by the Hebrew Union College–Jewish Institute of Religion in New York City. For the next nine years I directed the Hillel Foundation at the University of Virginia, and since 1988 I have served as rabbi to Charlottesville's one synagogue, Congregation Beth Israel. As these things go, thirty-three years in the same town represents considerable constancy of place and community.

Another constant of my career has been a sense that at the core of my rabbinic mission resides a persistent striving to find ways to navigate life's mysteries, to explore them as fully as I am able, and then to share the fruits of those explorations with others, to seek paths "out of the forest" together, as it were. Over the years, the writing and delivering of sermons have served me as primary opportunities to share those fruits. This collection of forty-five has been culled from sermons first presented to members of Congregation Beth Israel in Charlottesville, most during High Holidays and a few on various Shabbat occasions during the year. As originally oral presentations, with standards of citation suitable for that setting, I have made an effort to provide complete citations for this volume and, where appropriate, permissions. However, some sources were received orally or secondhand. Where it has not been possible to provide full citations, I have provided as much detail as I could locate.

When I consider how I tend to engage Jewish tradition, I find that the location of my greatest energy and excitement is in the process itself, in the journey rather than in reaching a destination, in the search for the way rather than in finding it, in seeking the way out of the forest rather than in getting out. In this regard, I have noticed that several influential Jewish teachers, Rabbi Lawrence Hoffman and Rabbi Steven Sager among them, have lately begun to employ the term "conversation" when referring to the essence of the Jewish enterprise. I am attracted to the idea that one authentically engages the traditions of Judaism by entering into a conversation that has been going on for many generations and, God willing, will continue to go on for many more, rather than, say, by arriving at a common set of dogmas or affirmations. Entry into the conversation does not presuppose a particular grounding in one set of propositions or another but merely a certain seriousness of purpose, a willingness to listen carefully to the language of discussion without prejudging it, and the freedom to raise questions, make associations, and allow the experiences of one's own life to be the filter for the appropriation of ideas. That is, although I have not always had the precise rubric of "conversation" in mind, I think it describes well the animating vision for the endeavor of composing and offering these sermons. They manifest my efforts to engage in the Jewish conversation.

As I consider my sermonic output, as represented by this volume, I find that since I myself am usually far more apt to gain inspiration from a story or a poem than from even the most persuasive didactic argument, I have tended to traverse the terrain of awakened or deepened spiritual awareness with a heavy reliance on implied lessons, virtues demonstrated anecdotally, or by means of the deliberately ambiguous language of poetic allusion. I hope that these personal preferences and the manner in which they have been carried out find favor in the eyes of others.

What might one make of the forty-five sermons in this volume, forty-five efforts to seek a way out of the forest of mystery and confusion that constitutes the human condition, forty-five manifestations of engaging in the Jewish conversation? One notes that the number forty-five can be rendered by the Hebrew letters *mem* and *hay*, which in turn form a word that indicates the question "what?" or the comparative "just as." I hope and pray that you who read into this collection will feel invited by what you find in it to engage in your own process of questioning and comparing, that it will open pathways for meaningful engagement in traditions that can inform and enrich the spiritual journey of your life. With God's help, may it be so.

THE HEAD I
Matters of Theology

BELIEF AND DOUBT
Rosh Hashanah 5768/2007

News flash: Mother Teresa had radical doubt. According to her letters in the recently published book *Come Be My Light*, for many years Mother Teresa experienced a sense of separation from God. Apparently she often lacked certainty about God's presence in her life, and for many years she felt a kind of distance that greatly bothered her. In one letter, she wrote: "I have no faith—I dare not utter the words and thoughts that crowd in my heart—and make me suffer untold agony" (quoted in Biema, "Mother Teresa's Crisis," *Time*). Apparently, some hear the revelations about Mother Teresa's doubts as unsettling, casting a pall on a reputedly saintly life. Others, myself among them, receive the reports about her struggles with faith as confirmations of her humanity and as affirmations that our own inner conflicts of faith do not negate the possibility of spiritual integrity.

As a young rabbinic student, I delivered one of my first sermons in response to the film *Winter Light* by the recently deceased director Ingmar Bergman. The film depicts three hours in the life of a Lutheran pastor in a bleak Swedish town. The pastor has struggled with wrenching theological doubts ever since his wife died some years earlier. Now he can barely tolerate the hypocrisies implied by his own attempts to minister to his tiny flock while beset by those doubts. In my youthful sermon, I contrasted the self-loathing of the pastor due to what I then viewed as his preoccupation with matters of theology with what I then regarded as a more Jewish approach to faith, faith rooted not as much in belief as in practice. "Faith," I wrote back in 1975, "for the Jew is a verb. It entails engagement to life without opiates. It entails the supreme acts of trust inherent in marriage and child-bearing. And it entails an ongoing relationship with our living tradition."

I still more or less agree with my youthful self, but I have to admit that, in the thirty-two intervening years, I have acquired much more sympathy for the fictional pastor and for the real-life pastors and rabbis and regular folks, Jews and non-Jews, who struggle with issues of belief and doubt.

On Rosh Hashanah, the beginning of a new Jewish year, a time of coming home, of turning within, of returning to core commitments, of reflecting on the values, principles, and beliefs by which we live or wish to live, I would have us pose the question: "Do we Jews believe?"

Do we Jews believe in God? According to a recent Harris poll, most Jews do not. The data from that poll reveal that only 30 percent of North American Jews declare "absolute certainty" in the existence of God compared with 64 percent of Catholics, 76 percent of Protestants, and 93 percent of Evangelical Protestants. What should one make of this data? More importantly, where do we situate ourselves in the conversation about belief, a conversation that for some of us includes the prominent voices of a group of prominent neo-atheists like Richard Dawkins, Daniel Dennett, Sam Harris, and Christopher Hitchens, the latter who now claims Mother Teresa was a closet atheist?

One is reminded of the Hasid who is said to have approached his rebbe, Menachem Mendel of Kotkz.

> "Rabbi," he complained, "I keep brooding and brooding, and don't seem to be able to stop."
>
> "What do you brood about?" asked the rabbi.
>
> "I keep brooding about whether there really is a judgment and a judge."
>
> "What does it matter to you?"
>
> "Rabbi! If there is no judge and no judgment, then what does all creation mean!"
>
> "What does that matter to you!"
>
> "Rabbi! If there is no judgment and no judge, then what do the words of Torah mean!"
>
> "What does that matter to you?"
>
> "Rabbi! What does it matter to me? What does the rabbi think? What else could matter to me?"
>
> "Well, if it matters to you as much as all that," said the rabbi of Kotzk, "then you are a good Jew after all—and it is quite all right for a good Jew to brodd: nothing can go wrong with him."

(Buber, *Tales of the Hasidim: Later Masters*, p. 280)

I am sure there are those among us who, like the troubled Hassid, do not actually deny God but rather have issues with God, serious ones. In other words, out of an experience of personal tragedy or our observation of significant unfairness in the world, we may well feel anger or confusion out of which may grow rejection. Thus does Rabbi Shmueli Boteach explain the low 30 percent level of Jewish belief. Rabbi Boteach regards Jewish disbelief as a transmutation of ethical sensitivity.

In a recent issue of the *World Jewish Digest*, Rabbi Niles Goldstein similarly points to Rabbi Abraham Isaac Kuk, the first Ashkenazic chief rabbi of Palestine in the twentieth century, who coined the term "temporary atheism" to explain the proper response to the human condition. According to Rav Kuk, one who perceives the world with all its violence, suffering, and injustice and does not experience this kind of disbelief would be guilty of sin. "…having serious doubts about God's active presence or existence, according to Rav Kuk, is not only acceptable—it is a sign of an insightful, caring, and empathic soul." ("Let's Get Over Ourselves," p. 7) In this view, some of us who reject God may do so not out of disbelief but out of profound disappointment, even unrequited longing for a caring God who often appears or feels absent, in the way apparently experienced by Mother Teresa.

In a second approach to the question of Jewish belief and the lack thereof, in an article in the same issue of the *World Jewish Digest*, Vanessa Ochs reframes the question by asking: "Do Jews believe in God less than Christians? Or does God figure differently in Christianity than Judaism?" ("Keeping Faith Without Faith," p. 4) Her artful reframing provides perspective on one facet of a recent Catholic-Jewish dialogue between members of the local synagogue and a Catholic parish. In small groups, members of each congregation were asked to respond to the question: "Do you feel loved by God?"

As I recall, most of the Catholics easily responded in the affirmative while most of the Jews seemed bewildered by the question. That is, it would seem that most of our Catholic neighbors do see themselves in a personal relationship with God, who gives and receives love. Most local Jews, on the other hand, see themselves in a relationship with a tradition, one that may have arisen from encounters with God in the past, but that now stands on its own. While belief in God surely occupies a part of our Jewish tradition, many Jewish theologians would argue that in a serious

Jewish life it is the teachings of Torah to which we Jews relate and which give our lives their highest purpose, not the divine Author of those teachings.

Ochs illustrates this point of view by graphically contrasting two fictional phone calls from adult children to their Jewish parents. If the child on the first call discloses that he has dropped all trappings of Jewish identity— holiday and Shabbat observance, synagogue involvement, relationship to Israel, et cetera—but declares to his parents, as if in compensation: "I now believe in God!" most Jewish parents of that child, says Ochs, would be less than thrilled. However, if the adult child on the second call were to describe to her parents a clear determination to raise her children with strong Jewish identities, to continue her involvement in a Torah study group and give to causes of social justice, support for Israel and the local synagogue, but then declares, "By the way, I recently realized I do not believe in God (and you know what, I probably never did)," the parents, says Ochs, would be unambiguously pleased, without a grain of regret, over the theological demurral. ("Keeping Faith without Faith," p. 4) Ochs's point is that sociology trumps theology in the way most Jews think about Jewish identity for themselves and for their children.

This notion of Jewish faith absent belief evokes the famous tale of Rabbi Nachman:

> A royal prince once became mad and thought he was a turkey. He feels compelled to sit naked under the table, pecking at bones and pieces of bread like a turkey. The royal physicians all give up hope of ever curing him of this madness, and the king, as a result, suffers tremendous grief.
>
> A sage then comes and says, "I will undertake to cure him."
> The sage undresses and sits under the table next to the prince, picking crumbs and bones. "Who are you?" asks the prince" "What are you doing here?"
> "And you?" replies the sage. "What are you doing here?"
> "I am a turkey," answers the prince.
> "I am also a turkey," answers the sage.
> The two "turkeys" sit together like this for some time, until they become good friends. One day, the sage signals the king's servants

to throw him shirts. He then says to the prince, "What makes you think that a turkey can't wear a shirt? You can wear a shirt and still be a turkey." With that the two of them put on shirts.

After a while he signals them again and they throw him a couple pairs of pants. Just as before, he says, "What makes you think that you can't be a turkey if you wear pants?"

The sage continues in this manner until they are completely dressed. Then he signals again, and they are given regular food from the table. Again the sage says, "What makes you think that you will stop being a turkey if you eat good food? You can eat whatever you want and still be a turkey!"

They both eat the food. Finally the sage says, "What makes you think a turkey must sit under the table? A turkey can sit at the table. The sage continues in this manner until the prince is completely cured. (revised from *The Seven Beggars and Other Kabbalistic Tales of Rebbe Nachman of Breslov*, pp. 123-124.)

In Rabbi Nachman's parable, God is the King and we Jews are the prince who has forgotten his true nature and constantly wanders off in turkey-ish directions. Rabbi Nachman and those like him are the wise sages who can coax us wayward turkey-princes back to our better selves, our true humanity. The sage's technique is not theological argument, not to persuade the prince that he is not a turkey, not to insist that he think of the grief he is causing his poor old dad, the king (i.e., God), but rather to cajole him toward civilized (i.e., Jewish) behavior and then to trust that transformed commitment and proper belief will follow changed behavior. That is, Rabbi Nachman teaches the behavior modification school of theological argument. To put it bluntly, when we resume acting like good Jews, we will eventually come to think and believe like good Jews. But until we reach that ideal stage where behavior and theology coincide, we should at least behave properly. We should, in this view, engage our tradition fully even if we have not reached the ideal stage where we can generate certainty about its ultimate Source.

A supporting line of reflection on the nature of Jewish belief and doubt arises out of a consideration about how we Jews speak to and about God. As the Prophet Isaiah declares:

> To whom can you compare Me or declare Me similar?
> To whom can you liken Me, so that we seem comparable? (*Isaiah 46:5*)

I would think most of us could easily agree with Isaiah that the God in whom we either believe or do not believe is really different from us, so different as to be beyond compare, beyond our ability to make attribution in the limited language that contains our limited thoughts. As Moses Maimonides, the famous Jewish theologian, recognized back in the twelfth century, there is no positive quality a human can correctly and accurately attribute to God because all attributions imply some limitation that would be false as applied to God. That being the case, we might then wonder what to make of all the Biblical and liturgical passages that not only attribute qualities to God—such as mightiness or justice or mercy or loving-kindness or forgiveness—but also describe God's body parts—feet, outstretched arms, nose, eyes, and head—and even God's emotions—sympathy, compassion, anger, jealousy, uncertainty, decisiveness, or loneliness.

We could each open our prayer book at random and find many examples of vivid, anthropomorphic representations of God and human longing for God. "You are our shepherd ... Sovereign ... Shield of Abraham ... Help of Sarah ... our Father ... our Keeper ... our Friend," to name only a few of these liturgical representations of God.

In line with the vivid images for God that Jews sometimes utilize, a rabbinic student at the Jewish Theological Seminary once referred to God as Fred Astaire to her Ginger Rogers. She wrote:

> When we miss a step it is always my fault. He dances in flats; I have to dance in heels; he is on the ceiling; I'm on the floor; he can be late; I can't. He pinches me in the clinches; I mustn't. And Cyd Charisse is waiting for me to fail. But when we get it together, it's sheer ecstasy. (quoted in *The Way into Encountering God in Judaism*, p. 13)

What are we to make of the assertion that we cannot use language to say anything truthful about God, on the one hand, while on the other hand we have inherited a tradition that says lots of things about God and God's qualities and encourages us to come up with more of the same? What does this odd juxtaposition say about Jewish belief?

The contemporary Jewish theologian Rabbi Neil Gillman writes:

> To think and talk about God is to think and talk metaphorically. We must make our peace with that conclusion and trace its implications. **The first implication** is that in regard to God's intrinsic nature **we are all agnostics**. . . . Torah is how our ancestors understood God's will, not God per se. . . . **The second implication** is that the image of God in the Bible and, even more, in the later tradition, is a complex metaphorical system. The primary characteristics of this system are its pluralism and its fluidity. (*The Way into Encountering God in Judaism*, pp. 10–11)

Gillman is saying not that Jews are agnostics but that essentially Judaism is agnostic. That is, because we admit our inability to know God's fundamental nature, we determine to maintain a stance of extreme theological humility, a stance that does not permit us to make certain claims about God. And because of that theological humility, we Jews regard our theological language as metaphorical, allusive, multifaceted, changeable, complex, and inconsistent. Because the object of Jewish belief is ultimately mysterious, we have evolved a multivocal religious system that emphasizes the implications of belief over the content and language of belief itself.

The following story of uncertain origin reflects the nature of Jewish belief:

> Once a famous atheist came to deliver a lecture at a shul in the old country. The lecture, a decisively persuasive argument for atheism, was brilliant but a tad long. As the minutes dragged on, the shamash started to signal to the lecturer to bring his remarks to a close but the lecturer failed to heed the signals. Finally, the shamash simply strode to the front of the room and interrupted, saying, "professor, we want to thank you for your brilliant and convincing remarks. Indeed we are all persuaded by your arguments for atheism. But we must now draw this session to a close because it is time to davven minchah, to pray the afternoon service.

Do we Jews believe? When all is said and done, after we Jews have heard the arguments of theists and those of atheists, it is, so to speak, time to *davven minchah*. It is time to get out from under the table, to root ourselves in our heritage of humble theological pronouncements and richly metaphorical, theological language, including the language of angry disappointment at a God often experienced as absent, to engage in learning and living Torah and passing on its teachings to the next generation, to work at deepening our spiritual lives, building Jewish community, both where we reside and in Israel, and to promote a more just and peaceful world. For therein do we demonstrate authentic Jewish belief and honest Jewish doubt.

GIVING LIFE TO THE DEAD
Rosh Hashanah 5758/1997

Turn the midrashic lens once again and take another look at the strange and mysterious Biblical tale we know so well and understand so little, the Binding of Isaac. A composite midrash:

> There have never been longer days than those three during which Abraham treks with his son and, for part of the trip, with two servants, to Mt. Moriah. On the first day, Abraham gazes up at the vast heavens and recalls with irony and bitterness God's promise to him that his progeny would be as numerous as the stars in those heavens and as the sands of the seashore. What would become of that promise now?
>
> On the following day, the two servants, anticipating Isaac's demise, argue over which of them would replace him as Abraham's heir. Meanwhile Satan appears in all manner of disguises, alternately to Abraham, and then to Isaac, with arguments, good, logical arguments, seeking to dissuade them from this mission. Satan then turns into a vast ocean blocking their path. But, into the water trudge Abraham and Isaac undeterred even as the water reaches their throats. Finally, at Abraham's rebuke, Satan flees.
>
> As the third day arrives, Abraham raises his eyes to see a pillar of fire extending from the mountaintop to heaven. Abraham and Isaac now climb alone; Isaac turns to his father and asks, "Where is the lamb for the burnt offering?" "God will provide it," comes the atonal reply. The two, father and son, construct the altar together with stones and mortar. The altar complete, Abraham binds his son upon it.
>
> Abraham, then, raises the knife, its cutting edge honed to a fine sharpness, glistening in the last rays of the day's sunlight. Time

moves slowly as Abraham pulls the blade downward. A voice calls out, "Abraham," and again, "Abraham." But, the voice is too late. Isaac's blood drains onto the ground. The sacrifice has been performed.

Heaven is in an uproar. It cannot be. The test has gone too far. The bearer of Abraham's seed, the inheritor of the covenantal legacy, lies lifeless amid stone and blood. Staring dumbfounded from their heavenly abode, the ministering angels burst into tears of shock and grief. The Holy One also watches in dismay: as the angelic tears fall to the earth, the Holy One directs them into the eyes and onto the wounds of the now still Isaac. The tears are restorative tears, tears of revival, tears of renewal. Isaac blinks, his life force returns, and he utters these words: "*Baruch Attah Adonai Mechayai Hametim*—Blessed are You Lord who gives life to the dead." (Rose, "Praying What We Mean," pp. 62--63)

Since the midrashic Isaac spoke those words of prayerful thanks for God's power to overcome death, the words have fixed themselves into the second bracha of the sequence that comprises the Amidah. Every time a Jew prays the established liturgy of our tradition, he or she praises God for giving life to the dead, unless he or she uses one of the rites influenced by the unflinchingly rationalistic Jewish Reformers of the nineteenth century, the Reformers who insisted on believing what we pray and praying what we believe. I do not fault those Reformers; I am one of their spiritual descendants; they acted on their convictions as one must. As we learn in the famous Talmudic account of Daniel, Jeremiah, and the Men of the Great Assembly, one must act on one's convictions, even if those convictions require a departure from traditional practice, particularly in matters of applied theology, the language of prayer.

The Talmud reports that both Jeremiah and Daniel were unable to completely retain the prayer language established by the venerable Moses where it contradicted their experience and understanding. Specifically, they could not bring themselves to describe God as respectively "mighty" and "awesome," because one (Jeremiah) witnessed the absence of God's might in allowing the destruction of Jerusalem. The other (Daniel) witnessed the absence of awesomeness when God failed to prevent the exile of the Israelites to Babylonia. "How could Jeremiah and Daniel (great prophets that they were) simply alter a sacred liturgical formulation?" the Talmud asks. They could do so because, says the Talmud, God insists on truthfulness.

God insists on the truth. We are not expected to pray with words we do not believe. On the other hand, along came the so-called Men of the Great Assembly who restored the Mosaic language not because they denied the perspectives of Daniel and Jeremiah, but because, from their own perspective, they were able to hold onto the ancient words by means of reinterpretation. "Mighty" is seen by them as God's ability to patiently forbear the enemies of Israel. "Awesome" is viewed as the manner in which God has enabled the single, tiny nation of Israel to survive amid nations more numerous and powerful.

In the same way, I sense that we, like the Men of the Great Assembly, have arrived on the scene at a time when we may face our theological challenges without the severe limitations imposed by nineteenth-century rationalism. That is what I propose we do with the difficult language and concepts of our tradition that enable us to face our deepest human needs.

The traditional language of resurrection is difficult for many of us, and yet, in my view, the doctrine of bodily resurrection touches on the most profound of human mysteries. It pertains to that which lies beyond the edge of our perception and maps a direction for endowing our lives with meaning beyond the grave. In doing so, it addresses the existential angst that often accompanies an awareness of personal mortality. That is, Isaac's prayer for resurrection becomes part of the daily liturgy of Jews not because it reflects certain belief in an odd but comforting idea, but because it addresses a primary human quest for putting a frame on the picture that is one's life.

Be that as it may, the bracha for bodily resurrection is problematic for many. It describes one of the eschatological doctrines of classical, rabbinic Judaism, those end-of-days ideas that include immortality of the soul, heaven, also known as *Olam Ha-Ba* (the World-to-Come), hell, and the Messiah, God's anointed one who will come to herald significant changes in the world order and, possibly, the end of history. Often, when I speak of these things, Jewish concepts relating to the end of days, I get quizzical looks from Jewish listeners and sometimes comments like, "I didn't know we believed those things," or, "I thought those were Christian ideas."

In truth, these ideas are little known among many Jews these days, nor necessarily believed even when they are known. Hence, I am on a minor mission to raise the collective Jewish awareness of these concepts, to return them to positions on our theological maps. With regard specifically to the resurrection language, my mission has taken the form of trying to convince Reform Jews to reinstate the traditional language back into Isaac's prayer, at least as one option, rather than the bland and, in my view, not very meaningful, formulation *Mechaya Hakol*—Who imparts life to all things. In the world of Conservative Judaism, where I am just a visitor, not a card-carrying member, I would simply note that whereas the Reform approach to problematic prayer language usually impels modification or deletion, the Conservative approach often involves retention of the language in Hebrew (which few understand) and English translation that obfuscates. I would like to see in the standard liturgies of the Reform Movement the traditional language of resurrection in Hebrew and straightforward translations.

In recent years, there has been an explosion of published books and articles concerning death and afterlife. As the twentieth century draws to a close, it would appear that the human impulse to probe these mysteries has withstood the rationalist's claim that belief in an afterlife is a mere illusion, a futile exercise in wish fulfillment. No less than others, contemporary Jews are driven to seek understanding about what lies beyond the grave. No less than others do we aspire to transcend the finite span from birth to death.

As contemporary Jews, our spiritual quest begins with essential features of our humanity that remain unchanged despite a great many technologically driven changes that characterize contemporary life. As humans, we distinguish ourselves among members of the animal kingdom by virtue of our awareness of our mortality. As such, like both our premodern and our modern ancestors, we crave the means to overcome the anticipated annihilation of our selves.

That the constraints of nineteenth-century rationalism no longer bind us could and should free us to take a second look at resurrection, among other premodern concepts and myths of our tradition, formerly rejected as nonscientific and irrational. As we withdraw from the modernist's reliance on rationalism, as we become more attuned to the multifaceted nature of ritual and myth, as we take note of the increasingly documented relationship between spiritual discipline and both physical and emotional health, many of us have come to seek spiritual growth that draws on nonrational realms without abandoning the rational.

As one proposing greater attention to and usage of the traditional language of bodily resurrection [*Techiyat Hametim*] but without faith in its literal truth, I had wondered about the dimensions of early rabbinic thinking about the concept of bodily resurrection. In what ways did they find the idea challenging, and how did they address those challenges? A review of Talmudic and midrashic literature reveals that these rabbis, the same ones responsible for encoding the idea in liturgical language, raise many of the issues that bother those of subsequent generations, as follows:

(1) Noting the lack of obvious Biblical basis for the idea of resurrection, and regarding that lack as intolerable, the rabbis cleverly interpret certain Biblical verses to yield that basis. For example, in one Talmudic passage, the rabbis offer:

> How is resurrection to be derived from the Torah? As it is written, "And you shall give thereof of the Lord's offerings to Aaron the priest" (*Numbers 18:28*). But would Aaron live for ever; he did not even enter Palestine, that *terumah* should be given him. Rather, it teaches that he would be resurrected, and Israel give him *terumah*. Thus resurrection is derived from the Torah.

(2) They raise and confront the challenge that the doctrine of bodily resurrection contradicts their understanding of science and the natural world. A two-part, Talmudic treatment of this dilemma:

> A. A Caesar questioned Rabban Gamaliel, "You maintain that the dead will come back to life. But they turn to dust. Can dust come back to life?" Caesar's daughter said to Rabban Gamaliel, "Let me answer him. In our town are two potters. One fashions his wares from liquid, and the other from clay. Which deserves greater praise?" Caesar replied, "The one who fashions from liquid." His daughter then said, "If He can fashion His wares (human beings) from liquid (the primal genetic soup), He can surely fashion them from clay."

> B. In the school of Rabbi Ishmael it is taught: The inference [to bodily resurrection] may be drawn from glassware. If glassware, which is made by the breath of human beings, may be mended when broken, how much more so flesh and blood made by the breath of the Holy One Blessed be He. (Each of the three above

from the *Babylonian Talmud Sanhedrin 90b–91a*)

Furthermore, the rabbis of Talmud and midrash address numerous other issues about the mysterious details concerning how resurrection might work: when, by what means, who will be affected, and who not? Will the resurrected return clothed or unclothed? When will resurrection take place, what will be its timing, and how will it be coordinated with the coming of the Messiah and the ingathering of the exiles (other classical Jewish concepts concerning future time)?

I mention these rabbinic passages not to suggest that old solutions to our skepticism are available, but to point out that the skepticism itself is old. I for one take considerable comfort when realizing that my issues with an aspect of tradition have precedent; this awareness enables me to feel a sense of comradeship with my similarly troubled ancestors even when their resolutions fail to impress me. Even then, we remain transgenerational colleagues, bound up together in a fellowship of questioning. Moreover, the more I study rabbinic midrash, the more I suspect that the contemporary inability to transcend skepticism may stem not from greater wisdom and sophistication on our part but from insufficient interpretive skill and from an overly rigid reflex in our reading of traditional language.

Near the end of our Passover seders, we sing "*Chad Gadya,*" the ditty about the little goat "my father bought for two zuzzim . . . then came the cat that ate the kid . . . then came the dog that ate the cat" until the Angel of Death comes and finally the Holy One of Blessing who slays the Angel of Death. After a long seder and four cups of wine, we probably do not pause to reflect thoughtfully on the theology of "*Chad Gadya,*" but, if we were to pause and reflect, I wonder whether if at that moment we really would believe that God can and will slay the Angel of Death in any literal or metaphorical sense whatsoever.

Is the concept of resurrection of the dead true? Is it real? Do I believe it? Do I believe it in any sense? The psychiatrist Robert Jay Lifton writes: "We live on images. As human beings we know our bodies and our minds only through what we can imagine" (*Broken Connection,* p. 3).

Thus, I am drawn to the image of bodily resurrection in spite of my uncertainty about its reality because it sparks my imagination. Because it promotes a confrontation with death and because it projects a vision in which one will overcome death, the notion remains vital. Because it describes that which transcends life, it enables one to engage life more profoundly. Is God stronger than death? I cannot answer with scientific certainty, but I do know that I want to speak the words that our father, Isaac of midrash, spoke, and thereby attend to the myth in which the question can be posed.

I BELIEVE WITH PERFECT FAITH
Yom Kippur 5761/2000

"I believe with perfect faith in the coming of the Messiah, and though he may tarry yet do I await his coming." *"Ani Ma-amin B'emunah Sh'leima B'viat Hamashiach; V'Af Al Pi Sh'yitmamei-ah, Im Kal Zeh Achakeh Lo."* This declaration of classical Jewish faith in a divinely appointed personality who would usher in an age of radical improvement of the world, this central element of Judaism, was I lesson I learned years ago as a prayer with a haunting melody. I learned it in connection with the Holocaust and, in particular, in connection with the determined spiritual resistance—when spiritual resistance was the only kind available—of some Jews who were unable to escape the Nazi onslaught. It seemed to me then as now that to maintain this traditional belief, to have hope for a better future, was a form of resistance suited for a condition of extremity; there could be none greater. Only later did I learn that *Ani Ma-amin* is but one of thirteen beliefs enumerated by Moses Maimonides, the great twelfth-century philosopher, as the essential beliefs or dogmas of Judaism.

Whether dogma or prayer, how about us? Does the ancient idea of Messiah in any of its several permutations speak to us? Do we believe with perfect or even imperfect faith in any sort of messianic idea? And, if we do, how does it operate for us? How does it inspire us? Where are the potentially dangerous pitfalls of this potent concept, and how may we avoid them? Where did the idea begin?

The idea of Messiah is as old as the Bible but not as old as the Torah. The first of the prophets called Isaiah presents the fullest Biblical depiction of the messianic concept. Isaiah lives in Jerusalem during the first decades of the eighth century BCE and witnesses two wars against his nation as well as the destruction of the Northern Kingdom. He articulates his hopeful vision in Chapter 11 of the Biblical book that bears his name: "A shoot shall grow out of the stump of Jesse [David's father]" (*Isaiah 11:1*). The prophet then goes on to characterize the messianic personality as one who will be wise, insightful, righteous, reverent of God, faithful, and an impartial judge of rich and poor.

In Isaiah's conception, the universal peace ushered in by this Messiah will even encompass the animal kingdom: "The wolf shall lie down with the lamb, the leopard lie down with the kid" (*Isaiah 1:6*).

Above all, the messianic age will be characterized by Israelite resurgence: "In that day, the stock of Jesse that has remained standing shall become a standard to peoples—nations shall seek his counsel. And his abode shall be honored.... In that day, He will hold up a signal to the nations and assemble the banished of Israel and gather the dispersed of Judah from the four corners of the earth" (*Isaiah 1:10*).

Isaiah's vision leaves much room for the imagination and raises as many questions as it answers. Is the messianic vision to be taken literally? Is it a conception about an ideal society, or is it a prediction? If the latter, is it a social goal for which people should actively work or a condition for which people should passively wait, brought about by God according to a divinely ordained timetable? Will the messianic age happen in real time, in history? Or will it signal the end of history? Will the messianic age affect only Jews, primarily Jews, or everyone? Can one separate the idea of a personal Messiah from the idea of a messianic age? Or is the one required to bring on the other? Will the messianic age happen soon, at any moment, or is it something for the far-distant future? For each of these questions one can find at least two, mutually exclusive, views within Jewish traditional sources. Thus, while the idea of the Messiah has been with us for a long time, moving Jewish hearts and stirring Jewish souls, it is an idea fraught with ambivalence and ambiguity.

Regardless of such ambiguities and variations concerning the initial messianic vision, the idea begins to take particular shape as mainstream Jewish theology prominently encodes it in traditional liturgy. Every Jewish prayer book gives voice to this concept in some form. How so? The traditional Siddur gives it prominence in several prayers. Just before reciting the Shema, during the morning service, one customarily gathers together the fringes of one's tallit and utters words that evoke the messianic future of ingathering exiles, saying: "*V'Havi-enu L'shalom Me-arba Kanfot Ha-aretz, V'tolichenu Kom'miyut L'artzenu*—Gather us in peace from the four corners of the earth and lead us upright into our land."

We further reinforce our messianic hope in the daily group of prayers, the Amidah, said thrice daily by traditionally observant Jews. Included among the thirteen petitionary prayers in its midsection are these four, each an evocation of restoration of an imagined stable and secure past in a messianic future: "Sound the great Shofar to herald our freedom. . . . Gather the dispersed from the ends of the earth"; "Restore our judges as in the days of old, restore our counselors as in former times. Remove from us sorrow and anguish. Reign alone over us with loving-kindness"; "Have mercy and return to Jerusalem, Your city. May Your presence dwell there as You have promised. . . . Re-establish there the majesty of David Your servant"; and "Bring to flower the shoot of Your servant David. Hasten the advent of messianic redemption. Each and every day we hope for Your deliverance."

Taken as a group, these prayers have three characteristics:

(1) They assume that we Jews live in a state of exile, that we are not in our homeland. The historical condition of exile goes back to the destruction of the First Temple by the Babylonians over 2,500 years ago and is reimposed by the Romans who destroy Jerusalem and its Second Temple in 70 CE. Ever since, the messianic idea has featured a longing for a return to the "good old days" when there was a Temple and priests and sacrifices and a Sanhedrin, "the judges and counselors as of old." Thus, the idea is restorative; those who affirm it hope to restore a preferable condition that, at least in the imagination, did exist at one time.

(2) These prayers also articulate Isaiah's conception that this restoration will involve a descendent of King David. This personality is the Messiah, a term that simply means one anointed by God in the way kings and certain prophets are anointed. The Messiah himself may be a charismatic leader, but no superhuman or supernatural qualities are herein attributed.

(3) Even though these prayers present a restorative kind of messianism, they also contain at least a hint of its opposite type, which is utopian. If God's reign is to be established and if sorrow and anguish are to be removed, this sounds like a radical departure from the world we know; there is at least an intimation of utopia here, beyond merely a restoration of the good old days, days that presumably contained some sorrow and anguish and the like.

As for discomfort with the idea of messianism: not every Jew in every age has placed messianic aspiration at the center of her or his system of belief. Some, including some of us, no doubt, may well feel downright uncomfortable with some of its facets or with the idea altogether. As we know, for example, Reform Jewish thinkers of the nineteenth century reject some aspects of the messianic idea and emphasize others.First, the Reformers of the nineteenth century reject the idea that Jews in the West live in exile. Rather they optimistically embrace the Enlightenment spirit of universalism and liberalism, regarding Western civilization as a movement in the direction of peace and prosperity for all. Thus, the nineteenth century Reformers deemphasize the idea of a personal Messiah who would reestablish better times for Jewish people alone and also deemphasize the idea of any kind of restoration or return to an ancient homeland. Instead, they stress a this-worldly, utopian ideal captured by the phrase "prophetic Judaism," whereby Jews would light up the way toward a society of universal blessing for everyone everywhere.

This universalist, messianic ideal is liturgically expressed most poignantly in the English rendering of the second half of the Alenu, familiar to all of us who grew up attending Reform synagogues:

> May the time not be distant, O God, when Your name shall be established in all the earth, when unbelief shall disappear and error be no more. Fervently we pray that the day may come when all shall turn to you in love ... when all who dwell on earth shall know that You alone are God. O, may all created in Your image become one in spirit and one in friendship, for ever united in Your service. Then shall Your kingdom be established on earth, and the word of Your prophet fulfilled: "The Lord will reign for ever and ever." On that day the Lord shall be One and His name shall be one.

I will admit that I still find these words stirring. They provide prayerful articulation to the proud Reform record of political and social activism. However, historical events of the century just ended preclude a simple confidence that their fulfillment is well under way. Following a century marked by technology gone awry, massively destructive wars, and nearly successful genocide, what messianic hopes are still possible for us? And what pitfalls must we see so that we can avoid them? For Jews living in the beginning of the twenty-first century, what could constitute a clear vision of messianism, one that retains its power? At the same time, we must insist that any contemporary messianic vision avoid the three potentially dangerous pitfalls of which we are aware, as follows:

Potentially Dangerous Pitfall #1: The idea of an identifiable personal Messiah who is living and breathing. This is what has come to be known as false messianism. The impulse to crown someone with the messianic title becomes nearly irresistible when times are tough, when suffering is great, when communities are demoralized, when the future looks unremittingly bleak. It is not an accident that the receptivity to Shabbtai Zevi as Messiah by millions of Eastern European Jews in the middle of the seventeenth century followed by only a few short years the devastating pogroms at the hands of the Ukrainian warlord Bogdan Chelmnitzky. It is perhaps even understandable why, a generation or so following the Holocaust, many among today's Lubavitcher Hasidim claim messianic status for their now-deceased rebbe, a dynamic leader who left no heir to the dynastic throne he inhabited. The persistent messianic claim on the part of these Lubavitchers strikes one as oddly similar to that of early Christianity, a claim over which Jews and Christians parted company. Thus, it does not come as a total surprise to hear that some among the Lubavitch have been altering the formulation for the rebbe as King Messiah to the rebbe as divinity whose return is expected immanently. To me, such thinking, for a Jew, is both delusional and idolatrous.

Potentially Dangerous Pitfall #2: Imminent messianism, the idea that the Messiah will arrive very soon, especially if such thinking assumes an end-of-history scenario, is a pitfall that is understandable for those who are desperate or suffering. However, if I truly believe that the Messiah is just around the corner, then I need not worry about the poor or the hungry or the homeless or the disenfranchised or the marginalized. After all, the Messiah will soon be here and he will take care of it or will create the conditions in which we may all deal easily with these otherwise intractable problems. The idea of an imminent Messiah inhibits people from taking responsibility and, in that sense, contradicts the prophetic vision that never sought abdication from human responsibility but always insisted on joining moral and ritual life.

With regard to this potential pitfall, Rabbi Yochanan ben Zakkai, the great first-century sage, is famously reported to have said that if you are holding a sapling in your hand (ready to plant it) and are told, "Look, the Messiah is here," first finish planting the sapling, then go out and greet the Messiah. More than an affirmation about the importance of trees, the tale urges us not to relinquish the human obligation to prepare for the future, to take care of one another, and the planet, even when the new age has begun, even if the Messiah has arrived

Potentially Dangerous Pitfall #3: The idea that the messianic age will come only if and when God wants it and that humans should avoid, at all costs, any move that might prematurely trigger the messianic advent. There is a strain of extreme messianic passivism in Jewish tradition that, for example, leads some to oppose political Zionism on the grounds that it illicitly absconds with the divine prerogative of returning the exiles "from the four corners of the earth." Since we do not know when or how God intends to bring the Messiah, to do anything to hasten his arrival constitutes grievous sin, goes such thinking.

As for me, I greatly prefer the strain of Jewish teaching encapsulated by Rabbi Tarfon's famous dictum: "One is not obligated to complete the task but neither is one at liberty to abstain from it." Overwhelmingly, the weight of Torah leans toward human action that would move us closer to a messianic reality rather than toward a fear of prematurely triggering its arrival.

Those are the pitfalls I wish us to avoid. But what is the messianic idea I wish us to affirm? I believe in a pragmatic, active, nonpersonal, nonimminent, messianic idea. I hold this belief because it gives us hope, even when despair comes more easily. I hold it because it precludes our investing all hope in any human savior. I hold it because it prevents us from evading our responsibilities in the world. And I hold it because it animates us to find ways, small and large, to make a positive impact, to engage in the task of perfecting God's creation even though completing that task is beyond our capacity.

Recently, I read a mother's account of a shopping outing with her eleven-year-old daughter, an account that embodies this idea of pragmatic messianism as follows:

> We parted ways at the front of the store, she off to do school supply shopping, and I to hunt down a ton of groceries. When I went to check

out, all 15 cashiers were busy with at least two shoppers in each line. I couldn't believe that I'd finished before Amanda and looked around for her. She got into another line and I watched her as she checked out. It's a mother thing, observing your children to see how they handle themselves when they think their parents are nowhere around.

Her eyes followed an elderly gentleman walking back and forth. He wore shower slippers. She watched him stop in front of a row of cookies. He counted the change in his pocket and then re-shelved the cookies.

I watched as she searched her purse for some money.... My beautiful daughter waited until the man turned to walk away, then walked up behind him and silently dropped the rolled up dollar bills on the floor. She tapped him on the shoulder and then bent to retrieve the money.

Both faces were smiling as Amanda skipped back to her place in line. I wiped my eyes and cleared my throat before I waved to get her attention. On the drive home, she said, "Mom, there was a homeless man in the store and he was hungry." "Well, did you give him some money or buy him something to eat?" I quizzed her.

"I did give him some money, but I pretended like I found it on the floor so he wouldn't be embarrassed. I told him that I thought the money was his, but he said it wasn't. But I handed it to him anyway. He said 'bless you.' and I do feel blessed, Mom." (Ledbetter, "A Child's Gift," http://www.heroicstories.org/ [story since removed from site])

Amanda, the eleven-year-old girl, did not end world hunger; she did not even end the hunger of the elderly man in the store. However, I am convinced that she did bring the messianic age one small step closer than it had been.

The Talmud itself embodies this kind of pragmatic messianism in recounting a legend about Rabbi Joshua ben Levi, an important sage of the early second century. Once Rabbi Joshua met his friend and teacher, Elijah the Prophet, who is said to be the one who will return and herald the messianic arrival. Rabbi Joshua asks, "When will the Messiah really come?"

Elijah replies, "Go and ask him yourself."
"And where can I find him?'
"He is sitting near the entrance of the town," Elijah answers.
"And how will I recognize him?" asks Rabbi Joshua.
Elijah answers this way: "The Messiah sits among the poor people

and the beggars who are suffering from various diseases and illnesses. Every one of them takes off and then ties up their wounds at the same time. The Messiah, on the other hand, takes off the bandages one by one, wipes the single wound and then ties it up with bandages before he goes on to the next. He does not treat all the sores at one time because, the Messiah says, 'If I will be asked to bring redemption, in this way, I will not be delayed.'"

Rabbi Joshua arrives at the gate and finds such a man tending his wounds. He approaches and said, "*Shalom Aleichem*, my rabbi and teacher."

"*Aleichem Shalom*, ben Levi," the Messiah answers.

"And when will you come?" asks Rabbi Joshua.

"Tell the people I will arrive today," replies the Messiah.

When Rabbi Joshua returns to Elijah, Elijah asks, "What did the Messiah say to you?"

"The Messiah says that he will come today, but he lies, for he has not arrived."

Elijah responds with some telling Biblical exegesis: "This is what he means: '*Today* if you hearken to My voice.'" (*Psalm 95:7*) (*Sanhedrin 98a*)

Thus, from the perspective of this rabbinic text, the messianic idea remains potent as a goad to strive toward our ideals concerning what the world could be. It does little good to calculate the time of arrival or the color of the horse the Anointed one will ride or even the nature of the changes he will bring. He may not be a he at all. He may be a movement rather than a person. The messianic age is the embodiment of redemption from the ills and evils of the world; its arrival is only as imminent as we make it, and, in that sense, could be very near. It could be in the encounter between a little girl and a hungry man in the grocery store. It could be today if we hearken to God's voice.

In a similar mood, the poet Ruth Brin depicts a messianic vision in the poem "Discovery":

No one ever told me the coming of the Messiah
Could be an inner thing.
No one ever told me a change of heart
Might be as quiet as new-fallen snow.

No one ever told me that redemption
Was as simple as Springtime and as wonderful

As birds returning after a long winter,
Rose-breasted grosbeaks singing in the swaying branches
Of a newly budded tree.

No one ever told me that salvation
Might be like a fresh spring wind
Blowing away the dried, withered leaves of another year,
Carrying the scent of flowers, the promise of fruition.

What I found for myself I try to tell you:
Redemption and salvation are very near,
And the taste of them is in the world
That God created and laid before us (*Harvest: Collected Poems and Prayers*, p. 206).

Thus, I do believe with perfect faith in the coming of the Messiah whose arrival I do not expect soon, though he may be very near. I believe in a messianic time that will not end history but is an ideal vision of an improved world that beckons all people. I believe that Jews have a particular obligation to help turn that vision into a reality through prayer, study, and deeds by which the world, or at least a small slice of it, becomes a gentler, more welcoming, and benign place for all. I believe, in short, that the Messiah shall arrive at precisely the moment he or she is no longer needed.

With God's help and ours, may that time come soon and in our day.

STANDING BEFORE GOD
Rosh Hashanah 5755/1994

I often have occasion to speak to non-Jewish groups in the sanctuary of our synagogue about Judaism or some of its aspects. Sometimes, I begin by noting the essential similarities between Judaism and Christianity, their shared values and beliefs. Then, I will often add, with a nod in the direction of the plaque that rests above our ark, that the two religions are virtually identical in all essentials with the singular exception that Christians pray to God and we Jews pray to the memory of Ida Shapero.

Most synagogues do not have memorial plaques above their arks (and the one that used to be above ours has since been moved to a less obtrusive spot). Many do, however, display the Hebrew phrase of Talmudic origin, *Da Lifnai Mi Atah Omed*—Know before Whom you stand! Whenever entering a synagogue, and really at all other times as well, a Jew is bidden to "know before Whom he or she stands." At no time of year more than during the Days of Awe is the image of standing before the Holy One so sharp, so pronounced, so emphatic.

What does it mean to have an awareness of standing before the Holy One of Blessing? What does it mean have a sense of standing before *Melech Malchei Hamlachim*, the One who rules over all earthly sovereigns? It seems to me that there are three major prongs to this awareness of standing before God: reverence, human accountability, and God's protecting care. Each of these prongs impels us to gather as a worshiping community.

Yirat Shamayim—Reverence. Regarding reverence, if you are like me, you will admit that a posture of reverence is not as familiar or as comfortably acquired as it might be. I often do not consciously appreciate the presence of divinity, nor do I always conduct myself in reverential awareness of my standing before God. I suspect it is, in part, the human propensity to avoid this awareness of our standing before God that impels our particular attachment to the *Yamim Noraim*, the Days of Awe. For, during the ten-day period from Rosh Hashanah through Yom Kippur, we strive to overcome our reluctance to see ourselves as Om-dim *Lifnai Hashem*, people standing before the Almighty.

Moreover, not only do we humans have a propensity for avoiding this perception, but we live at a particular junction in history that conspires against a religious posture, that would restrain us from knowing before Whom we stand, and that has distanced us from such an appreciation.

There is a story about two adventurers in the Pacific Northwest who, struck by the majestic beauty of Mount Rainier, felt compelled to conquer it, to attain its peak. When they sought to engage an Indian guide from one of the local tribes, but were told that the Indians considered it sacrilegious to climb the mountain. Furthermore, they were told, it was a sacred mountain with a lake of fire at its top. No native guide would violate its sanctity by treading upon it. Not to be deterred, the climbers offered more and more money until finally they prevailed upon one Indian guide to lead them up the mountain. However, the guide tried to misdirect them, leading them along circuitous paths, hoping to tire them out. But the two climbers remained stubborn and undeterred. Finally the guide led them a short way up the slopes of Mt. Rainier but declined to go further, saying to them, "I am forbidden to go any higher. From here on, you must go alone." Bravely, the men continued up the mountain, determined to reach the top. Finally, they did. They planted a flag there, took pictures of themselves, and returned to the base.

While praising these adventurers for their courage and perseverance, Rabbi Harold Kushner wonders about their respect for the sacred. He writes, "One of the things that modern men and women seem to do best is put out sacred fires, extending the domain of men and shrinking the domain of God." (*Who Needs God*, pp. 50-51) It's not that technology and science are irrevocably at odds with religion. The existence of many religious scientists testifies to the contrary. Yet it would appear that science, which once seemed to raise to great prominence the role of the human—to the point where God's shrunken domain was of no consequence—now has left us bereft, less sure of our own capacity to conquer worlds but without the faith of the premoderns to fall back on.

When Samuel Morse heard the first-ever message transmitted electrically, he is said to have responded, "What hath God wrought?" In our age, in another milestone event of technological mastery and conquest, Neil Armstrong stepped onto the surface of the moon and pronounced, "One small step for man, one large step for mankind." Where has our sense of reverence gone? Can we recover it? Does it matter?

In large measure, that is what the Days of Awe are about. That is what the Jewish calendar of holiday ritual is about, as are Shabbat (especially Shabbat) and daily prayer and the rituals marking the passages of our lives, and the simple *brachot*, the blessings that are available to us when we wash our hands or break bread or see a rainbow. All these ritual acts and words expand our sense of wonder, broaden our capacity for reverence, remind us of the One before Whom we stand at all times and in all places.

Albert Einstein once said: "There are only two ways to live your life. One is as though nothing is a miracle. The other is as though everything is a miracle." In this regard, I have always derived a perverse pleasure from violence in nature: thunderstorms, snowstorms, earthquakes, volcanic eruptions, hurricanes. It's not that I enjoy their tragic results. God forbid. But to the extent that these events inconvenience us, disrupt our routine or merely amaze us with displays of power so far beyond what humans can generate or control, they stop me short, reminding me that neither I nor my species collectively are totally in charge.

Al Neesekha Sh'bechol Yom Imanu—We thank You, God, for Your miracles that are with us every day. The prayer for thanksgiving, the penultimate prayer in the series of prayers known as *Amidah*, said by observant Jews thrice daily, thanks God for the miracles, the wonders, and good gifts which He showers upon us daily. Admittedly, I am not always sensitized to the miracles of daily life. It should not take thunder and lightning for me to appreciate the miraculous in the rising and setting of the sun, in the periodic rain and dew, in the magnificent array of flora and fauna that occupies even small patches of our gardens and our lawns, my respiring lungs and the beating heart sending blood coursing through vessels, eyes that can see, a nervous system that can sense, a mind that can think. It certainly does not, should not, take such a display to enable me to cherish laughter and warmth, compassion and generosity, bravery and nobility, friendship and love, or to realize that these are the most precious of miracles. Expressions of these human qualities are with us daily. They are gifts imbued with divinity, which, if we open our hearts to it, we see. Religion is, after all, a way of seeing. Not primarily a system of thought or beliefs, religion is a way of seeing the world, a way that acknowledges the wonder and mystery that inheres in the mundane.

Da Lifnai Mi Atah Omed—Know before Whom you stand, implies more than reverence. It connotes accountability, as well.

G. Peter Fleck, a Unitarian minister, describes the television portrayal of the following scene: a man dies and finds himself standing on line, addressed by a bored usher who tells him he can choose either door, the one on the right leading to heaven or the one the left leading to hell.

> "You mean I can choose?" the man asks. "There is no judgment, no taking account of how I lived?"
>
> "That's right," the usher says. "Now move along, people are dying and lining up behind you. Choose one door and keep the line moving."
>
> "But I want to confess, I want to come clean, I want to be judged."
>
> "I'm sorry. We don't have time for that. Just choose a door and move along."
>
> The man pauses and then chooses to walk through the door on the left, leading to hell. (quoted in Kushner, *Who Needs God*, p. 75)

Innately, most of us believe most of the time that morality is not simply a matter of personal preference, that standards of right and wrong behavior exist outside of ourselves. Whether to kill or maim or torture or steal is not, should not, simply be a matter of personal desire or even an expression of democratic will. (Sometimes the majority is wrong.) Most of us want to live in the awareness that we and others are being held accountable for our deeds according to some recognized set of ethical standards. The realization of a morality that obligates us to choose the good even when we might get away with the evil or selfish option— that too is part of what it means to live knowing before Whom you stand.

My final point emerges from a story told by a retired pastor to his student:

> When my son was small, we often walked together through the fields and neighboring pastures behind the parsonage. At first the little fellow would hold onto my little finger, but he found that when he stumbled over something, his grip would fail and down he'd go in the dust or snow. Not giving it much thought, my mind on other matters, I'd stop and he'd get up, brush himself off, and grab my little finger, gripping a little harder this time. Needless to say, this occurred frequently until one day, as he was brushing himself off he looked at me and said,

"Daddy." I replied, "Yes, son what is it?" He said, "I think if you would hold my hand I wouldn't fall."

The retired pastor then turned to his student and, with a tear in his eye, he said, "You know, he stumbled many times after that, but he never hit the ground. Now, as you walk with God, don't try to hold onto God, let God hold onto you. You may stumble but God will never let you fall." (Musser, "The Tabernacle," p. 244)

At the conclusion of most Jewish worship, we express the same sentiment:

B'yado Afkid Ruchi, B'eyt Ishan V'a-erah.
V'im Ruchi Geviyati, Adonai Li V'lo Ira.

The last stanza of Adon Olam says:

Into God's hands I entrust my spirit, when I sleep and when I wake. And with my spirit my body also. The Lord is with me, I will not fear.

"Know before Whom you stand" means not only a sense of reverence, not only an awareness of God's miraculous gifts each and every moment, not only an abiding judgment that personal piety depends on accountability to a moral authority higher than the human, but the understanding that when I know that I stand before God, I recognize God as the ultimate source of my comfort and caring.

When at night the parent goes in to comfort his or her crying child who has been awakened by some nightmare, and holds the child and says, "Shhhhh. Don't worry. Don't be afraid. Daddy's here. Mommy's here. Everything's all right," is the parent lying? Is everything really all right? I believe that if we truly know before Whom we stand, then, all appearances to the contrary, in an ultimate way, everything really is all right.

Da Lifnai Mi Atah Omed means that there is a hearing ear and a seeing eye and a caring presence in the universe. We would do well to cultivate this awareness and allow it to find expression in the sincerity of our prayers, in the righteousness of our deeds, and in our existential sense of well-being.

UNIVERSALISM FROM WITHIN PARTICULARISM
Yom Kippur 5752/1991

A story is told about Henry Cohen, a rabbi who served Congregation B.nai Israel in Galveston, Texas, for over sixty years from 1888 until 1949. During 1911, Rabbi Cohen leaped suddenly and briefly into prominence and was awarded a prize for humanitarianism in America. During that period, Galveston was one of the main ports of entry for immigrants and refugees during the flood of immigration into the United States, and among those immigrants was a Russian who, when he landed at the port, was immediately arrested by police, and an extradition order was issued against him at the request of the Tsarist government. Rabbi Cohen visited the prison and, learning of the man's plight, visited him and was convinced that he was not a criminal but a political refugee entitled to political asylum. With this conviction, Rabbi Cohen sought out immigration authorities, but none were responsive. Undeterred, Rabbi Cohen entered a formal appeal against the decision, but lost the case. Still undaunted, he then took the case to the governor of Texas and on to the Supreme Court, but with the same negative result. At last he decided to seek an interview with the president of the United States himself, President Theodore Roosevelt. After many frustrations, he was at last granted the interview where he pleaded the cause of the unfortunate detainee. Roosevelt listened to him and then shook his head. "I'm sorry, Rabbi," he said, "much as I admire the way you Jews stick together and try to help one another, I cannot see any reason for intervening."

"Jew?" said the Rabbi. "Who said he was a Jew? He's not a Jew. He's a Russian Christian."

"A Christian?" echoed the president in astonishment. "But why are you concerning yourself with him?"

"But he's a human being, isn't he?" retorted the rabbi. And so impressed was President Roosevelt that he directed the cancelation of the extradition order.

The account of Rabbi Cohen's intervention on behalf of the Russian Christian refugee, a Jew taking on a non-Jewish cause, comes to mind in connection with the Haftarah of Yom Kippur morning, the reading from the Prophet Second Isaiah. Just as we begin to feel self-satisfied at our pious observance of this day, at our marvelous self-denial, we hear the famous admonition that our fast alone is insufficient, that our prayers do not count, that all of the rituals of this Yom Kippur do not amount to a hill of beans if they do not inspire substantial acts of *gemilut hassadim*, deeds of human kindness. Isaiah addressed the Jews cast adrift in Babylonia in the mid-sixth century BCE. His words hit the mark for Jews adrift in North Central Virginia at the close of the second millennium CE. They obviously left an impression on Rabbi Cohen.

I wish to address two aspects of Isaiah's message, the universalism that leaps out at us, and the more faint, but undeniable particularism that provides the context for his universalist pronouncements. What does Isaiah really demand from us? What exactly is the nature of his universalism? Does it urge us toward political correctness or in some other direction?

Let's be clear about the terms of discourse, the main outlines of this universalist-particularist dichotomy, and what is at stake for us as Jews. There are those who would say, in line with major trends in nineteenth-century liberal thought, that all particularist traditions, such as Judaism, ought to and will ultimately yield to the overarching thrust of history in its march of progress. Particular civilizations, nationalities, religions will remain only insofar as they support and partake of these overarching themes. Marxism and Leninism epitomize this line of thinking. Many Jews have been and continue to be won over, as well, to this extreme universalist perspective. Felix Adler, some one hundred years ago, founded the Society for Ethical Culture, which stripped Judaism of all its unique trappings and boiled it down to the qualities he perceived as ethically or culturally advanced, according to the standards of the day. Unitarianism makes similar claims and continues to attract Jews. What is at stake, then, is the nature of Judaism and perhaps its very survival. Some would see the choice as follows: either get with it intellectually and become a Unitarian or an Ethical Culturist, or else be Jewish and, hence, deeply mired in atavistic, primitive, and uncool particularism.

Did Isaiah prefigure Felix Adler? Was Isaiah an extreme universalist? One might argue the case. Isaiah not only rails against empty piety. He does put forth a universal vision, the regard for the other, for those not of one's own particular family, tribe, caste, or ethnic group. Isaiah insists that we combat wickedness, find and feed the hungry, help the poor, clothe the naked, that we acknowledge the needs of our neighbors and lend a hand. He never says "the Jewish hungry," "the Hebrew naked," "the poor from among the children of Israel," or the "needy Israelites." Isaiah's universalism goes so far that he almost does become politically correct. Almost.

But he does not, in my view, because at its core, his universalism is framed by particularism. In the same speech in which Isaiah sets out his program of universal social action, he also bids us to properly observe the Sabbath day. In doing so, does Isaiah contradict himself? Why does he even bother to speak at all about ritual practice if he mainly cares about righteous action?

Isaiah assumes, as some of us may not, that ritual observance is obligatory. It would never have occurred to him to suggest otherwise. However, he also knows that observance may be sincere and wholehearted or it may be hypocritical and false (such as the fast that fails to raise one's awareness of those in need). Isaiah's point is not that we give up ritual for social action, but that when we pray, especially on this day, we do so not only for ourselves, not only for our families, not only for the Jewish people, but that our prayer include all our neighbors in the localities in which we reside and on the planet from whose atmosphere we all draw breath. His point is that prayer must not only be an inner experience. It must not only be communion with the divine. It must yield social impact. Our rituals, in part, must guide and goad us toward social action.

The first-century sage Hillel said: "If I am not for myself, who will be for me? If I am only for myself, what am I? If not now, when?" In epigrammatic fashion, Hillel captures the conceptual underpinning of Isaiah's diatribe. Hillel's three points could be restated as follows:

(1) Ethics must arise concentrically from the center; one must first look out for oneself and for one's own, lest no one else do so, and also because if one fails to care for oneself, one conveys the message that no one else need care either.

(2) Ethics must proceed quickly to the outer circles, to the other, to a concern for those whose humanity we share, but from whose particular ethnicity we may differ. To be preoccupied only with oneself or only with one's tribe is to fail the Jewish test of menschlichkeit, of what it means to be truly human.

(3) Tomorrow is too late. Hunger, homelessness, extreme poverty, severe anguish are urgent matters and must not be put off.

Thus, universalism is a value that emerges from within the particularisms of Judaism. To insist, as some do, that one abandon all forms of Jewish ethnic particularity, to give up tradition for the sake of universal ideals, is to throw out the baby with the bathwater; it is a destructive and unnecessary tradeoff.

Consider a prayer that is familiar to all of us, *Alenu*, with which most Jewish public worship is concluded. Its first paragraph acknowledges God for setting before the Jewish nation a unique destiny, a framework for making our way distinct (not necessarily superior) from those set before the other nations of the earth. Its second paragraph calls us to direct ourselves to the goals of the future-time, "when the world will be perfected under the Almighty, when all humankind will call upon God's name." It is a universal vision that encompasses all people and all the world. Thus, *Alenu* should remind us, every time we speak or sing its words with intentionality, that Jewish ethics begins within the framework of our particular tradition, out of which universal aspirations receive expression.

From the first Jew, Abraham, who argued with God to preserve the righteous Gentiles of Sodom, to Abraham Joshua Heschel, towering rabbi of our century, who stood beside Martin Luther King, Jr., on the march to Montgomery, and who spoke out eloquently for the Jewish imperative to aid the civil rights movement, Jewish history sports an impressive record of concern for the other, concern that emerges out of the ethical system contained by the Jewish tradition.

Recently, a periodical in the United Kingdom reported:

If the world were a village of 1,000 people:
700 of them would be nonwhite,

300 of them would be white,
60 people would own over half of the total wealth,
500 would not have enough to eat,
600 would live in slums,
700 would be illiterate.

If this village were our village, we would want it to change. This morning, Isaiah reminds us that this village is our village, since it is the world. Even in Charlottesville, where the statistics are better, there are poor, homeless, hungry, and undereducated people. There are others, Jews and non-Jews, who desperately require help of some sort: caring, comfort, a listening ear, or a friendly voice.

On this Yom Kippur, we recall Rabbi Henry Cohen, a latter-day Isaiah, and his example of the ethics of universalism that springs out of the particularism of our tradition. That example confronts us with the Jewish obligation to raise our sights and extend our efforts beyond ourselves, beyond our families, beyond our community, until they reach the general community, and beyond, to the human family.

In the new year, as we consider those in our own community, or elsewhere, who are hungry or homeless or in anguish or needy in any way, be they Jewish or not, let us consider it as a particularly Jewish obligation that we seek them out and lend them a hand. Let each of us resolve to find one new way to help, one new area in which to express our concern.

Ken Y'hi Ratzon. With God's help, may it be so.

IN THE IMAGE
Rosh Hashanah 5757/1998

No more dramatic account of creation has been recorded than that of Torah. The very rhythm of its repeated phrases and metered verses lends emphasis to its content, its orientation, purpose, and climax. We reach that climax in the description of the sixth day. After substantial accomplishments early in the day featuring the creation of all manner of land-dwelling animals, cattle, reptiles, wild and domestic beasts, and having pronounced that work "good," God issues a bulletin announcing further developments:

> And God said: Let us make a being in our image, after our likeness, and let them have dominion over the fish of the sea and the birds of the air, and over the cattle, over the earth and over every creature that crawls upon it. *(Genesis 1:26)*

Never before had God sent out prior notice of the intention to create anything. During the first days of creation, God simply did it. This broadcast of contemplated labor signals to the listener, in the words of Monty Python, "And now for something completely different." The advance notice calls the listener to apply heightened attention to the subsequent proclamation:

> Thus God created the human being in the divine image, creating it in the image of God, creating it male and female. (*Genesis 1:27*)

Unlike every other known account in the ancient world and unlike any account of creation proposed by modern science, the account in the Torah has the distinct purpose of defining the nature of the human essence in exalted terms. In the key phrase, *B'tzelem Elohim*, in the image of God, as applied to the singular, unique first human being, lies a bold affirmation at the core of Judaism. The meta-principle of human creation *B'tzelem Elohim* has far-reaching implications.

On the creation of the first human being, midrashim abound. Some go to the heart of the Torah's daring claim that humans contain within them something of their Creator. In one midrash, the heavenly angels, forewarned about God's plan to make a being in the divine image, become jealous. "What a waste. What could God possibly be thinking?" Appalled by the proposed plan, the angels decide to hide the divine image. But where could they hide it? One angel suggests: "Let's place it on the top of the tallest mountain." Another offers: "Let's hide it under the deepest of the seas." Finally, the most clever angel of all proposes: "This human is ambitious. He will search high and low for this treasure. Let us hide it within the soul of the human being. That is the last place that he will think to look for it."

The soul of each human being is that which contains the divine spark. If only we would see it in ourselves and in others. If only we would realize how close, how attainable is the greatest treasure of all, the divinity within our humanity. For if we would see it, we would realize how precious are our own lives and the lives of all others. If we would discover that spark of divinity within, then the notion of life's sanctity would become primary in our constellation of values.

In the description of the creation, the phrase *Tzelem*—image—occurs twice. Are there two facets to the divinity implanted in the human being? Perhaps. Consider a second midrash:

> Hillel the Elder has concluded his Torah studies for the day and walks away from the Beit Midrash accompanied by his students. They ask him, "Master, where are you going?" "To perform a religious obligation," he responds. "And what religious duty is that?" they inquire. "To wash in the bath house," he responds. "That's a religious obligation!" "Yes," replies Hillel. "If the statues of kings which are erected in theaters and circuses are scoured and washed by the man appointed and paid to look after them and who is honored for the high status of his role, then how much more I, who am formed in the Image and Likeness." (*Leviticus Rabbah 34:3*)

Not only is the soul the repository of divinity, but so too is the body. If so, then we must take seriously the injunctions of our tradition to care for our own, not only because doing so is good for us but because care and respect for our bodies befits the royalty they inherently deserve. So too must great respect be paid to the physical requirements of others. If divinity rests in the human body then the body is sacred in and of itself. The physical and material needs of our fellow earth-dwellers become sacred obligations.

Another way to draw out the implications of the Torah's account of the creation of our singular ancestor highlights the singularity itself in combination with the quality of divinity. As Nechama Leibowitz puts it: "Every individual is equally significant before God, since every [person] was created in [God's] image" (*Studies in the Book of Genesis*, p. 3). As the Talmud relates:

> Therefore Adam was created on his own, to teach you that whoever destroys one soul is regarded by the Torah as if he had destroyed a whole world and whoever saves one soul, is regarded as if he had saved a whole world. (*Mishnah Sanhedrin* 4:5)

I remember reading that economists had once ascertained that the body of a human being had a market value of about $2.63. No doubt, inflation has since increased the amount. However, the Torah teaches us to ignore market conditions when placing a value on human life. Among its dimensions, sanctity of life implies the infinite worth of each and every human being.

Furthermore, the singularity of the first human points to at least one more pivotal concept. As the same Talmud passage tells us:

> For this reason Adam was created alone, for the sake of peace among people, so that one person should not say to his/her fellow: my ancestor was superior to yours. (*Mishnah Sanhedrin* 4:5)

Among the challenges facing one seeking to reclaim and revitalize our faith are some very human traits, tendencies that in fact find supportive expression in the teachings of our sacred literature. When studied under too dim a light, such teachings can yield virulent results. Specifically, when regarding the other, the one not of our group, two interrelated human tendencies emerge: the assertion of superiority and the stigmatization or debasing of the other.

When we Jews tell our story, we assign to our ancestors and to ourselves a unique relationship with God, characterized by the notions of chosenness and covenant. By these concepts we see ourselves as especially privileged and particularly obligated. As for the Gentile, one can find in our tradition both universal, positive expressions (that most of us would applaud) and also those that are exclusivist (and to which many would take exception). All of these can be better appreciated and understood with an analysis of the historical circumstances that produced them.

To take just one difficult and problematic example: when we quote the Psalms at our Passover Seder, calling on God, "Pour out Your wrath on the nations who knew You not," the words strike most of us as harsh and dissonant. Most of us live comfortably with our non-Jewish neighbors and do not constantly fear for our property or our lives. But imagine if our village had just been ransacked by Ukrainian peasants, if our synagogue had recently been burned once again by government-supported thugs, if our daughters had been violated and our sons murdered before our eyes. In such a setting, the angry words quoted in the Haggadah would not seem too harsh. If so, then even in the comfort of my cozy split-level home, I might repeat the angry words not because I mistrust or fear my neighbor, but because I remember the powerlessness, pain, and desperation of my ancestors who required such prayers.

Thus, it should not surprise us that the Biblical and rabbinic literature of our tradition contains assertions of Jewish superiority and the other's inferiority. Weak and impotent, often isolated and persecuted, and too frequently attacked by those in power throughout much of our history, some of the teachings of our tradition reflect these circumstances. Amazingly, the stronger and broader thrusts of Jewish teaching reflect not these voices of the powerless, but rather a deeper and confident faith in God and trust in humankind.

The teaching that the first human being was created in God's image is, I believe, the most significant, broad meta-principle of our tradition. It overwhelms and supersedes the tendencies to build ourselves up by putting down the other. Set in the ethical foundation of Jewish thought, the idea of creation *Tzelem Elohim* cannot but help us see in the faces of our fellow humans, whether Jew or Gentile, men, women, or children, the image of the Holy One who fashioned us all. It cannot help but enable us to see the world of potential in each and every one of us. It cannot help but frustrate the impulse to demean, deny, harm, or kill one of our fellows, no matter how strongly we oppose what they think or what they do.

WHEN LIFE IS UNFAIR
Rosh Hashanah 5762/2001

On the morning of the first day of Rosh Hashanah, in keeping with its dominant theme of remembrance, we Jews study *Genesis Chapter 21*, no doubt because of the opening phrase: *"Adonai Pakad Et Sara*—God remembered Sarah." That is to say, God remembered that if God is to make good on the covenantal promise to Abraham and Sarah by blessing them through progeny, and if that promise means a child other than Ishmael, then He had better arrange a miraculous pregnancy for Mother Sarah. Such remembering of promises, blessing, and covenant fulfilled fits nicely into the master equation of these Days of Awe whereby we strive to turn and return and repent while, at the same time, we seek to trip the divine memory switch and stimulate the release of God's affection and mercy.

In zeroing in on the positive holiday themes embedded in this narrative, our rabbinic ancestors did not ignore other, more challenging and problematic thematic elements related to the unseemly dismissal by Abraham and Sarah of Hagar and her son Ishmael, apparently for reasons of jealousy. One cannot help but feel sympathy for the mistreated Hagar, on the one hand, and disappointment in the flawed characters of our ancestors, on the other.

But there it is for all to see: Hagar receives unfair and cruel treatment at the hands of prominent Biblical heroes. The foreign woman has suddenly outlived her usefulness and is now subject to expulsion. Hagar cannot help but ache at the unfairness of her situation as she cries out, "Let me not look on as the child dies." We, the readers, witnesses to the scene, sympathize with her plight; we are on her side.

As one reads the tale, one finds in it historical resonance with the unfairness experienced by mothers and fathers across the generations, beginning even before Hagar with the first parents, Adam and Eve, who had to look on as one son perished at the hand of another. In the case of Hagar, God opens her eyes and she sees the well of rescue. But for Adam and Eve and for far too many parents down through the ages, there has been no well of rescue, no saving response to the anguished cry. Can we read this narrative of anguish and pain without thinking of those we know, relatives, friends, and neighbors, who have suffered painful and unanticipated losses?

How does one make sense of life's unfairness? How does one respond to it? The narrative of today's Torah portion raises the question but provides no clear answers. We are left with a deep sense of existential unease, exaggerated, it seems to me, by the holiday's central theme of judgment by God and by self, judgment that assumes a universe of fairness. How are we to respond when life seems devoid of fairness?

The Jewish theologian Neil Gillman once questioned a friend, a Catholic priest who had just retired after over five decades as a church pastor, "What have you learned in all your years of listening to your people emptying their hearts to you in confession?" Replied the priest: "I have learned two things that I did not anticipate when, as a youth, I was called to the priesthood: I learned that there is a great deal more pain and suffering in the world than I had ever imagined. I also learned that no one is an adult."

The Torah sometimes presents us with a world of ideals, where good will be rewarded with a bountiful life and evil will be punished. But we often do not experience such a world. As seven-year-old Sam Lamott, son of author Anne Lamott, once said, "I think I already understand about life: pretty good, some problems" (*Traveling Mercies*, p. 145). And, one might add, at times the problems seem to outweigh the "pretty good." The pain and suffering of the world abound. In the face of it, we do not feel any sense of adult competence. Rather, it befuddles us, overwhelms us, even threatens at times to bring us down into the depths of unremitting despair.

There is an old folk tale that tells of a sorrowing woman who came to a wise man with the heartrending plea that he restore to her the life of her only son who had suddenly died.

> The wise man told her he could consider her tragic request on one condition. She would have to bring him a mustard seed taken from a home entirely free from sorrow. The woman set out at once on her quest. She went from house to house, from family to family, from city to city. Years elapsed and she did not return.
>
> One day the wise man chanced upon her, but he hardly recognized her, for now she looked so radiant. He greeted her and then asked her

why she had never kept their appointment. "Oh!" she said in a tone of voice indicating she had completely forgotten about it. "Well, this is what happened. I went everywhere searching for that mustard seed you told me about. And wherever I went, I came into homes so burdened with sorrow and trouble that I just could not walk out. Who better than I to understand how heavy was the burden they bore? I felt I knew what they were going through. Who better than I could offer the sympathy they needed? So I stayed on in each home as long as I could be of service." Then she added apologetically: "Please don't be angry, but once I saw what other people were going through, I forgot all about the mustard seed and our appointment."

Well, Jewish tradition also addresses the awareness of life's unfairness. Whereas the Torah often asserts a simple system of divine retribution—do what God wants and you shall prosper; fail to obey and your crops will dry up—the Book of Job puts the matter quite differently. When the pious Job becomes stricken with more undeserved suffering than anyone could possibly bear, his friends seek to "comfort" him by insisting that his suffering must signal his sinfulness. Their logic is unassailable: it derives from the Torah, which they know well and which teaches that those who sin will suffer and that those who live according to God's way will prosper; if so, suffering must signal sin and prosperity must signal piety. QED. Job's friends are not illogical; they are simply wrong.

I enter dangerous waters. There are those who say, "Suffering has purpose." Christianity, as you know, builds a theological universe on the value of suffering and the ultimate salvation that comes from suffering. Even in Judaism, there is room for suffering valued positively. A Talmudic idea, *Isurim shel Ahaval* the afflictions of love, refers to the suffering of the pious as God's application of suffering to those who can handle it and who will, in some unplanned and unexpected way, benefit from it. When suffering is valued in such a fashion, at least we do not blame the victim for the pain she or he endures. And yet I join those who reject the notion that God tinkers with our lives in such a manner, by doling out bounty or suffering as the case may warrant. As I regard the small section of the universe I occupy, suffering seems much more random and completely devoid of moral value. Honesty compels me to say that suffering has no meaning in and of itself.

Yet if suffering has no purpose, no meaning, as I claim, how does one address those in pain, the Hagars among us? Rabbi Hirshel Jaffe, a rabbi who, in the peak of physical conditioning, used to run marathons, was suddenly stricken with leukemia. He wrote a book entitled *Why Me? Why Anyone?* Jaffee found in his suffering much learning, about himself, about the capacity for human beings to care for one another, about the normal "miracles" performed every day by those who practice medicine and those who advance its potential to cure or relieve physical pain, and about the many noble dimensions of the human spirit. In his own suffering, Jaffee became more attuned to the pain of others and to the significance of every moment of every day. He writes: "I didn't choose my illness; I didn't ask for this painful experience. But I can choose my attitude toward it; I can forge my own response to it. Since it is happening to me, I can choose to make the best of it; I can use it and learn from it and grow from it, shape it into a positive force in my life" (p. 192).

Suffering, I claim, has no inherent meaning. However, in the response to suffering there can be tremendous growth and purpose. Even in cases of extremis. The famous psychiatrist Victor Frankl observed his fellow inmates in the Dachau concentration camp. By and large, those inmates had little control over the suffering they incurred; in fact, they had little control over any aspect of their lives. They could, however, choose the attitude by which they would respond to the horrendous conditions in which they found themselves; attitude is a small thing, invisible, but it makes all the difference.

"*Hakol Netunah V'reshut Panui*—All is foreseen and free will is given." The most enigmatic of the teachings found in *Pirke Avot* obtains. *All is foreseen*—there is an overlay of divine perspective into which all things fit, but *free will* is given—we human beings, even when circumstances confine us, can choose to respond by our actions or, at the very least, by our attitudes. By our choosing, we express our freedom and our humanity.

Ultimately, we err when we try to explain the aspects of experience that fall in the realm of mystery. Job knew that his friends failed to understand the cause of his pain, but neither could he grasp it. Nor do we. The beauty of the Book of Job and, in my opinion, the reason it resonates still is that to the insistent demand "Give me the meaning of my suffering!" no simplistic answers come forth, no answers at all. No answers are presented because none that could be given would match the lived human experience. In appearing out of the whirlwind, God provides Job with the comfort of divine presence but fails to satisfy the eager seeker after ultimate meaning. "Where were you when I laid the foundations of the earth?" hardly explains why Job had to endure years of pain and agony or if his suffering had cause or purpose. Rather it strikes one as the classroom teacher responding to a premature question: "Excellent question, but we're not going to go there; you haven't taken Advanced Calculus or Organic Chemistry yet. The language in which a response could be provided is not one you yet comprehend."

So life is unfair in large measure; people suffer without deserving their suffering. And yet, as Rabbi Morris Adler once put it:

> Sorrow can enlarge the domain of our life. Our sorrow can bring understanding as well as pain, breadth as well as the contraction that comes with pain. Out of love and sorrow can come a compassion that endures. . . . Sorrow can enlarge the domain of our lives so that we may now understand the triviality of the things many pursue. . . . What is important is not luxury but love; not wealth but wisdom not gold but goodness.

Finally, says Adler:

> Our sorrow may so clear our vision that we may, more brightly than before, see the God of Whom it was said "The Lord is close to them that are of a broken heart. . . ." There is a God in a world in which human beings could experience tenderness. There is a God in a world in which two lives can be bound together by a tie stronger than death.
>
> Out of that vision will come a sense of obligation . . . to spread love . . . to share joy . . . to ease pain. . . . There is work to be done and in work there is consolation. Out of love may come sorrow. But out of sorrow can come light for others who dwell in darkness. And out of the light we bring to others will come light for ourselves—the light of solace, of strength, of transfiguring and consecrating purpose. ("Sorrow Can Enlarge the Domain of our Life," *Lights from Jewish Lamps*, pp. 312–313)

For the Hagars of the world, life contains pain, suffering, and unfairness. During these Days of Awe and always, may our response to their suffering and our own be one that enlarges us and brings us clarity of vision about what truly matters.

REGARDING THE LAW
Shabbat Mishpatim 5763/2003

Parashat Yitro describes the receiving of the Ten Utterances (or Commandments). As an experience of high drama, stark power, and pyrotechnics, one would be hard-pressed to top the Sinaitic revelation. Yet, following the high drama at Mount Sinai, the Torah continues to spin out narrative and to elaborate mitzvot in the form of rules and regulations, laws and precepts, until we arrive at 613 of those mitzvot. Hence, in Parashat Mishpatim, the section that immediately follows Yitro, we encounter numerous laws dealing with a wide range of subjects, including the treatment of slaves, the consequences of murder, individual liability in cases of damage or neglect, concern for the stranger and the poor, the standards of fairness required of judges, and on and on.

Taken all together, the array of laws found throughout the Torah invites one to consider one's attitude toward the totality of law, in all of its breadth and complexity, as it has evolved in Jewish tradition. In large measure it is the nature of one's attitude toward Torah Law that defines one as a Jew. Hence, what follows is a brief exploration of some texts that reveal some of the attitudes toward the law as it found in Jewish tradition.

By way of literary foil, one might recall the famous passage from Franz Kafka's novel *The Trial*. In a section called "Before the Law," Kafka's protagonist journeys a long way in order to get to the Law. When he arrives, however, he finds it blocked by a gate guarded by a gatekeeper. Subsequently, with each and every entreaty to gain admittance, the gatekeeper demurs and does so for the remainder of the protagonist's life, which is spent in the same spot, just outside that gate. As his final moments draw near, the protagonist, who has tried every means to bribe his way in, asks why, in all the years of waiting for admission, he has never seen anyone else approach the gate. The gatekeeper bends down to the dying man and informs him that the gate is his personal gate and that it will now be shut.

To Kafka's wretched protagonist, the Law, though it beckons with enticing mystery, remains forever maddeningly inaccessible, foreboding and depressingly remote, qualities that snuff out any possibility of attaining purpose or understanding in a finite life. Kafka's Law exists in a world of extreme isolation; the door that blocks one's admission is uniquely constructed for social isolation. In this world, one stands alone in insufferable waiting and longing. Kafka's Law is oppressive and arbitrary, a source of misery and suffering. By comparison, how does Jewish tradition regard the imposition of Torah Law? What qualities does it impute to that law, and how does Torah Law impact the life of the one who submits to it?

Not surprisingly, Moses ascribes to the Torah qualities that diametrically oppose those of Kafka's Law. In *Deuteronomy 30*, Moses asserts, "This instruction which I enjoin upon you this day is not too baffling for you, nor is it beyond reach. It is not in heaven.... Neither is it beyond the sea. ... No, the thing is very close to you, in your mouth and in your heart, to observe it." The rabbis of Talmud expand on this Mosaic idea of accessibility as follows:

> "As for God, His word is purifying" (*Psalms 18:31*). Rav said: Precepts were given only so that mortals might be purified by them. For of what concern can it be to the Holy One whether, in [preparing his meat], a man slaughters an animal at the windpipe or at the gullet? Or of what concern is it to Him whether a man eats animals that are unclean or animals that are clean? Hence, precepts were given only so that mortals might be purified by them. *(Babylonian Talmud, Shabbat 130a)*

`In my role as a rabbi who often encounters skepticism about the value of ritual observance, I sometimes hear comments such as "Why would God possibly care whether I eat a Big Mac or not?" or "What difference does it make to God whether or not I say a *bracha* over candles as Shabbat begins?" The question can be posed about any ritual observance: "How can my ritual observance possibly serve any function whatsoever for God who is completely self-sufficient?" To such a question, passages such as the one above reply that the rituals benefit not God but us. As Rambam put it: "The purpose of the *mitzvot* is ... to promote compassion, loving-kindness, and peace in the world."

Another rabbinic passage expands further:

The precepts were given to Israel for no reason other than for Israel to stay alive, for it is said of the precepts, "Which if a man do, he shall live by them" (Leviticus 18:5)—live by them and not die by them. Therefore, when there is danger to life, no precept is to be insisted on except those prohibiting idolatry, unchastity, and murder. (*Tosefta Shabbat 16:17*)

This passage famously extends and interprets the phrase *V'Chai Bahem*—and you shall live by them, so that it forms the basis for one of the meta-principles of Jewish Law. Namely, when life is endangered, one may suspend one's obligations to perform all but three of the mitzvot. That is to say, the laws of Torah are meant to enhance life not to diminish it or to impose harsh or confining restrictions upon it.

And further:

"He declares His word unto Jacob" (*Psalms 147:19*). . . . Rabbi Shimon said in the name of Rabbi Hanina: What God did may be illustrated by the parable of a king who had before him a table set out with all kinds of dishes. When his first servant entered, he gave him a slice [of meat]; to the second he gave an egg, to the third some vegetables, and likewise to each of the others. But when his son came in, he gave him all that was on the table before him, saying to him, "To the others I gave only single portions; to you I put all that is here at your disposal." So also the Holy One gave to the nations only some commandments, but when Israel arose, He said to them, Behold, the whole Torah is yours," as Scripture affirms: "He has not dealt so with any nation." (*Psalms 147:20*) (*Exodus Rabbah 30:9*)

That is to say, the rabbis regard the Torah not as a burden but as is a gift. Its abundance ought to be regarded as the happy result of familial inheritance. Mitzvot, like food, provide sustenance. In the image of the midrash above, other peoples received some morsels of food, but the people of Jacob/Israel was given the keys to the cupboard. For that, we Jews should feel overwhelming gratitude.

A final rabbinic text pertaining to attitudes toward the Torah and its laws:

Rabbi Abba said: In the Torah there are two hundred and forty-eight positive commandments, as many as the parts of the human body. Each and every one of these body parts cries out to the individual, saying: Perform through me the commandment that applies to me, so that by its merit you will stay alive and your days will be long. And [in the Torah are] three hundred and sixty-five negative precepts, as many as the days in the solar year. Every day that the sun shines, and until it sets, the sun cries out, saying to the individual: I decree upon you in the name of Him who has brought your days to this day, do not commit a transgression during my span of hours, lest you tilt the scale for yourself and the entire world, all of it, toward the side of guilt. Thus you come to a total of six hundred and thirteen Commandments. (*Midrash Tanchuma*)

Thus, the rabbis see in the numeric 613 a symbol of total spatial and temporal commitment out of which arises vast potential for transcending life's pitfalls. Far from regarding the Torah's law as oppressive or isolating, the rabbis view it as the means for seeking life's highest and most fulfilling purpose. We too may come to view it not as Kafka's protagonist standing before a cold and foreboding Law, but as a precious and life-enhancing gift that is "very close," in our mouths and in our hearts.

FROM THE DIARY OF ABRAHAM
Parashat Noach 5764/2003

It is over. The discussion, that is. If it really was a discussion where one talks and the other listens and then responds, back and forth until each concurs or disagrees or just grows tired. I never really know for sure if my discussions with the Holy One, Blessed be He, are real discussions. Sometimes I sense that my speech has been scripted for me, that what feels like an expression of choice or desire are simply the lines of dialogue that go with my role.

But this time it did feel different, like I, Abraham, engaged in a real discussion with God. I, Abraham, the first and only one to recognize the unifying force in the universe, the supreme power beyond all the natural bodies, behind all the human fabrications in front of which others bow and pay homage, I know that God is not a planet, not the moon, not the sun, and not a statue or anything we humans can see or touch.

This time, as I said, I had a real discussion with the *Ribbono Shel Olam*, the Master of the universe. When the Supreme Being informed me of the divine intention to destroy the city of Sodom and all its inhabitants, I spoke up in a flash, delivering inspired words that arose from deep within me: "*Ha-af Tispeh Tzadik Im Ha-rasha?*" Will You sweep away the righteous with the wicked?" (*Genesis 18:23*).

I don't know what possessed me. I had never before challenged the Almighty. Now that I think of it, who did I think I was to suggest that God might have made an error of discernment? Ah, the arrogance of youth! But I didn't stop with a simple challenge. No, I could not stop myself. I began to bargain with the Creator of the universe on behalf of the innocent and righteous people who might get caught in the carnage. "What if there are fifty righteous people in the city?" I asked. "Will you wipe out the place and not spare it for the sake of the fifty? *Chalila L'cha Mei-asot Kadavar Hazeh L'hameet Tzadik Karasha; Chalila L'cha Hashofet Kol Ha-aretz Lo Ya-aseh Mishpat?!* God forbid that You should do such a thing, destroying the righteous and wicked alike! God forbid that the Judge of all the earth should not act justly!"

I love that last line: God forbid that the Judge of all the earth should not act justly! But amazingly, the Master of the universe seemed to accept my gambit and agree to its terms: if fifty righteous could be found in Sodom, the divine hand would be stayed. I felt so empowered, you cannot imagine! So I persisted: what if there are not fifty righteous but only forty-five? Okay? How about sparing the city for forty? It was a deal. For thirty? Again, a deal. I was on a roll. For twenty? How about for ten? For the sake of only ten righteous people, God would withhold His wrath and spare the city of Sodom.

I stopped at ten. I felt that my point had been made and I could stop pressing: God should spare the city for the sake of a community, minimally ten, of righteous people. It does not matter that, with the exception of my nephew Lot and his family, not one righteous person would be found in all of the city. The lesson had to come out: the Judge must act justly. As earlier reported, the story ends there.

What had not previously been reported and what I shall now reveal is the follow-up, the conversation that never made it into the sacred text. During several successive nights of fitfulness and unease, I began to think I had let the matter drop too soon. Rather than forcing the issue, I had given in. Rather than make a case for righteousness, I had missed an opportunity at spiritual growth.

And so, in my distress, I called out once more to the Holy One of Blessing: "Why must the city be destroyed at all? Even if no righteous people dwell in Sodom, why must You destroy the city?

"Did You not teach me that in the distant future a prophet would arise, Ezekiel by name, and declare in Your name: 'as I live, says the Lord God, it is not the death of the wicked I seek but that they turn from their ways and live. Turn back, turn back from your evil ways!' (*Ezekiel 33:11*)? True, Ezekiel addresses the House of Israel and not Gentiles, much less barbaric pagans like those residing in Sodom. But I also recall that at another time, You taught me about another prophet who would come onto the scene, not someone of great stature or gravitas like Ezekiel or Isaiah or Jeremiah, but a more ordinary member of the prophetic guild. I forget his name. No, I remember. It is Jonah. You intended to send Jonah to prophesy to the wicked pagans of Nineveh, that they would be destroyed for their evil ways.

"But here's the thing: they don't die. They repented and You spared them. Jonah, meanwhile, tried to escape the whole business in the first place because he anticipated the outcome: he would prophesy doom, the people would repent, and You would lighten up and show mercy; his reputation would be 'down the tubes.'

"So the question remains: why not give the dwellers of Sodom the same chance to repent? You told me once that there were a small number of things, six I think, that preexisted the creation of the world: one of those preexistent things was repentance, the capacity to change and then be forgiven. That means that even before the world and before human beings, You planned for human failings, shortcomings, failures, wickedness, and sin. Even before there were people, You created a process for the weak and the wicked to turn away from their misguided wickedness and find a pathway back to You. That is the message of Ezekiel. That is the lesson of Jonah's story. So why, then, did Sodom have to be destroyed without a chance at repentance?"

I was not bargaining this time. I was not trying to turn a clever phrase. I really wanted to know why the wicked could not be given a second chance.

"Abraham, Abraham," came the weary but gentle voice. "With all your clarity of vision and all your instincts for kindness and generosity, there is so much you do not know and cannot know. You sound like another of my children, Job, who sought answers for some of life's most difficult questions, for unexplained and unjustified suffering. If you would like a glimpse of what is at stake, turn around and you shall see!"

So I turned around and found myself on a railroad platform. Stern-faced soldiers stood on the platform speaking a language I knew somehow to be German. The soldiers shouted at the prisoners who tumbled out of tightly packed freight cars of the train that had just pulled up to the station. The disheveled and frightened prisoners wore yellow, six-pointed stars. I asked one of them who they were and why they were being treated so roughly. In furtive whispers, he told me that they were Jews, children of Abraham, and that the German soldiers were Nazis who meant to rob them of their human dignity and then their lives. Before I could learn any more, one of the soldiers yelled, "No talking!" He then lifted his rifle and shot. The man, who minutes before had spoken nervous words, crumpled to the ground.

As I stood on the railroad platform, I witnessed many other horrors, but the pain of their recollection is too great and I would rather not call them to mind. Suddenly, I found myself in my own place and time.

Before I could say a word or ask a question or demand an explanation for the cruelty I had just seen, the calm, quiet voice of the Almighty murmured in my ear: "Abraham, some human evil is so great, some cruelty so harsh, some immorality so extreme as to place the perpetrators beyond the power of repentance. More than that, you may not know. More than that, I will not say."

FATHER JACOB AND UNCLE HO
Shabbat Toldot 5771/2011

Many commentators have pointed out that rather than provide us with exemplary mythic ancestors, characters with consistently high moral fiber, steadfast faith, gentle hearts, and heroic spirits, the Torah instead depicts the founding fathers and mothers of our Jewish faith in many colorations, some positive, some negative, with some noble, gentle, and heroic attributes, but also with many other qualities far less flattering, including examples of selfish, greedy, ungenerous, and morally obtuse behavior.

The Torah reserves its least flattering patriarchal portrayal for Jacob, whose story begins in Parshat Toldot with the description of Jacob and Esau's birth. The Torah's account commences with struggle and conflict—as the twin brothers strive with each other even while still in the womb of their mother—and then turns on deceit and cunning, themes that play and replay throughout Jacob's life. Hence, one cannot help but observe that the Torah establishes in its foundational narration heroes with obvious defects of character. If so, Jacob, who as Israel will give his name to the entire people, surely manifests the most noticeable flaws of character. I wish to reflect on some implications of possessing a foundation myth whose central player displays such flaws by contrasting it with an alternate image of a founding father, one that lingers in my consciousness after a recent visit to Vietnam.

As a point of contrasting reference, then, let me characterize the public representations of Ho Chi Minh, the founding father of Vietnam, as I experienced them in various museums in Hanoi and through the countryside of the north. Before his death in 1969, Ho successfully led the Viet Minh communists in overthrowing the French and later masterminded the war against the United States and its allied regime in South Vietnam. Obviously, one's opinions of his accomplishments and personal character may well depend on one's predilections and political persuasions. However, anyone would admit that this man led an extraordinary life, accomplished many of his goals, and may well have improved the lives of many Vietnamese. However, he also engaged in violent purges directed at rival organizations in the 1940s and, in the 1950s, following the defeat of the French, imposed a harsh program of Maoist- and Stalinist-inspired land reform in which thousands of his fellow countrymen were persecuted, murdered, or forced to flee. Many Vietnamese remember him as a brutal despot. That is to say, not surprisingly for a revolutionary leader contending for power and ideological control in a period of political turmoil, a dispassionate portrait would include mixed and complex colorations.

However, as presented in national museums and other public displays, Ho Chi Minh, who is often referred to as "Uncle Ho," is remembered as a morally pure and benign leader, a scholar in the tradition of Confucius and an idealized pre-Confucian heritage, and a prescient proponent of universal education and technological development; indeed, he is treated as if he were still alive and overseeing a revived national culture. His brutality, when mentioned at all, is presented as uniquely directed toward the colonialist and imperialist foreign powers—France, China, Japan, and the United States—and at the local feudal potentates who illegitimately accepted their largess. Scholarly books that have presented Ho as a complex man, including his various liaisons, for example, have been censored. Furthermore, his body rests within an immense mausoleum where both Vietnamese pilgrims and tourists come to pay their respects (except during the months of October and November when it is removed to Russia for reembalming). It seems that Ho, in his death, has achieved mythic, if not semideistic, status. In its public representations, the myth of a pure, noble, and benign Uncle Ho has surely replaced the not quite so pure historic man.

Returning to the flawed patriarch, Jacob, and the implication of his flaws for the self image of those who regard him as his spiritual descendants, I would refer to the Hasidic commentary known as *Sefat Emet*, composed by Rabbi Yehudah Leib Alter, the third rebbe of Gerer Hasidim. It picks up on the two mentions of "love" in Genesis 25:28, which reads: "Isaac loved Esau, for he relished his venison, but Rebecca loved Jacob." Sefat Emet writes:

> Scripture gives a reason for Isaac's love; it was not true love, for it depended upon a particular thing. If that thing were to disappear, so would the love. Therefore when Jacob approached him with venison, his love for Esau disappeared.
>
> But Rebecca loved Jacob without reason, and her love lasted for ever.

... God's love for Israel is of the same sort. It does not depend on anything, not even ... deeds. God has simply chosen Israel.... Wherefore, Scripture [records the following dialogue]: "'I love you,' says the Lord. But you say, 'In what do you love us?' 'Was not Esau Jacob's brother,' says the Lord, 'but I loved Jacob'" (*Malachi 1:2*). This love does not depend on any reason. Israel [here meaning, Israel, the people] are just attached to God in their root. (*Language of Truth*, pp. 39–40)

As understood in Sefat Emet, God chooses Jacob not out of a conditional love akin to Isaac's love of Esau for his venison, but out of an unconditional love akin to Rebecca's love of Jacob. Jacob, in this view, brings nothing of merit or value to the table. God loves him in the way a parent loves a newborn who has as yet demonstrated no characteristics of worth. On the downside of this sort of love: because it is not grounded in any conditions, the subsequent covenantal choosing of Israel, the man, and Israel, the people, implies no special status. God does not love us for our venison or our righteous deeds or our dimples or any other attributes. The Jewish quality of chosenness, then, is simply a root condition for which we might offer thanks but have no cause to allow it to get to our heads. We may not even include it as an accomplishment or a skill on our resumes.

It would appear that the cost of asserting the purity of a founding father, at least in the case of contemporary Vietnam, is the requirement to suppress the truth about a complex and necessarily flawed human being. As we observed its representations, the love of dear Uncle Ho seems conditioned on a false image of the man and is maintained only by denying free and open inquiry. By contrast, since the God of Torah embraces our mythic but impure ancestors and, by extension, contemporary Jews, without conditions, without reservations, and without qualifications, no such suppression of inquiry obtains. As such, we may now count ourselves as fortunate recipients of a tradition that emerges from a flawed Father Jacob rather than one that requires a sanitized Uncle Ho.

EZEKIEL'S DRY BONES
Shabbat Chol Hamoed Pesach 5764/2004

The Haftarah for Shabbat Chol Hamoed Pesach, *Ezekiel 37*, with its famous image of the Valley of Dry Bones, arouses many questions, among them these two:

(1) The two verses before the vision speak of the reestablishment of the festivals of pilgrimage to Jerusalem. But the connection between the central image of the Valley of Dry Bones and the Pesach season is less obvious. What are the possible points of connection?

(2) With regard to its theme of resurrection, is the image in Ezekiel 37 meant by its author to be taken literally or nonliterally, as a parable or a metaphor?

Ezekiel probably lived a few years after the fall of Jerusalem in 586 BCE. It seems that he accompanied those who went into exile and that he subsequently prophesied among the exiles in Babylonia. Many regard his image of dry bones taking on life as reflective of optimism, a prophetic promise of national restoration and renewal. One might well regard Ezekiel's prophetic promise as parallel to the Exodus story of redemption. And if one understands Ezekiel's portrayal as less historical and more messianic, then we have a link between redemptions past and future, between paradigm and prophecy.

Digging a bit more deeply, one finds that the Binding of Isaac, as depicted in some midrashic traditions, becomes a connective link between the theme of resurrection and the Pesach season. First, Isaac's birth and binding are said to have taken place at this season. The tears of angels, in some midrashim, revive an Isaac already sacrificed. Hence, these reviving angelic tears both foreshadow and enable the redemption from Egypt. They both release the bound Isaac and allow for the generational continuity that leads up to the Exodus story.

Heavenly tears may evoke the supersessionist image from Mel Gibson's film *The Passion*, where the heavenly tear shed over the crucifixion cracks the foundation of the Jerusalem Temple, causing destruction and havoc for disbelieving Jews and an end to the favorable status they once enjoyed. In the Jewish parallel found in midrash, the heavenly tears shed over the bound Isaac perform a powerful healing as they prevent a tragic outcome and even intimate the possibility of ultimate victory over death itself. Extending this comparison further, one sees how the binding of Isaac becomes a vehicle for salvation in the rabbinic imagination much as does the crucifixion for Christians. Both images, according to Jon Levenson (in his *The Death and Resurrection of the Beloved Son: The Transformation of Child Sacrifice in Judaism and Christianity*) serve similar theological goals within their respective religious systems.

Continuing the theme of resurrection, seasonal Jewish liturgical insertions call attention to the dew of the spring season. One includes prayers for dew beginning with Pesach because as the rainy season in Israel ends, the much-appreciated dew is required for natural sustenance. Thus, even as the dew harkens back to those angelic tears, midrashically imagined, and in doing so, reminds one of resurrection past, it also symbolizes the cycle of rebirth and renewal in nature. When our daughter arrived a couple of days before Pesach, my wife and I had such associations in mind when we chose for her the name Talia, meaning "dew of God."

With resurrection and springtime dew, I would add the other important American symbol of rebirth, namely, baseball. I am among those for whom the renewal of spring is inextricably bound up with baseball. On opening day, the possibilities of a successful season loom large; my hopes for my beloved Giants have not yet been squashed by the long, hot summer of competition against superior teams, by subpar performances of key players, by injuries, or by other such disappointments that accompany most seasons. With the sunshine, warmth, and flowers of April come youthful optimism, joy, and hope born anew, resurrection of a sort, dry bones coming to life.

With the seasonal theme of resurrection, one might pair the observation that human passivity characterizes the Haggadah's telling of the redemption from Egypt. That is, the traditional text of the Haggadah emphasizes the role of God and God's outstretched and mighty arm and God's miraculous deeds. Even the heroic Moses has nearly no mention in the traditional Haggadah.

On the other hand, the ethical teachings that emerge from the exodus story insist on vigorous and active human agency in recognizing injustice in our time, in engaging in efforts to reduce injustice, to increase kindness, and to improve the world according to a godly vision. However, even here, even amid such lessons of active human agency, the theological metaphor behind this activism is one of human passivity and divine control: as slaves, we require God's strong hand to rescue us. We cannot do it on our own. So too with Ezekiel's optimistic vision of national revival: God will enact it as we stand by.

Two thoughts on the relative human passivity in these metaphors of revival, by way of conclusion. Firstly, Pesach tells of disenfranchised, bound, and powerless humans who require rescue by an outside Power. However, having achieved that freedom, the predicate that necessitates and enables the possibility of Torah is established. That is, the freedom passively acquired permits the active reception of Torah, by which freedom achieves purpose. In receiving Torah, the former slaves acquire responsibility for carrying on redemptive work. The next chapter in the story, the beginning of responsibility and human assertiveness, is told seven weeks later during the holiday of Shavuot.

Secondly, it is difficult for those of us living in relative comfort and freedom to fully appreciate, much less empathize with, the limited choices available to those striving to retain their human dignity when their mere survival is in doubt. One Haggadah records the story of a father and his son still interred in one of the Nazi concentration camps toward the end of World War II:

> The father suggested a pact between them to save part of what little bread they received. After several days, the father reported to his son sheepishly: "I am sorry but I have given away our whole store of bread to a new arrival." "Why?" asked the son in desperation. The father explained: "There are two reasons: first, he needed food even more than we and second, I exchanged the bread for a miniature haggadah." Several days later using this haggadah, the father conducted a seder for many of the inmates. Even though matza was unavailable, the seder gave everyone a special kind of nourishment—hope. (Zion and Dishon, *A Different Night*, p. 49)

From a perspective of comfortable distance, the act of the father, trading bread for a book, may seem foolish, or inconsequential. But, inside that camp, it may well have supplied the key to both survival and human dignity. As for us, American Jews dwelling in considerable ease yet also in the shadow of 9/11 and with anti-Jewish sentiment growing alarmingly throughout much of the world, I feel that we do sometimes regard ourselves as beaten and withered, spiritually akin to Ezekiel's vision of dry bones awaiting revival. If so, it is possible that the image of God's strong arm stretched out toward our tired bones could have particular appeal. Without it, from where would our hope for redemption come?

Baruch Attah Adonai Mechayai Hametim—Blessed are You Lord who gives life to the dead.

THE FINAL EXAM: DEALING IN FAITH
Rosh Hashanah 5758/1997

One question remains constant: we all want to know what will be on the final exam. According to the Babylonian scholar known as Rabbah, of the six questions that everyone will be asked during the final examination, on the day of judgment, the first will be: *Nasata V'nattata B'emunah*—Did you deal in good faith? Did you conduct yourself in matters of business and in personal relations in a trusting and fair manner? Did you conduct your affairs based on an awareness of the larger picture, the one constructed according to divinely determined dimensions? Did you live in such a way that faithfulness increased in the world? *Nasata V'nattata B'emunah*—Did you deal in good faith?

At first blush, it would seem that the question of dealing in faith is related to and perhaps depends on possessing certainty of faith itself. Surely, if one is to act faithfully it would help to have faith. It would seem that a nice, clear, simple, and reliable faith would really help. It shouldn't be too much to ask. It is the way most people understand the first of the Ten Commandments. But, for most of us, simple, clear, and reliable faith is not in the cards. We are either just not wired that way or the times conspire against it. As modernists, we require scientific certainties, proofs that are not forthcoming in this nonscientific realm. As postmodernists, even the "proofs" of science, were they available, would not suffice because we would deconstruct them out of existence.

We will discover, however, that not only do the doubts and worries that beset us not constitute final breaks with the Jewish community of faith, but they may even constitute something quite the opposite; they may signal the beginning of a kind of faith that encompasses doubt. We speak of the High Holiday season as one of *teshuvah*, of repentance, or more literally, turning, turning within to reflect and examine the state of our lives and our souls. But, the word *teshuvah* also means "response" or "answer," "the words returned in response to a question." Playing on these multiple meanings, then, I propose that the real task of this season, as in Rabbi David Hartman's conception, may not be to become a *Chozer B'teshuvah* (literally one who comes to the answers, and, colloquially, one who has become newly observant) but rather a *Chozer B'she-alah* (one who comes with the real questions).

Thus, I would opine that acting on faith or dealing in faith is certainly related to having faith and yet not being dependent upon it. In this vein, consider this legend about dealing in faith in the absence of faith:

> There was once an exceedingly evil and ugly king who was in love with an extremely beautiful and virtuous young woman whom he wished to marry. The evil king realized that in order to win the heart of the young woman, he would need to make certain changes for the sake of appearances. This he was more than willing to do, so in love with her was he.
>
> So first, the evil and ugly king obtained a mask, a handsome one, of course. Then, the king set out, against his nature, to do good deeds, not out of conviction, mind you, but solely in order to win the heart of the beautiful and virtuous young woman with whom he was madly in love. He began to visit sick people in the hospital and elderly people in the old age home; he set up a soup kitchen for the hungry and a subsidized housing project for the homeless; he established a jobs program for people who had no jobs (working with the private sector, of course) and a loan system so whoever needed a loan could obtain one. He smiled at children and helped infirm people to cross the road.
>
> Well, it worked like a charm. The young woman, unable to see beyond the mask, and not knowing that the good and kind deeds of the king were only "for show," grew to admire, respect, and, yes, even to love the seemingly righteous king. And so they got married. The king continued the charade of wearing the mask and doing kind deeds, because he still wanted the beautiful and virtuous young woman, now his wife, the queen, to love him.
>
> And so it went, for days, weeks, months, and years . . . until one day, the king felt that the charade could go on no longer. He could no longer live with the hypocrisy of his own evil and ugly true nature and the pretend exterior he had been living these past years. So, that very day, he called his wife to him and said, "I regret to tell you that I have been living a lie all these years, and the time has come to remove my mask so

I can reveal who I really am."

With that, he tore off the mask, only to find that his face, the face underneath the mask, had taken the shape and form of the mask; it was kindly and handsome. And the king and the queen lived happily and virtuously ever after.

It is often the case that commitment follows action, faith follows faithful deed. *"Na-aseh V'nishmah,"* said our ancestors in counterintuitive response to the commanding voice at Mount Sinai: "We will do and then we will understand—we will act as we must, and later on, we hope, we will internalize the message; we will first deal faithfully and, in time, we will acquire faith."

For many of us much of the time and for all of us some of the time, if our faithful actions had to depend on certain and solid faith, we would sink into a deep rut of paralyzing inaction, rendered impotent by the inability to know for sure what we ought to do with the opportunities that life affords.

To put this all a bit differently, consider the question posed bluntly: "Do you believe in God?" Now, consider this question: "When do you believe in God?" I have found that for many, the second question is much easier to answer in the affirmative. For some, it will call forth peak moments of our lives: thrilling moments of accomplishment, flashes of insight, profound experiences of friendship or love, miraculous experiences of creation, healing, beauty. Many people have been touched by an encounter with another, an encounter that leaves one with a sense of faith in humanity and even a sense of faith that, beyond all the evidence to the contrary, there is a transcendent presence just beyond one's ability to perceive it, a presence that somehow endows life with meaning and purpose.

Once, I was visiting our friend Joan in Seattle. We made plans to attend Friday night services, and she would drive. We set out with no time to spare for our twenty-five-minute drive, and we had just pulled out onto the highway, when I noticed the gas gauge was quite low. "Joan," I asked, "do we have enough gas to get there?" "I hope so," she replied, as I recalled that our friend Joan can be wonderfully oblivious to prosaic realities and has on several occasions run out of gas. This turned out to be one of those occasions. As the car sputtered to a halt, we coasted to the road's shoulder. I remember going through stages of disappointment at missing one of the rare and treasured opportunities I have to attend a Friday service as a congregant, then annoyance at Joan for her blithe disregard for the practical, and then, after sitting along the highway for about ten minutes, concern for how we were going to get back to Joan's house.

A moment later, a middle-aged woman pulled over to offer assistance. Gratefully, we accepted her kindness, and she drove Joan to a gas station while I remained with the car. Joan and the middle-aged woman were gone about twenty minutes, long enough for me to fantasize about all the dire scenarios that might ensue for Joan or me, yet they returned uneventfully with a container of gas. The kind stranger waited to make sure we could start the car and then drove off, but not before refusing our offer to pay her for her help, with the words, "What comes around goes around."

Indeed. What comes around goes around. I did not get to Kabbalat Shabbat services that evening, but I did witness a simple faithful act based not on any desire for reward but on the assumption that if individuals act in faith, then faithful action is spread in the world and the world thus becomes a more godly place. What comes around goes around.

Rabbi Harold Kushner tells of visiting with a rabbi in Puerto Rico and seeing a painting of Moses holding the Ten Commandments. When Kushner admired the painting and asked about its origins, he heard the following story:

> One day, years ago, the rabbi, then a rabbinic student in Israel, went into an art gallery in Jerusalem, saw the painting and liked it. He asked how much it cost, and when the owner told him, he said, "I'm sorry, that's more than I can afford." The owner reduced the price by about a third, but he still could not manage it. He explained, "I'm a rabbinical student from Buenos Aires. I'm here for a year of study. I'm not working. I won't earn any money until I get back home and go back to teaching Hebrew school." The owner said, "Fine, take the painting; when you get back home, you can send me the money." The student said, "How can you do that? You never met me until ten minutes ago. I live on the other side of the world. How can you be sure you'll ever be paid?" The owner said, "I can tell you are not the sort of man who will be able to look up at this painting every day, with Moses holding the tablet that says, 'thou shalt not steal!' and think to yourself, 'Ha, ha, I cheated a gallery owner out of a few hundred dollars.'"

And, sure enough, as soon as that rabbinic student returned home, he hung up the picture and sent the money off to Israel.

And there's a postscript. Years later, after taking a congregational post, a woman came up to the rabbi after a Friday night service and said, "I love this prayerbook. It's the best I've ever seen. I'd love to buy a copy and use it at home every Friday night." The rabbi replied, "no problem; come back Sunday morning, and get one at our gift shop." "That's the problem," said the woman. "We're only visiting here, and tomorrow we're leaving the country." The rabbi said to her. "OK, take the siddur and send us a check when you get home." The woman said, "You trust me to do that?" And he answered, "An art gallery owner in Jerusalem taught me that lesson. Someone who loves a Shabbat prayerbook that much isn't going to cheat a synagogue out of a few dollars."

Dealing in faith, then, is about acting in faith even in the absence of faith; it's about increasing trust and harmony in the world with no thought of reward; dealing in faith is taking a stand against cynicism, against triumphalism, against insularity, and against despair, traits to which most of us are prone from time to time or often. Dealing in faith is also self-replicating. What comes around goes around. Moreover, *Na-aseh V-nishmah*; by acting in faith, even in its absence, one often comes to the experiential awareness that there is a Source to the human impulse to act with generosity, with nobility, or with simple decency.

Did you ever notice how few academic Jewish theologians there are? Theologians are professionals who think about the nature of God. I wonder if that paucity has something to do with a quality of Jewish culture, a culture that does not include questions about the nature of God on the final exam. That is not to say that belief in God or faith in God is not a Jewish concern; it is. There are many of us like the Hasid with Rabbi Menachem Mendel who worry about the presence of evil and tragedy and a Judge and Judgment and how it all works. And that's good, but it won't be on the final exam.

We do want to prepare for the exam, though. Yet do so, must get to the realm of the pragmatic. However, at least one more lingering theoretical concern remains. Acting in faith in the absence of certain faith I can live with. However, I want to know: Just how good do I have to be? If I do not want high honors, just a passing grade, will I be expelled at the outset? About this, the Talmud (in *Tractate Makkot 24a*) makes a radical claim.

King David came and declared that 613 commandments were too many. He reduced them to eleven, which are enumerated in *Psalm 15*. We breathe more easily. The list of eleven concludes with the phrase: "the one who does these things will not be moved"; that is, will acquire a place in the World-to-Come. The Talmud then goes on to report that when the first-century sage Rabban ben Gamliel read this psalm, he would cry and say, "One who has done *all* these things shall not be moved?! It's still too much. No one can live up to the standard." His colleagues, though, comforted him, saying, "'The one who does these things' means one of these things, not *all* of these things."

Despite what some may claim, Judaism is not, and has never been, an all-or-nothing religion, one with inhumanly high standards. Therefore, starting today, simply act in faith! How? Pick a mitzvah; almost any one will do. Pick prayer. Okay, not all of Jewish prayer. Just one prayer will suffice. Okay, not the whole prayer. Pick, for example, "*Baruch Attah Adonai*." In all seriousness, a routine contemplation of this oft-repeated but challenging and mysterious phrase embodying a direct address to the Source of creation would be quite sufficient.

The last two summers while in Jerusalem, I stayed in the Scottish hospice, overlooking Mount Zion and the old city. On most mornings when I arose to davven in front of my window, I faced that magnificent scene. With the morning's first golden rays sparkling on the ancient stones before me, how could I not pause and consider anew the words I then uttered, the words preceding the Shema: "*Or Chadash al Tzion Ta-ir*—May a new light shine upon Zion." I could not get beyond those words. So too may you pick a phrase of prayer to own on any given day.

Or one may pick another mitzvah as a vehicle for dealing in faith. Regarding *tzedakah*, one might ask: "What would it mean to give charitably and live righteously?" Or one might pick *kashrut* and recall Marshall McLuhan's claim, "We are what we eat." What could it mean to eat as a Jew who wishes to conduct herself in faith?

One may pick even a peculiar mitzvah, like *shatnez*. About the largely neglected mitzvah of *shatnez*, of avoiding garments made of a linen-wool mixture, Rabbi Charles Arian once said to me, "When I buy new clothes, I read the label and pay attention to the material, the origin of the cloth and the place of manufacture, what I know about conditions for workers in that place, and not just the price." Even an odd and remote mitzvah may be worth considering. Perhaps *shatnez* may point us toward a Jewish way to consecrate the act of purchasing clothes. Imagine, shopping as an act of faith!

Visit a sick friend! Offer hospitality to a stranger! Join a Caring Committee of a synagogue! Help plan or implement a social action project! Look into the face of a stranger and give him or her the benefit of the doubt!

Preparation for the final exam requires ownership of mitzvot, not all of them, but at least one. So, pick one! Absorb it! Own it!

Even though faith itself will not be tested, dealing in faith will count heavily, even as it is appreciated by all who experience its capacity to enhance society and uplift its members. Not only will it count on the final exam, but ultimately, when all is said and done, it will lead to a faith-infused community, full of folks who have come to experience the trust that follows faithful deeds, who have removed the masks, as one day we all must, revealing the faces beneath, of kind and gentle shape.

THE HEAD II
The Binding of Isaac

THE FAILURE OF ABRAHAM
Rosh Hashanah 5754/1993

Broadly speaking, there are two approaches by which Jewish tradition interprets *Akedat Yitzhak*, the Binding of Isaac, that intriguingly difficult and problematic passage that we Jews read on the morning of the second day of Rosh Hashanah. From the perspective of the first approach, Abraham passes the tenth and last test of his faith with flying colors. Abraham's performance, according to this view, which demands the suppression of his fatherly inclinations in favor of obedience, becomes the paradigm for faith of the absolute variety. As such, we recall and evoke this tale, especially during the season of repentance, hoping to acquire some zechut avot, some of the merit of our faithful ancestor, seeking thereby to get on God's merciful side as these days of judgment unfold. No doubt we can use all the help we can get.

In this vein, the Danish philosopher Soren Kierkegaard applies the epithet "Knight of faith" to Abraham and refers to his act of supreme obedience as the archetypical "leap of faith." To Kierkegaard, Abraham's "leap of faith" sets the standard against which all religious faith must be measured.

The other approach, admittedly a narrower stream of our tradition, asserts that Abraham fails the test. In this view, God is not looking for Abraham's faithful obedience, but rather for his plucky refusal to commit a most heinous act, even if directed to do so by the Commander-in-Chief.

Thus, if one reads the passage according to the second perspective, one could then consider the "evidence" that lends credence to the notion that the binding of Isaac is a test that Abraham fails. And one could weigh the lessons or messages that emerge from that line of interpretation.

Among those who interpret *Akedat Yitzhak* as Abraham's failure are Andre Neher, Rabbi Harold Kushner, Woody Allen, and before them, the first rebbe of Ger, known by the title of his Torah commentary, *Sefas Emes*.

Kushner and Neher recall that this Abraham is the self-same fellow who argues vociferously against God when God announces His intention to annihilate the wicked city of Sodom. In that case, Abraham sets a bold example for all subsequent ages. In crying out for justice, in arguing against the One who established the principle of justice, Abraham inaugurates a tradition of religious protest, a tradition of contending with God for the sake of what is perceived as God's teachings. In the case of the *Akedah*, Kushner and Neher propose, God expects and hopes Abraham will refuse, will again protest, will storm the rafters of heaven, shouting for the same application of justice he had earlier demanded in the case of Sodom. Only when God sees that Abraham remains steadfast in his obedience, in his failure to object, does He move to intervene. In the humorous retelling of Woody Allen, God becomes appalled that Abraham could fall into mindless submission to a disembodied voice from heaven, just because it is deeply toned and resonant.

Sensitive to the subtleties of text, the Gerer rebbe observes that up until the *Akedah*, God and Abraham are on rather intimate terms, speaking to each other often. But from this event on, God never speaks to Abraham again. And at the scene of the *Akedah* itself, it is an angel, not God directly, who intervenes. Thus, on Mount Moriah, it may be said that God draws away from Abraham, as if in disapproval, ceasing to be his intimate companion, severing the lines of direct communication. If not an outright punishment for failing to adhere to clear principles of righteousness, it would appear that this distancing is at the very least a consequence. It is as if to say: God is close to those who behave in a godly fashion and distant from those who do not.

Understood in this manner, Abraham's failure, his silence, suggests what he ought to have done. He ought to have stood up; he ought to have refused; he ought to have shouted at God that what God was requesting was too much, unfair, more than a human should be asked to bear. He should have said that it is not fair or just to demand the sacrifice of a child, to set aside the interests of the child, for the visions or the dreams of the parent. He should have protested that the God to whom he pays allegiance could not possibly command this heinous act, this violation of a core principle of justice.

If Abraham had stood up in refusal of the unjust command, he would have maintained his tradition of protest. He would have continued to stand tall with Moses, Job, the Hasidic master Reb Levi Yitzhak of Berditchev, and others who have come to personify the Jewish tradition of protest, the proud tradition of contending with God.

How does Moses come to exemplify the proud tradition of contending with God? One might take the example of the golden calf scene in

Exodus 32. In that scene, when a disappointed God regards the Israelites dancing around the golden calf, He determines His intention to destroy them and informs His servant, Moses, of the plan that includes providing Moses with a substitute nation, presumably one better behaved, for him to lead to high honor and glory. Rejecting the idea of a better-behaved people to lead, Moses instead enters into argument and debate with God, employing numerous strategies, as if unsure of which, if any, will convince the Holy One to employ restraint, to curb the divine wrath. After considerable back-and-forth bickering comes the verse that prompts midrashic attention: "And now [God says,] let Me be, that My wrath may wax hot against them that I may destroy them" (*Exodus 32:10*). That is, God tells Moses to leave Him alone, to get out of His way, to stop arguing with Him so He can carry out the destructive goal.

The midrash starts out by addressing its concern that the merely human Moses could possibly be construed as being in almighty God's way. It reads:

> Does the verse imply that Moses was physically holding the Holy One, so that He had to say, "Let Me alone?" How may the matter be understood? By a parable of a king who became angry with his son and brought him into a chamber for punishment. There, as he began preparing himself to beat his son, he kept shouting loudly, "Let me alone, that I may beat him!"—so loudly that the boy's tutor, standing outside the chamber, heard. The tutor said to himself, "The king and his son are alone inside the chamber. Why does the king keep shouting, 'Let me alone,' unless he wants me to hear and to come in and plead on behalf of his son? That is why he keeps shouting, 'Let me alone!' Likewise, when the Holy One said, "Now let Me alone," Moses reasoned: Because the Holy One wishes Me to plead on Israel's behalf, He said: "Now therefore let Me alone." At once, Moses besought mercy on their behalf, leaving no corner of Heaven upon which he did not prostrate himself. (*Exodus Rabbah 42:9*)

That is to say, in the midrashic imagination, even in the midst of divine wrath, God really is on the side of humanity and really wants us to stick up for each other and for what is right, even if doing so requires standing in opposition to God Himself. On Mount Sinai, Moses, ever sophisticated in human and divine psychology, correctly perceives his role as advocate for the defense of Israel. On Mount Moriah, by contrast, in equating belief with blind observance, Abraham missed an opportunity to advocate for his own son and, in that failure, missed an opportunity to exemplify justified protest.

On Yom Kippur, Reb Levi Yitzhak of Berditchev would stand before the ark and cry out: "Ribono Shel Olam, Master of the Universe, what do You want from the people of Israel? Why do you pick on the people of Israel? Wherever one looks in the Torah it says, 'Command the people of Israel this way and command the people Israel that way!' It is enough already, Ribono Shel Olam. I, Levi Yitzhak son of Sarah, will not move from this spot until You say you are going to help the people of Israel!"

Much of what the Days of Awe are about is reengagement with, turning toward, opening up to the Source of life, the Fountain of existence, the Foundation of the cosmos. These days are about seeking and searching for hints of the Divine. These days are about awareness of God's presence, hidden as it may often seem. I would assert that turning, reengagement, opening up, and faith, do not preclude arguing and protesting. There is much to protest before God and humankind. Our list may differ in detail from that of Levi Yitzhak, but it should compel the same vehemence on our part. Should we not rail against the slaughter of innocent people, among them many children, in places like Bosnia, Somalia, Angola, Liberia, and Brazil? Should we not protest to God the destruction of property and lives by natural causes like flooding in the Midwest of our country or by typhoon in the Far East? Should we not protest against those who commit crimes of the intellect, those deniers of history who would rewrite the past for their own virulent aims, who would doubly victimize both the martyrs and the survivors of the Holocaust? Should we not argue against a world where children are born into a life without caring, without love, to teenage mothers and unknown fathers, a world full of drug abuse and physical violence? That world, everyone should realize, is an active subculture of our very own community. And we should protest. Faith demands that we do.

I am not saying that all of these are all primarily God's fault. Nor am I saying that all we should do is argue with and protest to God. Rather, I am saying, in all of these trials of life, among others, we can and ought to cry out in anguish, in protest, and in refusal to accept what sometimes seems to be God's decree, even as we admit our need for sources or the Source of inspiration, wisdom, guidance, strength, and perseverance, for the wherewithal to cope with a seemingly endless morass of trouble and woe.

And what if, and I guess here is the danger of protest against God, what if our protest should lead to denial? What if we should become so upset with God, with the plate of problems served up to us, that we decide simply to ignore Him or reject Her? Very quietly, I would suggest that such rejections of God may not be all bad. If they result from a dynamic engagement with the world, with a seeking after truth, then such rejections of what one perceives to be God might well serve as a healthy cleansing of the slate.

No less an eminent sage than the remarkable former chief rabbi of Palestine, Rav Abraham Isaac Kuk, once wrote an essay boldly praising the value and truth of atheism. For the most part, he declares, the god rejected by atheists is a god that ought to be rejected. Such rejection of false gods paves the way for a fuller, more sophisticated belief. Rejecting one's ideas of God may be a healthy and necessary step toward a more nuanced appreciation of the divine. Dynamic rejection or denial of God is, in this sense, says Rav Kuk, greatly preferable to unquestioning belief.

There was once a man who found himself drowning at sea. An ardent believer, he prayed to God for help. While he was praying, a coast guard boat came by and the captain offered the man a line. "No," insisted the man, "God will save me." And he continued to pray. A little later, a helicopter flew overhead and the pilot let down a line. "No thanks," said the man, "God will save me." The man drowned and went up to heaven, where he angrily confronted God. "Lord, I was drowning. I believed in you. Why didn't you save me?" Replied God, "But I tried. I tried to save you twice."

God desires and requires our active engagement, even if that engagement takes the form of protest or argument. Moreover, our arguments with God ought not stay in the passive, merely verbal realm. Particularly where the matter protested is close at hand, our protest can and ought to take the form of social action. We are, according to our tradition, called on to be God's partners and agents. Like Abraham at Sodom, like Moses witnessing the golden calf, like the people who prepare and serve food at the local soup kitchen, we garner divine approval, according to our tradition, when we articulate principles of righteousness and justice in our thoughts, in our words, and in our deeds, when we protest injustice, contending against God and humankind with every means at our disposal.

In this manner, from Abraham's failure to perceive the necessity of protest in the Binding of Isaac, emerges a lesson of righteous protest.

TWO PARADIGMS OF FAITH
Rosh Hashanah 5757/1996

Fire is dangerous and also extremely useful. Water is dangerous and also essential for life. So is air. In a similar fashion, the Torah is dangerous, even as it is both highly beneficial and essential to the life of a Jew.

That the Torah is necessary to the life of a Jew is axiomatic. To see that it can be dangerous, one need think no further than Yigal Amir, or Baruch Goldstein, or Meir Kahane, all Jews who took the Torah seriously and used it to justify extremist views or egregiously immoral deeds. If the Torah is dangerous, no text within it better illustrates its dangerous quality than that of the Torah portion in which Abraham heeds God's call to take his son Isaac up to the summit of Mount Moriah and there to bind him upon an altar as a sacrificial offering. The text is doubly dangerous because not only is it found in the heart of the narrative about the founding father of Judaism, but the passage comes to be highlighted and underlined by the post-Biblical tradition that assigns it a central place in the readings of these High Holy Days. Even the Reform *minhag* has retained its High Holiday usage, emphasizing it even more by moving it from Day Two to the center stage of Day One.

What makes a text dangerous? A text is dangerous if it promotes dangerous behavior on the part of those who take the text seriously. As such, the Binding of Isaac, on its face, justifies and lauds an act that, if it were to occur tomorrow in our locality, we would consider extreme, fanatical, barbaric, crazed, or all of the above. We would not applaud the contemporary parent who took his son or daughter for a sacrifice to God as a model of faith or piety.

How may one who takes Torah seriously render this dangerous text palatable? One might simply jettison it from the constellation of sacred literature. One might stop reading and studying it. Taking that approach, one would avoid its disturbing impact but would also miss the opportunity to continue the long and precious tradition of wrestling with disturbing sacred texts and allowing their valuable, but often hidden, dimensions to emerge.

One mode of textual redemption through reinterpretation was revealed to me this past summer by Yehuda Gelman, professor of philosophy at Ben Gurion University in Israel. Gelman picks up on some seemingly minuscule details found in several linked midrashim that bring Sarah into the narrative. One reads as follows:

> When Abraham returned from Mt. Moriah, Satan was angry because he saw that he had failed to achieve his desire to stop Abraham's attempted sacrifice. What did he do? He went and said to Sarah, "Oh Sarah! Have you not heard what has happened?" She said to him, "No." So he told her. "Your husband took the lad, Isaac, and brought him for a burnt offering, and the lad was crying and wailing that he could not be saved." Immediately, she began to cry and wail. She cried three cries corresponding to the three blasts [of the shofar] and three wails corresponding to the three ululations [of the shofar]. And her soul took flight and she died. (*Pirkei d'Rabbi Eliezer*)

This midrash draws a causal connection between the binding of Isaac and Sarah's death. It also relates our employment of the shofar on Rosh Hashanah not with the ram in the thicket, not with Abraham's faith (as do other midrashim), but with Sarah's anguished wail of protest against her husband and against God.

Another midrash puts Sarah's reaction as follows:

> When Isaac returned [after being bound on the altar] to be with his mother, she said to him, "Where have you been, my son?" He replied, "My father took me up mountains and down valleys, and took me up one of the mountains, built an altar, arranged the wood, prepared an offering place, and took a knife to slaughter me, and an angel called out to him [to stop]." And she said, "Woe unto my son! Were it not for the angel you would have already been slaughtered?" To which he answered, "Yes." At that moment she screamed six times corresponding to the six blasts [of the shofar]. (*Leviticus Rabbah*)

In the second midrash, Sarah does not die as a result of hearing of the binding of her son for a sacrifice, but she does let out a *geshrei*, a cry of protest against a horrible injustice committed in the name of piety. On the detail of Sarah's wail, Gelman hangs a theory about the religious faith one may derive from the narrative read side by side with these two midrashim. He derives two paradigms of religious faith, the paradigm of Abraham and that of Sarah. From Gelman's perspective, neither of the two taken alone will serve well as an adequate model for faith. When we focus on Sarah's faith, the faith embodied by her wail, we obtain a much-needed corrective to the faith of Abraham. Taken together, each provides a proper counterbalance to the other.

Consider Abraham. Gelman describes him as sacrificial man. He acts out the attribute of *chesed*, kindness or love, and takes that attribute to an extreme place, a place where most of us no longer recognize it as kindness or love at all. In its less extreme forms, Abraham is willing to deny his own pleasures in order to serve others. He does this in offering bountiful hospitality to the strangers who visit his tent. He does this when he defends his nephew Lot and when he takes up the cause of Sodom against God's intention to destroy it. The quality of *chesed* might produce a Mother Teresa or an Albert Schweitzer or a teacher in an inner-city school. Many of us could benefit from a healthy measure of the other-directedness entailed by *chesed*, a quality so foreign to a culture of narcissism.

However, taken to its extreme, raised to the level of absolute principle, *chesed*/love becomes self-denial, self-abnegation, even self-annihilation. Sacrificial man ultimately aims for self-transcendence, for union with the Almighty. To sacrificial man, transcendental union supersedes all other concerns or goals. As sacrificial man, out of absolute love of God, Abraham is willing to jump into the abyss, willing to offer up that which is even more precious to him than his own life, without thought of consequences or ramifications. In the same way, Yigal Amir was willing to spend his life in prison in order to achieve a high and, in his mind, divinely mandated purpose.

By contrast, Mother Sarah exhibits a faith based on *din*, on law and judgment. Sarah's highest goal is not union with the Almighty, but a recognition and validation of the multiplicity in creation. To live the attribute of *din* is to live in the fullness of each moment, to savor, know, and celebrate all of life's diversity, not to transcend self but to see eternity in a grain of sand and to make the most of each moment.

The author and essayist E. B. White once said: "If the world were merely seductive, that would be easy. If it were merely challenging, that would be no problem. But I arise in the morning torn between the desire to improve (or save) the world and a desire to enjoy (or savor) the world. That makes it hard to plan the day!" (Shenker, "E.B. White: Notes and Comment by Author")

If Abraham wants to "save" the world out his impulse for sacrifice, out of absolute love for the Almighty, then Sarah wants to savor the world by taking advantage of each and every moment. Sarah's wail is a protest against her husband, who would willingly toss away a future full of precious opportunities for beauty and mitzvah for the sake of a goal that negates the future.

I am reminded of a clergy meeting I once attended. We were planning a program on "spirituality and aging." One of the planners, a Presbyterian minister, objected to the term "spirituality," because, he said, in his denomination, the term had become a buzzword, evoking a heated conflict between two factions. One, the "pro-spirituality" faction, was primarily interested in addressing the inner void experienced by many, the sense that in all our busy-ness and with all that stimulates us, there is something seriously missing. And that something is encompassed by the term "spiritual." The "anti-spirituality" faction finds in the other group a hyperconcern for personal gratification at the expense of ethical concerns, too much concentration on the spirit of the self and not enough on the material and physical well-being of our fellow creatures.

Surely what is needed by the religious person is a balance between concern for the spirit of the self and a concern for the material welfare of the other. Surely what we want to attain is the ability to work at saving the world without giving up too many chances at savoring it. Surely what we require is both the ability to sacrifice and deny the self to some extent and also the ability to protest when the self or what is precious is being annihilated.

Jewish tradition sees the act of blowing the shofar on Rosh Hashanah and at the end of Yom Kippur as positively affecting our ability to do *teshuva*, to repent and to improve ourselves. It works in two ways. First, the shofar spurs the Jewish community to take the process of *teshuva* seriously. And, second, its sounds echo in the heavenly realms, causing the Almighty to render judgment with a kind eye. One midrash on the shofar's function describes the instruction to both *take* and *blow* the shofar (Vienna edition of *Pesikta Rabbati 166*). On this taking and blowing, Professor Gelman says that when we take the shofar, we call forth the image of Abraham *taking* Isaac, Sacrificial Man, Abraham, ready to go to the hilt for the sake of one kind of faith. However, when we blow the shofar, we imitate Sarah's wail against the intended death of her son. We imitate her cry to God to reject religious extremism that would sacrifice the future.

Thus, as Abraham has bequeathed to us the capacity to sacrifice, so has Sarah bequeathed to us the capacity to wail. Sarah has given us a faith rooted in the ability to cry out against injustice committed in the name of faith, against sacrificial man and his horrible deeds, against her much-regaled husband, and against the Yigal Amirs among us who claim to serve a higher cause.

Let the taking and sounding of the shofar inspire us to seek a faith of proportion and balance.

THE TEST OF THE TEXT:
THE BINDING OF ISAAC AND JEWISH LIVING IN THE POSTMODERN AGE
Rosh Hashanah 5756/1995

"*Va-Yehi Achar Ha-d'varim Ha-eleh*—There came a time when God put Abraham to the test." Thus begins a passage read in synagogues throughout the world every year at the beginning of a new Jewish year. Thus begins the disturbing, infinitely enigmatic tale about the first Jew and the binding of his son, Isaac, on the altar at Mount Moriah.

God tests Abraham the first Jew, but does Abraham pass the test or fail it? The test results are not reported, not clearly, and so commentators over the years have seen it both ways.

According to one perspective, Abraham, great visionary that he is, must pass the test— and with flying colors. You bet. He passes the test and demonstrates his unshakable faith in the process, and that's why we read the tale now. The story reminds both us and the Almighty of the nearly inconceivable willingness and the incomparable faith of Jew Number One. And that little matter of intended child sacrifice and the other about not bothering to mention to Sarah that father and son would not be home for dinner: well, we can explain these matters in at least two dozen clever ways.

However, according to a second perspective, Abraham fails. For surely, no principle looms larger in the Bible or in Jewish tradition than that of the sanctity of life. Indeed, God does test Abraham, and Abraham flunks badly, so badly that he has to be thwarted by an intervening angel. The Binding of Isaac depicts a great man committing a grave and terrible deed. No clever explanation can save Abraham from such a judgment.

"There came a time when God put Abraham to the test." Did he pass or did he fail?

From yet another perspective, it could be said that what is most important for those of us who hear the story once again is not the test results, but rather the notion that God tests Abraham at all. If so, then it would also be of great importance that those of us who hear the story yet again realize and take to heart that God who tests Abraham also tests us, that, as we encounter the tale yet again, the text tests us, each and every one of us.

How does God test us?

The Torah tells us: do justly, act righteously, be holy and serve as a light to the nations, love our neighbors, even the ones we dislike, and treat them with kindness and sensitivity. The Torah teaches us not to steal, not even by paying too little taxes to the IRS, not to worship the idols of material possessions or power or prestige or status, but rather to discipline ourselves in countless ways, in every aspect of our lives, in our eating, our speaking, our mode of dress, in our thoughts and in our deeds, at every moment of every day.

Not enough of a test? Okay, the Torah instructs us to live in the world and be of the world but also to celebrate our Jewish distinctness, using an ancient tongue and ancient rituals that are often inconvenient, uncomfortable, inaccessible, or otherwise simply strange.

Still not enough of a test? Okay, then, figure out how to be an authentic Jew in this postmodern age, an age that not only challenges the fundamental beliefs of Judaism, but that also challenges the very possibility of belief itself.

Let me elaborate the last point and the nature of the test that inheres as a quality of postmodern existence. As I understand it, postmodernism assumes that there is no reality beyond what humans artificially construe it to be. There is no reality beyond what humans construe it to be. If reality, then, is merely a social construction, then how may one affirm a belief in God? When God, like any affirmed truth, is regarded as no more than an artificial or arbitrary social construction, how can one affirm Him or Her, much less show passion for that affirmation? In other words, in an age when all reality has become virtual reality, socially constructed reality, how can one affirm, with intellectual honesty, a positive Jewish identity, rooted in faith, even if one were to wish to do so?

Furthermore, this prevailing unbelief does not promote even the certainty of clear denial. As G. K. Chesterton is often reputed to have said, "When a man stops believing in God he doesn't then believe in nothing, he believes anything." Whether or not Chesterton deserves credit for the quote, it remains the case that in our day, the "anything" in which people believe includes a bewildering and ever-increasing array of newly synthesized religions and quasi-religions and pseudo-religions and cults and self-help societies and esoterica of all types.

I do not mean any of this as a putdown. Rather, I wish to indicate that postmodernity has failed to shut down the religious impulse and instead has produced a huge bazaar of religious options, much of it easily accessible in catalogues, on the college campus, and, of course, on the information superhighway. Among the offerings, along with the expected interest in Islam and Yoga and Vedanta Hinduism and Theosophical Buddhism and Rosicrucians and Eckankar, are some that strike me as more exotic, including organized Satanic cults, shamanism, Celtic societies, Native American Indian groups populated by light-skinned Anglo-Saxons, witchcraft organizations (some allow men, others do not), JFK worshippers, and, a personal favorite, the Nudist Christian Church of the Blessed Virgin Jesus. There are hundreds more.

We are tested at every turn. Not only do some of the dominant intellectual currents of our age rob us of the foundation upon which Jewish faith has classically rested, but it then thrusts us into an unending and confusing marketplace of salvation systems.

In this regard, Walter Anderson, in *Reality Isn't What It Used to Be* (p. 29), points to *The Wizard of Oz* as a foundational myth for our time. At the conclusion of the story, after the long and arduous journey, after overcoming wicked witches and other challenges, Dorothy and her friends do return to the palace and find themselves in the awesome and mighty throne room full of flashing lights, billowing smoke, and a voice that thunders commands at them. Of course, Dorothy and her friend are properly terrified, until Dorothy's little dog, Toto, pulls away the curtain and reveals the disheartening truth: behind all the impressive special effects stands a mere human being, somewhat frazzled and bent, not exactly anyone's image of a grand wizard. Full of disappointment, Dorothy accuses the wizard of being a very bad man, to which he replies that he is actually a very good man, but a very bad wizard.

Abraham thought he had problems. His wizard may have put his belief to the test, but ours has been unmasked, leaving us without either belief or wizard. Now, that's a test.

How shall we regard the test of our day? In a poetic essay called "The Key," Edmond Jabes compares Judaism to authorship. He writes:

Like the writer, the Jew expects his identity from the book. He owes his

Jewishness less to the accident of his birth than to the future he strives to shape down to the smallest details. Here lies his genius.

Judaism is a faith based not on faith alone, but on the test to which the text of this faith forever puts it, on every word of this text which it accepts by putting it to the test in every turn.

Interminable challenge which only death can terminate.
(*Midrash and Literature*, p. 352)

I understand Jabes to mean that the text, all the texts that Judaism has deemed as sacred and even those traditions that are not formally set down in writing but that have come down to us nonetheless as traditions, oral reports, or customary ways of doing things, all these texts test us, challenge us, force us to confront ourselves and whom we have become. They insist that we hold ourselves up to their light. And we, in turn, put the test to the text. We hold the text and its components, usually words, to ever new and unfolding challenges. We demand that it both listen and speak to us. Such is the dynamic, interactive process upon which rests our Jewish faith.

"*Ma Nafka Mina?*" the rabbis of the Talmud often ask at the end of long, convoluted discussions. What is the practical implication of such theoretical musing about the texts of our tradition and the tests confronting us in the postmodern age? I think it may be something like this: as Jews of today we are being put to the test, like Abraham, in a most profound fashion. The very foundations of our faith, of all faith, have been undermined by an extreme and pervasive skepticism: there may be good people, but there are no good wizards to whom we may defer. How does one persevere in such an environment as an authentic, committed Jew?

In Jabes's characterization of Jewish faith lies a profound response. In my own reformulation, his response is "Get midrashic!" Return to the text, where, even today, especially today, the Jew may encounter in the words and in the spaces, in the sounds and in the silences, in the static and the unfolding, in the new and the ancient interpretations, echoes of the divine, revelatory voice.

When God commands Noah to begin his voyage, He says, "*Bo el Ha-teva*—Come to the ark." But at least one of our rabbinic ancestors notes that teva can mean "word" and says, "Don't read the phrase as 'Come into the ark,' rather read it as 'Come into the word!'"

Come into the word! Don't stay outside. Come into the word and let it reverberate for you, within you. Come into the word and get midrashic by noticing the shape of the letters and the spaces and that the word is found elsewhere and that the text is infinitely self-reflexive, endlessly full of possibilities—and if so, why should we fix our attention only on the most simple or crude understanding of a text? If, as Jabes says, we expect our identity from the book, then why should we accept a narrow view of how to apprehend it? Why should we accept the notion of Christians who call our Bible "Old Testament," implying as they do that we are an outmoded people with a superseded religion? If, after all, we do accept their view, then, instead of sitting in shul, we should be preparing our sheep and goats for the Levites who will sacrifice them on their altars!

Let's get midrashic and recognize and appreciate, as did our rabbinic ancestors, the essential paradox upon which Judaism rests: that an infinite, transcendent, Almighty God encountered six hundred thousand of us in a remote wilderness spot. That paradox at once confounds us and frees us to enter the words that emerged and continue to emerge out of that encounter; it frees us to fill their shapes with our flavors, and to augment them with words of our own that will put the test to the text and, in turn, will be tested themselves.

There came a time when God put Abraham to the test. And there comes a time when God puts the test to us. That time is now. The examination is under way.

FROM THE OTHER END OF THE KNIFE
Rosh Hashanah 5753/1992

One might read this famous and troubling passage, *Akedat Yitzhak*, the Binding of Isaac, from any number of different perspectives. One might imagine it from the viewpoints of the various mentioned or unmentioned characters of the story itself: Abraham, God, the angel, or Sarah. Each one would view the event uniquely. No doubt, each one would come away from this "peak experience" affected in some distinct fashion. Consider, then, the perspective of Isaac. How might Isaac experience his own binding? And how, having gone under the knife, might he be affected after the fact?

The recent film *The Doctor* involves a flashy heart surgeon who performs his surgical art at a prestigious teaching hospital. "Performs" is the word. During his surgeries, he has loud music filling the operating room; he jokes boisterously with the operating room staff and flirts with the female nurses. He treats the patient as mere props on a stage where he, the doctor, plays the leading role. When the doctor takes his residents on rounds he insists that they avoid references to the patients by name: it's not Mr. Harris but the valve replacement in Room 403. It's not Ms. Jones but rather the triple bypass in 411. The doctor insists that a good surgeon must maintain distance, must avoid seeing the patient as a person.

The doctor of the film is very wrapped up in himself, in his career, in the trappings of his success and the esteem in which he is held; he travels in a high-speed lane of life, has little time for his children or his wife; he often forgets social engagements, omissions for which he feels professionally entitled.

Then one day, the tables are turned. The doctor finds himself at the other end of the knife, literally and figuratively. He receives the diagnosis of throat cancer, a disease that threatens his career, his life, and his sense of self. I don't want to give away the entire plot except to say that the doctor's world turns inside out and upside down. Nothing seems the same. What was least important before becomes of utmost importance and vice versa. Two examples illustrate this transformation.

First example: before the illness, the doctor rarely spends time with his family, rarely talks with his wife and his children. After his surgery, when he is unable to speak for a time, he notices them as if for the first time; he desperately longs for communication with them, to be with them, to share in their lives, and to have them share in his.

Second example: made in Hollywood, the movie has a Hollywood-ish ending. In the last scene, finally able to return to work, the doctor instructs a new batch of residents on rounds. Before you can be a good doctor, he tells them, you need to know what it feels like to be a patient. He proceeds to have them, one by one, strip off their clothes, put on hospital gowns, lie on hospital beds, sit in waiting rooms, be inspected and poked, their control diminished, talked about, viewed as objects for study, ignored, and humiliated. The obvious message to doctors and all helping professionals: in order to help patients one must have compassion for them as people; in order to do that one must appreciate what they go through.

Having gone under the knife, having changed roles from doctor to patient, the doctor of the film undergoes profound personal transformation, teshuvah big-time. After a similar fashion, we might well imagine the transformation of Isaac, as he too faced and then survived his own near-death experience.

When one considers Isaac, one discovers the least of all the patriarchs and matriarchs. All the others overshadow him in prowess, in accomplishments about which one could write home, in force of personality. Isaac does not innovate a religious world view as did his father; he does not rail against God or kings. He does not direct events as does his wife Rebecca. Nor does he wrestle with an angel and become Israel like his son Jacob. Mostly, he serves as a link. He is a son, a father, and a husband to characters more notable in curricula vitae than he. And yet, when one inspects him through the eye of imagination, one discovers an altered character, a man whose life has taken an instructive turn after Mount Moriah.

After Isaac emerges from under the knife, one next regards him returning from a desert oasis to his settlement in the Negev. The Torah says, "And Isaac went out to meditate in the field" (*Genesis 24:63*). No one else in the entire Bible is said to have done so, to have gone out to meditate in a field. Not Abraham, not Jacob, not Rachel, not Moses, not Miriam. None of the great prophets is reported to have meditated. Only Isaac goes out to the field to meditate.

Meditation, then, could be regarded as a significant defining quality for Isaac. About what does he meditate? What can one learn about this quality? Unrevealing, the text allows one to imagine the details. I imagine that Isaac goes out to the field to be alone, to get away from the busy servants, from the noisy animals, and mostly from his patriarchal, domineering, famous father, in order to be with his own thoughts, to lick the wounds that will never fully heal, wounds from the trauma of his own near-death ordeal and, now, the new pain of grief over the recent death of his mother.

I imagine that Isaac feels plenty sorry for himself as he contemplates the fragility of life, its brevity, the still palpable sense of his own mortality. Isaac might reflect that if life is as precarious as it seems to be and all-too brief as well, then it must also be precious. And, if that is so, then it must not be wasted, and one ought to live well, not frivolously, but meaningfully, honestly, and without hypocrisy.

I imagine Isaac making some resolutions to himself in that field: "I will not try to be like my father because I am not my father. I do not want to change the world as he feels called to do. I will respect the memory of my mother in that, if I am fortunate enough to marry, I will try to build a relationship of love and trust with my wife. If we are fortunate enough to be blessed by children, I will try to appreciate them for who they are and will try to help them find their own distinctive ways in the world. I will not forget to enjoy simple pleasures. I will not allow lofty goals to overwhelm or negate the importance of living each day fully and well."

Concluding his meditation, I imagine Isaac composing this prayer to God:

> O God of my father and mother, hear my prayer even as you have heard theirs. Remember that I stood ready to be sacrificed for Your sake and am forever injured by that encounter, just as I am permanently grieved by the death of my dear mother. O God, do not expect me to be like Abraham, but help me to be myself, to be Isaac. Help me to love and be loved, to enjoy life and enable others to do so. Help me to contribute to the peace and well-being of the community and the region. As the Psalmist will someday say: "The years of our life ... are soon gone ... [so] teach ... [me] to number ... [my] days that ... [I] may possess a heart of wisdom." (*Psalm 90:10–12*)

Thus, I imagine Isaac meditating alone in the field, as the servant Eliezer approaches with Rebecca prepared for marriage.

And we read further that Isaac loves Rebecca and is comforted by her at the death of his mother, Sarah (*Genesis 24:67*). The emotion "love" is not ascribed to many other Biblical couples. Later, feeling Rebecca's pain, Isaac pleads on her behalf (*Genesis 25:21*). We recall that Abraham did plead for the residents of Sodom, but the Torah reports no empathy for the pain Sarah must have felt when the son of her old age became a near sacrifice. Elsewhere, the Torah depicts Isaac frolicking with Rebecca (*Genesis 26:8*). These two enjoy one another, have fun together, spend unstructured, quality time together. In short, though devoid of great distinction, one might imagine Isaac, after going under the knife, transformed into a loving, devoted husband and a decent family man.

In his career as tribal head, Isaac becomes entangled in disputes with Philistine bands over the rights to wells in the Negev region on three occasions. Each and every time, he defuses the conflict by backing away, by moving on until, eventually, he comes to a well that is big enough for everyone to share. He exhibits a reserved and cooperative spirit, an unusual ability to put peace-loving above personal comfort and wealth, an attitude that ultimately wins the respect of the Philistine king who eventually approaches Isaac, offering a permanent peace treaty.

Of course, Isaac and Rebecca are blessed by twin sons, each so different from the other, upon each of whom Isaac manages to confer the proper blessing, the qualities and ascriptions most appropriate to the recipient son. That is to say, after going under the knife, Isaac emerges as a man committed to reordering his life, a man devoted to his family above all else, a man with a loving, empathic, and playful nature, a man who puts peaceful relations above the desire for material gain, a father who treats his children according to their unique and distinct natures.

We know so many modern-day Isaacs, women and men who have emerged from under the knife with a changed perspective on what is truly important. Remember Lee Atwater, the hard-nosed former head of the Republican Party who orchestrated the 1988 presidential campaign, a campaign that even he admitted was mean-spirited and negative. After he was diagnosed with a fatal brain tumor, Lee Atwater apologized to Michael Dukakis for the manner in which he had conducted that campaign.

He did not have to apologize. But when the end closes in, there is no room for bluffing. It's time to settle accounts.

Last year one of our congregants had open heart surgery. He tells me that when he awoke in the recovery room, he cried and tried to reach for the hand of the nurse. She thought he was uncomfortable or wanted something, water perhaps. Only later could he tell her that he was crying from the sheer joy at finding himself alive; he wanted to kiss her hand to express his thankfulness. Life does not look the same after going under the knife.

Another man I know had been angling for a promotion in the large corporation in which he worked. For years he put in extra hours, took on extra assignments, arrived at work early, went home late, worked some weekends, all in order to be recognized for that promotion. After he had a heart attack, he decided, "If I don't get the promotion, so what?" He decided to work nearly normal hours so he could spend more time with his family and with his hobbies. Time, after all, is limited. Why not use it in the best way?

Indeed, finding oneself at the other end of the surgeon's knife may concentrate the mind and catalyze a process of serious self-reflection like nothing else. However, the potential for raised awareness holds even for those of us who have yet to experience such reminders of our own mortality. After all, each one of us is one year older than last year, one year further along the path of life. Thus, as we enter a new Jewish year, let us consider well and take to heart the lesson of our father Isaac, irrevocably sensitized by having been under the knife.

AND THE TWO WALKED ON TOGETHER
Rosh Hashanah 5755/1994

"*Vayailchu Shenaichem Yachdav*—And the two walked on together." So we read in the Binding of Isaac, the portion of Torah selected by tradition for reading on the second day of Rosh Hashanah. Much has been written and spoken about this difficult and intriguing passage. But, from a plain view, it tells of a parent and a child, a father and his son. "*Vayailchu Shenaichem Yachdav*—And the two walked on together."

Recently, with my son, I had the good fortune to visit the blacksmith shop of B. and Mike Hensley, father and son, in Spruce Pine, North Carolina. The image of the Hensley shop now resides in my memory as a vivid picture and as a point of comparison with the Biblical tale of father and son. Let me try to paint the scene.

According to the records of the Smithsonian Institute, the Hensley shop is one of only six in the country that employ traditional, medieval techniques to fashion andirons, intricate gates, light posts, fixtures, and anything else that might be formed by striking iron to anvil. Son of a Baptist minister, seventy-year-old B. began learning the blacksmith craft fifty-four years ago from his master, Daniel Boone VI, descendant of the famous Boone.

The son, Mike, now with forty-plus years of experience, had learned the trade from his own father. While we visited, father and son demonstrated their craft, evoking the early stages of the master-apprentice association.

B., the master, stood between the furnace and the anvil; Mike, the apprentice, positioned himself on the other side of the anvil, facing the master. Before beginning to pummel the red-hot metal, Mike first lifted the anvil and pushed some iron filings around and underneath, then struck the anvil several blows. Ping. Ping. Ping. He did this several times. Ping. Ping. Ping. I thought—at first—he was leveling the anvil. But, no, he informed us, he was rather "tuning the anvil" so it would deliver its song, speak its language-without-words, on pitch. Ping.

Words cannot do justice to the audio-visual, sensory experience of witnessing a father and son assume the master-apprentice pose in a blacksmith's shop: B. held the iron with his left hand while, with a constant rhythm, Mike beat his hammer, metal on metal, against the anvil. Meanwhile, B., too, pinged out metallic notes with his hammer in his right arm—signaling by tonal variations—created through nuance of placement—where and how the apprentice must proceed. The two worked rapidly and rhythmically, wordlessly, generating a dazzling image and a dizzyingly beautiful, musical sound.

Though now a master smith himself, Mike had apprenticed himself for the standard fourteen-year period: four years on the apprentice's side of the anvil, six years on the master's side under the watchful eye of another, then four more on his own anvil, his work still carefully supervised and inspected by the master, his father. In all ways, an apprentice shows deference to and respect for the master smith. He may not talk without explicit permission. Today, when working together, Mike always stands on the apprentice's side of the anvil, never, never on the master's side. According to rabbinic teaching, a student of Torah, even one who has attained the level of sage, should maintain a respectful silence in the presence of his own teacher. It would seem that the tradition of maintaining respect for one's teacher transcends time and culture.

Even as the training of a master blacksmith is rigorous and long, the daily work is hard and tedious. There are no shortcuts. Having witnessed the process, only now can I appreciate the muscle and sweat, the love, the patience, and the tradition, that goes into each exquisite piece of wrought iron work.

Vayailchu Shenaichem Yachdav—And the two walked on together. A father and a son join hands and carry on together with common purpose. A master and an apprentice, a parent and a child, wed themselves to an ancient, simple, yet complex craft, an old-fashioned way of working, unique in our day, and, in doing so, walk the pathways of their lives, for now, together. Like B. and Mike Hensley, Abraham and Isaac stride through a phase of their lives, a father and a son on a journey. Of course, theirs is not a fishing trip or a camping excursion. Nor are they going into business together—not exactly.

We read that the two servants do not make the entire journey. After the third day, Abraham and Isaac carry on without them. What happened to the servants? According to one midrash, on the third day, Abraham, gazing ahead, sees Mount Moriah rising in the distance. He asks the servants to look up and tell him what they see. They both look but see nothing. Abraham asks

Isaac to look. Isaac says, "Abba, I see a mountain. It is our destination, isn't it?" *Vayailchu Shenaichem Yachdav*—And the two walked on together.

According to the midrash, Isaac sees what Abraham sees, and unlike the servants and other people, comprehends the significance and therefore chooses to continue on with his father. This is Isaac's revelatory moment, that point where he first perceives the extraordinary nature of his father's spiritual journey and chooses to make it his own.

These days, adult children in America only rarely follow in their parents' footsteps. More rarely still do they walk together with them, sharing a vision, a sense of purpose, much less the adjacent physical space.

It amazes me that Mike and B. Hensley can spend so much time together. The bond between them must be as strong as the anvils they strike, their mutual respect and love as solid. Though fully aware of the wide world out there, they have embraced a craft from another era. They each selected it. They each love what they do. They each derive tremendous satisfaction from their mastery of that craft. They each possess a knowing admiration for the history and tradition of their craft. And they each derive palpable satisfaction from carrying forth that tradition and exposing it to the world as it passes in and out of their hospitable shop.

And the two walk on together. However, even in the best of cases, parents and children can only walk together so far. A story, which I remember first hearing from the rabbi of my childhood, Rabbi Jack Stern of blessed memory:

> The time for birds to migrate had arrived. For one particular mother bird, the migratory season caused a dilemma because she had two young ones who could not yet fly and because the migratory route crossed a wide body of water, an ocean. What did she do? She placed both on her back and began the journey. However, when they were well over water, the mother bird grew tired and realized she could carry only one of her children. And so she posed the question: "When I am old and unable to fly will you carry me across the ocean?" The first youngster said, "Yes, I will carry you across the ocean." The second young bird answered, "Mamma, I can't be sure I will be able to carry you across, for I may have young birds of my own to carry." That is the one the mother bird carried to safety on the far shore.

And the two walked on together, but only for a time did they physically walk side by side. After that, Isaac carried Abraham's legacy with him—he carried the inspiration, the values, and then the memory of who his father and mother were and how they had lived. And he continued to walk with them in that he became who he was, in part, because of who they were.

Some months before my mother died, I asked her to write an ethical will, a document of thoughts and wishes for her grandchildren. She thought about it, but declined, telling me that her life was her ethical will. Indeed it was.

The two walked on together.

We are all children. We are all Isaac. In part, we are the kind of people we are because of the kind of people our parents are and have been, not that we are restricted by their talents or confined by their dreams or excused by the limitations or faults of our parental models. But we do walk with them and they with us. And, in the best of cases, we walk together, in large measure, sharing values and visions.

And we who are blessed with the privilege of parenthood do well to appreciate and savor the period of time in which our children walk closely with us. For, in the not too distant future, our physical paths will diverge. As for our children, they may not climb our mountain, they may not beat our anvil. But they will, without a doubt, notice our generosity of spirit, our kindness, our compassion, our faithfulness to one another and to God, our honesty, our consideration—or the lack thereof. They will notice whether we proudly tell about how we haggled for a lower price or about how we returned change given us in error at the supermarket.

We walk together, parents and children, children and parents. As we do, may our values and our visions be worthy of emulation and respect.

TO HOLD AND LET GO
Rosh Hashanah 5760/1999

A boy and his dad wake up early one morning and go off on a three-day camping trip. They bring with them all the supplies they need and even a couple of hired porters so they don't have to carry everything. In the cool mornings they begin the day with breakfast cooked over an open fire. Later, they hike through the ravines and along the hillsides. As the day heats up, they pause to refresh themselves at a spring-fed pool. From time to time, the boy and his dad gaze in awe at the graceful ibex leaping from craggy ledge to craggy ledge and at the Egyptian eagles gliding magnificently through the unseen currents of air. Few words are said because words are not needed. What a great adventure! What a marvelous bonding experience for father and son! How could time have more quality than this?

With a hefty amount of redirected emphasis, that is the account we read in *Genesis 22*. Omitted above is the detail about the intended sacrifice of son by father, a facet of the telling that upsets the tale's otherwise idyllic quality. In all seriousness, one could read the tale of Abraham's outing with his son, Isaac, as idyllic and pastoral. For twice does the text report about Abraham and Isaac, "*Vayailchu Shenaichem Yachdav*—The two walked together." What the narrative repeats the reader must try to comprehend. Somehow, despite the ominous overlay, this father and son did set out together on this trip; they were close, a team, in sync, as one.

By focusing on the idyllic elements of *Akedat Yitzhak*, one picks up on the themes of children and generational continuity, strong themes throughout the liturgy of Rosh Hashanah and, to an extent, Yom Kippur. In both Torah and Haftarah readings of Rosh Hashanah, Day One, fathers and, even more, mothers anxious over their infertility are rewarded with the birth of sons. In the Torah reading of Day Two, the fulfillment of generational continuity—not to mention covenantal promise—is placed in jeopardy. The horror of the tale of Isaac's binding on the altar is poignant, in part, because we can imagine its coming to pass; we have seen and heard of parents losing their children, and not only in literature but also to the real-life ravages of war or disease or through acts of random violence and hatred or to accident or through neglect or abuse. Most of us would be hard-pressed to imagine a greater horror than the loss of a child by a parent.

And yet, all parents do lose their children, not through death—God forbid—but more benignly, as soon as children take their first independent steps. Remember that first step of your own first child or the first child of your friend or of your sibling or your neighbor? That step induces such a conglomeration of emotions: exhilaration, glee, fear, and sadness, all at the same time. That first, independent step foreshadows going off to child care where the caregiver becomes as significant as Mom and Dad, off to school where friends influence as much or more than parents, off to camp where, for a week or more, home is but a memory, off to college, a career, a spouse, and a family of his or her own. What is true for the first step is true for the first bike ride, the first swim, the first time behind the wheel of a car, and any number of other necessary transitions in the growth and development of our children.

The most poignant moment of my summer occurred at Newark Airport. Talia, our seventeen-year-old daughter, had been gone all summer, traveling in Eastern Europe and Israel with Camp Ramah. True, Dela and I did get to see her once, in Israel, for about three hours on a Shabbat afternoon, but still we were eager and excited to welcome her back home. So there we were, with Dela's mother and dozens of other parents and grandparents and siblings, waiting eagerly and expectantly to greet the young world travelers at International Arrivals. We stood in a large area divided by a plexiglass screen that separated the parents from the returning travelers. As the kids left the customs and baggage claim area and began to walk through an automatic door, we could see them before they could see us. Like most of the other parents, we had arrived at least an hour and a half before necessary.

Anticipation and anxiety were high by the time the first of the Ramah kids appeared. When they did appear, parents would jump up and down shrieking such things as, "There's Josh, there's Josh!" and then frantically wave their hands trying to get Josh's attention, urging him to hurry toward the automatic door. When I saw Talia, I immediately joined the screaming throng. Some parents whipped out their cell phones to call some relative not at the airport but eager for news of a sighting. It was basic pandemonium on the parents' side of the plexiglass.

Meanwhile, on the kids' side of the plexiglass barrier, all movements took place in slow motion. Kids would emerge from the baggage claim area, walk halfway toward the exit, and then stop and wait for the rest of their friends. For a time, I wondered if the plexiglass offered only one-way viewing. The teen travelers did not seem to see us. However, every now and then, an almost undetectable, reluctant wave in the direction of the parents was released, a sign that the nonacknowledgment was not a matter of perception but of intention or focus. We were eager to hug our kids. They were reluctant to leave one another. And that's the way it needs to be.

Letting go is very hard for most of us, and not just letting go of children, but of all the significant others in our lives: friends, siblings, relatives, spouses, and parents. Some years ago, Rabbi Milton Steinberg described this most significant of life's tasks as follows: "It does not ask of us that we hold life dear one moment and release it the next but that we do both simultaneously. Now, I can grasp something in my fist or let my hand lie open. I can embrace it, enfolding it in my arms, or let my arms hang loose. But how can I be expected to do both at once?"

But, difficult as it is, that is precisely what life demands, that we embrace it and those we love, but with open arms.

One of the most touching scenes of the year and of my life took place one afternoon some months ago in J. Marymore's hospital room in the hospice unit of UVA Medical Center, just a few days before J. died. J.'s two sons and his daughter were present as well as several good friends. Everyone knew, including J., that he did not have long. All of us hoped that a way could be found to manage his considerable pain. Adding to the physical pain was the necessary separation from his beloved Trudy, who was herself confined to a health-care facility and had at that time diminishing moments of mental acuity. So I was amazed, when that afternoon, into J.'s room, Trudy was wheeled. She came close enough to J.'s bed so that they could hold hands, which they did. J. grew calm and focused and Trudy seemed alert. They asked after each other's well-being and then J. continued to visit with others in the room, all the time holding hands with Trudy and smiling a smile of deep contentment. They were, it seems to me now, illustrating the art of holding on and letting go simultaneously, of embracing with open arms, each other and life itself.

I have educators describe parenting using the metaphor of a boat leaving a dock. The purpose of the boat is to leave the dock and sail off into the body of water, eventually finding another dock to tie in to, or, perhaps, even to return to the original dock for a time. The purpose of the dock is to supply the boat with a firm and secure place from which to set off and to which it may return. It isn't always easy to be the dock, but that is what we parents are in relation to our children especially, and to others as well. Sometimes, our task is to supply the firm and secure place from which they may push off and to which they may return, or not, as the case may be.

Abraham and Sarah set the pattern. In order to further their spiritual maturation, they needed to leave home: "Get yourself going and leave your homeland, your birthplace, and the home of your parents" (*Genesis 12:1*).

Of course, the task is not easier on the other side of the relational equation. Children, like parents, want and need to hold on and let go simultaneously. A woman named Treasure Cohen described her experience of transition at the celebration of her daughter's Bat Mitzvah:

> After sharing her personal thank-you's before the congregation, our daughter Esther addressed us [her parents] from the bimah with this plea: "Mom and Dad, please understand that I am getting older and at times want my space. So here's my deal—let me have my space, and most likely, when I get older, I might not want it so much." ("Between Parent and Child," *Lifecycles*, p. 262)

The same author also points out that the Hebrew word hand (or arm) is spelled *yud-dalet: yad*. Taking the same letters in reverse order yields the word dai, meaning enough. We may use our hands and our arms for embracing or for indicating when enough is enough, for holding on and for letting go. ("Between Parent and Child," p. 263)

Rabbi Harold Schulweis wrote this poem, a fitting coda for a consideration of the challenge of simultaneously holding on and letting go of those we love:

> Hold on and let go
> On the surface of things
>   contradictory counsel.

But one does not negate the other.
The two are complementary, dialectical
    two sides of one coin . . .

Hold on and let go
    a courageous duality
    that endows our life with meaning.

Neither denying the past
    nor foreclosing the future.

The flow of life
    the divine process
    gives and takes
    retains and creates.

Old and new yesterday and tomorrow
    Both in one embrace.

The Lord giveth and the Lord taketh
Blessed be the name of the Lord.
("Holding On and Letting Go," *In God's Mirror*, p. 304)

THE HEART I
Standing in the Doorway

STANDING IN THE DOORWAY
(Inspired by teachings of Rabbi Steven Sager)
Rosh Hashanah 5754/1993

We may view a new year as a threshold in time.

As we stand on that threshold, we are aware that living involves constant movement from place to place, from state to state, changing as we go, in physical, emotional, intellectual, and spiritual ways. Liturgically, we acknowledge one set of changes when intoning these words of Rabbi Alvin Fine:

> From childhood to maturity and youth to old age. From innocence to awareness and ignorance to knowing ... From weakness to strength or strength to weakness—and, often, back again. From health to sickness and back, we pray, to health again ... from fear to faith ... From birth to death ... ("Birth is a Beginning," *Gates of Repentance*, pp. 283–284)

And, then ... we know not. The ten days beginning with Rosh Hashanah and including Yom Kippur, variously called the Days of Awe or the Days of *Teshuvah*, of turning, of renewal, are served up to us unlike other Jewish holidays that recall events in the sacred story of our people's journey. More than the recollection of events in Jewish sacred history or their celebration, these days are given to us as a time of inward reflection, a time for opening up to the awesome Holy One who undergirds all things. The sacred event these days recall is cosmic creation. Hence, the days are universal, human, personal, and in a sense, at their core, not particularly Jewish.

It is a time of taking stock, a time when we are challenged to look realistically and with hard honesty at who we have become, at how we live, how we treat others, ourselves, and the world of nature, the environment that houses us.

It is also a time for admitting our limitations and our relative impotence. Over and over, during these days, we invoke God as *Melekh*, king/

sovereign, and God's sovereign rule. Ours is not a religion that emphasizes passivity, but at this time of year, we bow our heads more often, we even fall prostrate on our faces, we beat our breasts—humble postures reflecting the admission that, in the last analysis, our understanding is meager, our power slight, that, for all our electronic wizardry, for all our conquests of outer and subatomic space, we are finally dependent on *Melech Malchei Hamelachim*, the King who is sovereign of all sovereigns. For some, it takes a one billion dollar NASA blunder or the devastation of the flooding in the Midwest. But for us, for Jews, the arrival of this season of renewal suffices to make the point: we are not entirely in control.

On this day, as we stand on the threshold of a new year, we concentrate our attention on the ultimate values we wish to affirm in our lives and on the sense of holiness we wish to acquire and carry with us during our days. Standing between a year completed and one just under way, these Days of Awe rise like a temporal doorway before a room of uncertain hospitality, before a year of unknown fortune. "Who shall live and who shall die," intones our High Holiday liturgy. These are days of heightened liminality.

"Liminality" is the term anthropologists use to describe the condition of being in-between, of being no-longer in one state and at the same time not yet in the next. It is the position of standing in the doorway, anxious about what lies ahead, uncertain and unsettled, in limbo, needing support, assurance, comfort, protection.

Standing on the threshold of this new year, my thoughts fly back to the summer just ended and the surprisingly poignant doorway in which Dela and I left our children, Talia and Benjamin, at Ramah, a Jewish sleep-away summer camp. Trite as trite can be were my emotions of happy sadness: Could my children have grown so much so fast? Is that preteen girl diving into the lake the same as the seven-pound crying bundle I held moments after her birth? Has that much time flown by? Trite too the premonitions of separation to come: as we drove away, leaving them at camp, I could feel myself driving away, leaving them at college. I was momentarily engulfed by the bittersweet future emotions as I imagined myself, God willing, standing under the chuppahs at each of their weddings. "All in good time," I told myself rationally, but I could not help myself. And I think I understood, empathically, for the first time, how my own parents must have felt with each new distancing, each new separation from their three children.

Standing in the doorway of this new year, having been poised for some time to renegotiate the relationship with my own parents, I was poised, but not prepared, for the passing from life of my dear mother, an event still too recent for full acknowledgment or acceptance or sufficient grieving.

No doubt many in this congregation have undergone some encounter with liminality during the past year or will do so in the year under way, for these experiences accompany each of life's many transitions, and they carry with them deep emotions, among them: anxiety, pain, confusion, doubt, sadness, and aloneness. Standing on these liminal thresholds, one wonders: Is there a Torah for the experience of the doorway? Are there voices that speak to us from our collective Jewish past, speaking the words of instruction, healing, or hope we need in those moments of liminality? Are there echoes we can hear, stories we can retell, conceptual frameworks we can appropriate, to help us stand a little more securely, a little more confidently, a bit more comfortably in the doorways of our lives?

Torah comes from many sources. Regarding a Torah for doors, doorways, and passage through them, Robert Sardello writes:

> Doors have soul. They are the guardians of boundaries, they serve both to divide and connect the psychic topography of the house keeping its imagination multiple, and each part in direct or indirect relation with every other part. Doors make and mark tension between the diverse elements within the house.... The art of the door makes of arriving, departing, and returning a ritual process that assures that the house will not be taken for granted. Clothe your entrance with such images. (*Facing the World with Soul*, p. 36)

Does the notion "the art of the door" that "makes arriving, departing and returning a ritual process" not strike a very Jewish chord? "*U'chetavtem Al Mezuzot Baitecha Uveesharecha*— And you shall write them on the doorposts, the *mezuzot*, of your house and upon your gates." The mezuzah—that particularly Jewish ritual art form, that encased scroll, handwritten by a scribe, like a Torah scroll itself, containing the two paragraphs of the Shema in which mezuzot are mentioned, affixed to the upper third of the right side of doorways and entranceways of Jewish dwellings, with the top inclined inward, that traditional ritual object, much observed even by the otherwise nonobservant among us, whose staying power partakes of the mythic and the mysterious—must be the receptacle for an unfolding Torah of the door, one that we would do well to explore.

A midrash:

> Arteban [the last Parthian king] sent our teacher, Rav, a priceless gem, with the request, "let me have something in return as valuable as this." So our teacher sent him a mezuzah. Ardavan sent back word: "I gave you a priceless object and you sent me something worth but a folar [a coin of little value]." Rav responded, "the things you and I desire cannot be compared to her. Moreover, you sent me something which I must guard, whereas I sent you something which guards you while you lie asleep, as it is said, "When you walk, it shall lead you, when you lie down, it shall guard you." (*Proverbs 6:22*) (*Genesis Rabbah 35:16*)

Now, I do not for a moment believe literally that a mezuzah protects us in any magical fashion. I am much too much of a rationalist to believe in the efficacy of amulets, even though they abound in the folkways of our people. As it happens, I am appalled when I hear ultratraditionalist Jews "explain" tragic events like murders or the failure to achieve pregnancy by the presence of improperly inscribed *mezuzot*. The God I seek to affirm is no cosmic magician, doling out goodies only if the proper incantations have been uttered or the scrolls properly inscribed. And yet, on the other hand, could there be a nonmagical sense in which the mezuzah protects?

In his Law Code, the *Mishneh Torah*, the Rambam, Moses ben Maimon, presents his conception of the underlying rationale of the mitzvah of mezuzah, in stating:

> One should observe the precept of mezuzah, for it is a duty of all, continuously. Whenever a person enters or leaves a home provided with a mezuzah, he will meet with the Oneness of the Holy One, blessed be He, and will remember God's love. He will be aroused from his sleep and indulgence in temporal vanities. He will conceive that nothing endures forever and to all eternity except the knowledge of the Creator of the universe, and immediately he will return to his senses and walk in upright paths. ("Laws of Mezuzah 6:13" in *Mishneh Torah*)

Is the Rambam kidding? The little encased parchment rolled up, affixed to the upper third of our doorposts, inclining inward, is going to raise consciousness to such an extent! "Yes," says the Rambam, the little object (which one midrash refers to as one example of the "little that contains the much") can alter the minds of those who encounter it. The mezuzah of the doorpost can create a "mezuzah-consciousness," affixing itself in the upper third of our awareness and inclining inward. In the sense that raised awareness of God's loving and caring presence buffers one against the forces of despair, the mezuzah indeed may provide real protection.

Doors invite. Doors repel. Many midrashim refer to the obligations we bear toward our impoverished kinfolk employing the image of "the poor man standing in your doorway with the Holy One, Blessed be He, standing at his right." Impoverishment of the other, material, educational, and emotional, according to our tradition, are all matters requiring our concern. Thus, each and every time an opportunity for *tzedakah* knocks at our doors, we are watched and judged, judged well when we respond with charitable generosity to the needs of our fellow human, or judged ill when we react in miserly fashion.

The mezuzah that affixes itself in the upper third of human consciousness and inclines inward not only makes us cognizant that, as we enter a physical space, we tread on God's territory, as it were, but also that we are responsible for all manner of poor ones that stand in our doorways. The poor ones may even be ourselves.

But the heightened awareness comprising mezuzah-consciousness has further dimensions. I recently heard a colleague, now in his sixties, talk about his personal history vis-à-vis the mezuzah. When he was young his father had taught him to touch his hand to each mezuzah in their house and to kiss the hand, expressing awareness of God's loving presence, symbolized by the mezuzah. When he grew to the age of about ten, he realized that his father never touched the mezuzot, and he asked him about it. His father replied that he personally did not really believe in the custom, but that his own father had taught him to do it, and so he felt he should teach his son the same thing. He also felt that the custom helped provide a sense of security for a young child. As one might expect, from that moment, my colleague ceased the practice and further resolved not to be so hypocritical with his own children.

Sure enough, he grew up, married, had a son, and, breaking his resolution, taught him to touch and kiss the mezuzah, thinking of it as an enhancement to his son's sense of security. When the son reached the age of nine, he observed that his father did not practice what he had taught him and so he inquired about it. The man explained to his son that he really did not believe in the custom, but felt it would provide some security to him as a young child, and one more thing: when he was about the same age he had had the exact same conversation with his father. "Wow!" said the son.

The mezuzah really is the little that contains the much. If the doors of our hearts and minds are sufficiently open, then the little encased, rolled-up parchment anchored to the upper third of our doorways on the right side and inclined inward sparks an awareness that extends beyond the immediate temporal and spatial boundaries to a concern for the other, to the generations of past and future, to the purpose-giving Oneness underlying all creation, to an awareness of our treading on God's space, and to the obligations for the poor who stand in the doorway.

The mezuzah, the little that contains the much, marks our doorways for all to see. It declares: "We are Jews, descendants of Sarah, Rebecca, Rachel, and Leah, Moses, Miriam, Ruth, and Hillel and Rabbi Akiva and Beruriah and Rashi and Rambam, the Vilna Gaon, and the Baal Shem Tov, and Grandma and Grandpa. We mark our homes and our rooms as they did and in doing so are linked to them and their spiritual travels. They stand with us in the doorway."

When we stand in the doorway of a new year, just as we stand in the doorways of our homes, the little that contains the much is thick with the generations that have gone before. We join hands with them when we perform the rituals they performed, when we speak the words they spoke, when we tell the tales they told. We join hands with them and are less alone for their company and for the awareness that our journeys are bound up with theirs.

ALTERS OF THE HEART
Shabbat Ki Tissa 5765/2005

Does Judaism have a concept of original sin? Many Jews would probably answer no, and might further express the view that Judaism and Christianity diverge around this very topic. Such Jews might point out that Christians understand the story of the Garden of Eden and the Fall as one of original human transgression, a transgression forever after hardwired into our very natures and into the sinful means by which humans procreate. By contrast, Jews, they might submit, regard choice, not sin, as the hardwired condition of human beings, choice between the good and evil options always before us and between the good and evil tendencies always competing for primacy within us.

Truthfulness, however, and humility might have us admit that we Jews may not be qualified to characterize Christian beliefs, especially if in doing so, we tend to make ours seem more enlightened or more appealing. We may even be too quick in our self-characterizations as well.

It would not be an exaggeration to say that the sin of the golden calf, as recounted in the Torah portion Ki Tissa (*Exodus 30:11–34:35*) and as cited in rabbinic literature, constitutes the original sin of Judaism. Our ancestors regarded the golden calf as the paradigm for backsliding into false and idolatrous worship, a transgression numbered as one of the top three (with murder and sexual immorality) in many rabbinic texts. It is not an overstatement to say that Jewish tradition is obsessed with this sin. From the oft-repeated mention in the laws enumerated in Torah to an entire tractate of the Talmud (along with lengthy accompanying commentary) to the large sections in the major codes of Jewish law, our tradition devotes great attention to this specific category of prohibition.

"You shall have no other God before Me. You shall not make unto you a graven image, nor any manner of likeness. You shall not prostrate yourself unto them, nor serve them" (*Exodus 20:4*), says the second of the Ten Commandments, one of many instances where the Torah hammers home this message. "Make no mention of the name of other gods" (*Exodus 23:13*). "Do not turn to idols, nor make yourself molten gods" (*Leviticus 19:4*). "And that you do not go about after your own heart and your own eyes" (*Numbers 15:39*). These represent just a selection among those instances where the Torah addresses this theme.

The ancient rabbis built upon the Torah's obsession with false worship by layering on rules and further prohibitions designed to heighten the concern for avoiding idolatry or even the appearance of it lest one partake of or induce others to partake of this most abhorrent of transgressions.

The rabbis say that one who makes an idol or instructs another to make one is subject to flogging. One who deliberately worships an idol commits a capital offense, death by stoning. We properly understand these laws as efforts to inspire a healthy fear, to inhibit the undesired behavior, and to promote piety, but not to sanction punishments actually to be enforced. However, the rabbis also taught that one must be ready to sacrifice one's life rather than commit idolatry, a teaching that tragically had too frequent occasions for fulfillment during the Middle Ages.

I have often wondered why idolatry so preoccupied our ancestors and why this preoccupation seems so quaint to many of us, the products both of Enlightenment thinking with its emphasis on the capacity of the rational human mind, science, and technology, and now of post-Enlightenment thinking with its inability to accept either the truths of science or the pious assumptions of an earlier age. If I honestly try to identify my own idolatrous temptations, rarely do I recognize an impulse to bow to clay figurines or totemic statues. Admittedly, I do have material desires beyond those required for my sustenance. Those objects of material desire could take on an idolatrous spin that would be worth guarding against, but it seems to me that something deeper in the human psyche may have worried our ancestors.

The key to the mystery of idolatry may relate not to idolatry as a matter of external behavior so much as how it works as an inner phenomenon, as worship on the level of the heart. As Robert and Jane Alter have described the matter:

> Our true spiritual nature is a worshipful nature. Worship is its essential nature and its heart's desire. There is an altar in the heart, and we must place something on it as our object of worship because until that altar in our heart is occupied, our worshipful nature has nothing to worship

and we cannot rest. There are lots of things we can place on the altar of the heart for our worship.... Whatever we call it, we must place it on the altar of our heart and spend the rest of our days worshiping it through our thoughts, words, and actions because if we don't, if that altar stays empty, an addiction will eventually land on it. Then the worshipful energy of our nature will flow to the addiction instead of to the Spirit. (*How Long Till My Soul Gets It Right?*, p. 137)

If one accepts as a reality of human nature that something must occupy those interior altars of our hearts then we may now better understand the insight driving the ancient preoccupation with idolatry. As we read in the Torah portion Ki Tissa: "God said to Moses: 'Hurry down, for your people, whom you have brought out of the land of Egypt, have acted basely. They have been quick to turn aside [saru maher] from the way that I have commanded them'" (*Exodus 32:7–8*).

The verb "to turn aside" [*saru*] jumps out at us because it also appears in the second paragraph of the Shema: "Be careful lest your heart be tempted and you turn aside [v'sartem] to worship other gods and bow down to them" (*Deuteronomy 11:16*). Commenting on the juxtaposition of the verbs "turn aside" and "worship" in this passage—which in the Torah are not separated by any intervening words— the Baal Shem Tov says that the Torah means to teach us that it takes only an instant for us to stray from what is true and holy and good. We so quickly and easily turn aside and worship the false god. The interior altar cannot stand to be empty.

The issue of contemporary idolatry, then, is not one of clay figurines or other totems of ancient or primitive religion and their pull on our devotional energy but something far more primary, more personal, and exceedingly real. Avoiding idolatry is about cultivating our heart's desires so that these are wholesome and holy and true. How to do that, how to confront oneself with sufficient honesty, how to wisely choose the objects we place on the altars of our hearts without "turning aside" to pick up some dazzling alternative might seem terribly daunting and far more challenging than smashing mere idols of clay. But that is precisely the enterprise of idolatry avoidance toward which our tradition guides us.

LESSONS FROM THE NOLICHUCKY
Kol Nidre 5758/1997

One Kol Nidre at a very large synagogue in a very large city, as the evening service is nearing its conclusion, the rabbi stands at the podium, and in front of the entire congregation, in a voice laced with sincere piety, announces, "I feel myself to be but dust and ashes." Overcome with emotion, the rabbi resumes his seat. Hearing this uncommon display of humility, the president himself now approaches the podium, where he announces, "I too feel myself to be but dust and ashes." Now the shamash, the sexton, the man who cleans the synagogue, has observed these unusual public confessions, and he too is overcome by the spirit of the moment. He too strides to the podium and announces, "I too feel myself to be but dust and ashes," upon which the president leans over to the rabbi and whispers, "Look who thinks he's dust and ashes."

Obviously, the rabbi and the president, for all their mustering of pious humility, have missed something key about the egalitarian spirit of this day of Yom Kippur, in spite of the many symbolic cues to help them achieve that spirit. Whereas on other days of the year we often fall into a pattern of elevating or denigrating the status of others, at least on this day, if we heed the customs of tradition, we obliterate the distinctions between those who wear designer clothes and those who buy from the secondhand store. On this day, tradition would have us join together in a community donning simple white clothing. Some even wear the kittel, that plain white robe, garb of burial, reminder of the condition of mortality shared by all human beings. On this day, more than any other, Jewish tradition would have us alter our consciousness and recognize that, before the Almighty, all human beings possess equal status; differences of merit relate only to deeds, deeds that will be judged by the heavenly court.

On this solemn day of Yom Kippur, then, we gravitate toward white, recalling as we do Rabban Gamliel II, sage of the second century. A wealthy aristocrat, Rabban Gamliel learned that funerals had become so expensive and burdensome that many people would abandon their dead. So what did Rabban Gamliel do? He ordained an exceedingly simple funeral for himself; he was to be dressed in plain white linen shrouds, a practice that has become normative for Jewish burial ever since. Thus does our wearing of Yom Kippur white put us in touch with the radical egalitarianism of Rabban Gamliel's funeral prescription, an awareness that the rabbi, the president, the shamash, and all other members of the community share a common humanity.

But, alas, much conspires against the consciousness we would properly achieve on this day. Satan, in Jewish lore, is an active presence, seeking at every turn to thwart noble human impulses, to block our God-intended purpose of just and merciful living. Once, according to legend, Satan decided to convene a conference of his devilish colleagues to discuss the most effective ways of leading humans astray and foiling their desire to make life meaningful. One impish creature proposed this plan: "Let's tell them there is no God." Another came up with this idea: "Let's tell them there is no judgment for sin and that they can do whatever they want without consequences." A third suggested: "Let's tell them their sins are so many and so great that there is no possibility that they will ever be forgiven."

Finally, Satan himself said, "No, these ideas all have merit, but humans unfortunately are likely to reject each one of them. Rather, I propose we simply tell them they have lots of time. That they are likely to believe."

Central to Yom Kippur consciousness is a heightened awareness of the preciousness of time. It is the lesson of Rabbi Eliezer, who teaches, in Mishnah Avot, *Ethics of the Fathers:* "Repent one day before you die." "What!" his students complain, "no one knows for sure when death will come. So how can one know on which day to offer repentance?" "Exactly," replies Rabbi Eliezer, "let one repent today lest tomorrow he die, and repent tomorrow lest death come on the day after."

I had an intimation of Yom Kippur consciousness on one glorious day this past summer in a raft on the Nolichucky River as it flowed from North Carolina into Tennessee. It was sunny but not too humid and not too hot. For a first-time rafter like me, the Class-Four rapids were just right, a bit adventurous, but not more than my friends, other rabbis and their families, and I could handle. During the several hours we rafted on the crystalline, meandering river, we would paddle according to the directions of the young woman who guided us. "Paddle right!" meant just those of us on the right side should paddle. "All paddle" meant both sides should paddle in unison. She would yell at us when our strokes were out of sequence. She expressed no sympathy for our failures of coordination. Sometimes the young guide would direct one side or both sides to paddle in reverse in order to wind and spin our way through the rougher waters so that we would avoid hitting rocks and not flip over.

Rivers play major roles in the history of human civilization and also in the mythologies of those civilizations. They provide a means for livelihood, transportation, economic development, and the setting of political boundaries. In Jewish legal documents, places are identified with rivers, because it is assumed that whereas the political boundaries of cities and towns may come and go, rivers will remain.

Rivers assume larger-than-life, even sacred, dimension in folklore and myth. Consider the Nile for Egyptians, the Ganges for Indians, the Rubicon for Italians, the Congo for central Africans, the Amazon for Brazilians, the Tigris and Euphrates for Sumerians, the Rhine, Seine, Danube, or Thames for Europeans, the Mississippi, Ohio, Rio Grande, Hudson, Potomac, and Delaware for Americans—to name just a few. My college song referenced a river: "On the banks of the old Raritan." Rivers have taken on symbolic dimension also in Jewish myth: at the River Jabbok, our father Jacob emerged from the wrestling match with God's emissary a changed man with a new name and new identity, Israel. By the rivers of Babylon, our exiled ancestors wept in remembrance of their homeland.

One may regard a river as a macrocosmic mirror of human existence, a vessel of fluid crisscrossing the sinewy countryside carrying and removing life's necessities. Rivers to be crossed represent life's transitional moments, points of no return, or key stages of growth, maturation, or insight. Similarly, one may view a river as a microcosmic representation of life's stream: rivers to be traveled upon represent the continuous flow of life, whether gloriously rushing or trickling gently, from upriver to down, unremittingly steady and ineluctable. Rivers may also teach.

After about an hour of rafting, when we had all pretty well gotten the hang of it, one of my friends, also a rabbi, made the observation that our control of the raft seemed limited—that mostly the river did the work, while we merely tried to finesse the situation, and that the faster the rapids, the less in control we seemed to be. The guide responded, "Absolutely right. Out here, the river is boss. It's much bigger and stronger than us. We're mainly along for the ride."

In Jewish mysticism, there is a concept called *Bittul Hayesh*, meaning something like "making yourself small." That day, the river was offering lessons in the limitations of the human place on nature's scale.

As we rafted on down the Nolichucky, I found myself concentrating hard on the directions of our guide and on not falling out of the raft, always a distinct possibility. At one point, after we had snaked our way into a particularly deep and lovely gorge, surrounded by steep verdant walls and several sheer rock faces, I looked about and I allowed the unmitigated pleasure one feels in the presence of awesome natural beauty to wash over me, and with it, the accompanying sense of smallness and comfort. Rarely used muscles aching, we knew the delightful trip would soon come to an end, as all rafting trips must. The river is boss, not us, but the journey can be exhilarating and beautiful. Like a rafting trip, life's journey begins and ends, and, if lived with the awareness of both our smallness and our capacities, it too can be exhilarating and beautiful.

A tourist from America once came to visit the Chafetz Chaim, one of the great nineteenth-century sages of eastern Europe. The tourist arrived at the single room that comprised the home of the famous rabbi armed with questions he had intended to pose, questions only few could be expected to answer. The tourist entered the room and looked around. He saw a table, a desk, a bookcase, a closet, a bed, and a chair. His prepared questions flew out of his mind. Instead, he asked, "Where are your possessions?"

"Where are your possessions?" came the rabbi's reply.

"What do you mean, 'where are my possessions?' asked the tourist. "I'm just a visitor here."

"So am I," said the Chafetz Chaim.

We are all temporary visitors who sometimes require a Yom Kippur reminder that the quality of our lives will not be measured by the quantity of our possessions.

Rivers teach Yom Kippur consciousness, but we may also learn this lesson through other avenues. Consider the Israeli violinist Yitzhak Perlman who once gave a concert at Lincoln Center. Those who have seen Perlman play know that, unlike most violinists, he performs sitting down because of the polio with which he has lived since childhood. In fact, Perlman gets around by means of braces on his legs and crutches for his arms. He uses his powerful upper body to propel himself from backstage to center stage and then back again. He moves adeptly but slowly and with obvious effort. When he reaches his chair, Perlman sits down slowly, puts his crutches on the floor, undoes the clasps on his legs, tucks one leg under the chair, and extends the other foot forward. He then bends down and picks up the violin, places it under his chin and nods to the conductor.

Returning to that concert day last November: Perlman had made his way out onto the stage at Lincoln Center and had readied himself to play; he nodded, the conductor began, and the piece was under way, when all of a sudden one of the strings of Perlman's violin snapped in two, reverberating throughout the auditorium like gunfire.

The audience, already hushed, now gasped a nervous gasp and wondered what would happen next. Perlman paused a moment, closed his eyes, and then signaled to the conductor to begin again. The orchestra began, and Perlman played with passion and purity.

An eyewitness reported:

> Now I know that it is impossible to play a symphonic work with just three strings. I know it, and you know it, but that night Yitzhak Perlman refused to know that. You could see him modulating, changing, recomposing the piece in his head. At one point, it sounded like he was detuning the strings to get new sounds from them that they had never made before. When he finished, there was an awesome silence in the room. And then people rose and cheered. There was an extraordinary outburst of applause from every corner of the auditorium. We were all on our feet, screaming and cheering, doing everything we could to show how much we appreciated what he had done. He smiled, wiped the sweat from his brow, raised his bow to quiet us . . . and then he said . . . not boastfully, but in a quiet, pensive, reverent tone, "you know . . . sometimes it is the artist's task to find out how much music you can still make with what you have left." (King, "Making Music with Whatever Is Left," p.14)

Who among us has not bemoaned the declining eyesight and hearing, the expanding middles, the aches and pains that accompany our advancing years, while youth continues to be wasted on the young? Who among us has not bemoaned the increasing speed at which time seems to zip by as we grow older? What will it take if not the consciousness of Yom Kippur to go ahead and find out how much music we can make with what we have left? And so we read in *Psalm 90*: "Teach us to number our days that we may obtain a heart of wisdom." Teach us to make our days count, to use them and not waste them, to use them and not abuse them, to use them now and enjoy them and not delay every goal for an uncertain tomorrow, to use them even when we lack the ideal means or the perfect time.

In Robert Fulghum's book *From Beginning to End: The Rituals of Our Lives*, there is a black-and-white photograph with the caption, "A man sitting in a chair in a cemetery, as a light rain fell and the sun shone at the same time, on the fourth day of June in 1994." Fulghum goes on to write about the photograph:

> If you were there, standing close by, you would notice that the sod beneath his chair was laid down in small square sections, suggesting it had been removed and then carefully replaced.
>
> The man owns the property upon which he sits. He has paid for the site, paid to have the ground dug up, to have a cement vault installed, and to have the ground restored.
>
> He is sitting on his own grave. Not because his death is imminent—he's in pretty good shape, actually. And not because he was in a morbid state of mind—he was in a fine mood when the picture was taken. In fact, he has had one of the most affirmative afternoons of his life.
>
> Sitting for an afternoon on his own grave, he has had one of those potent experiences when the large pattern of his life has been unexpectedly reviewed: the past, birth, childhood, adolescence, marriage, career, the present, and the future. He has confronted finitude—the limits of life. The fact of his own death lies before him—raising questions of the when and the where and the how of it. What shall he do with his life between then and now? (pp. 29–30)

Of course, the man in the chair and the author who keeps the photograph posted in his study are one and the same. Fulghum explains how it is that he describes himself sometimes in the third person. He speaks of his morning ritual of looking at the man in the bathroom mirror. Fulghum recalls having been aware as an adolescent of the man in the mirror growing facial hair, growing taller, getting pimples. Lately, he has noticed him going through middle age, becoming wider, losing hair, developing wrinkles. He writes: "The man in the mirror is older than I am now. While I have been thirty for many years, he'll be fifty-eight next June." Fulghum adds: "I see his white hair and beard, the lines on his face, the liver spots and scars on his hands, the sagging of his flesh. And I wonder how far from making use of his gravesite he might be? He certainly looks closer to death than I am."

Robert Fulghum is a Unitarian minister who has devised a ritual for achieving Yom Kippur consciousness, an awareness of life in the context of its full sweep, an awareness that ought to empower and not be morbid. So too do we fast and pray and wear white and avoid leather, acts designed to heighten our awareness of the beauties and pitfalls, the challenges and opportunities that meet us on life's river excursion.

May the Yom Kippur consciousness of this day goad us toward a serious appraisal of just how much music we can make with what we have, with the limited but potent means at our disposal, in the finite and precious span of time allotted to us on our life's journey.

THE MEANING OF "I AM JEWISH"
Rosh Hashanah 5767/2006

History will record a tide of horror and madness that swept over our planet in the beginning of the third millennium. The basic rules of civilization were violated, and all theories of cognition, common sense, and human values laid shattered and betrayed. History will also record that, in the midst of this chaos, there was a young man who, in a moment of extreme crisis, looked straight into the eye of evil, and said, "My father is Jewish, my mother is Jewish, I am Jewish." (I am Jewish)

Thus did Judea Pearl address Congregation B'nai Jeshurun in New York City in February, 2003, on the first yahrzeit of his son, the *Wall Street Journal* reporter Daniel Pearl. The entire *yahrzeit* address comprises part of the introduction to the book *I Am Jewish*, in which over a hundred Jews from around the world were invited to reflect on the meaning of those words to them, the meaning of Jewish identity in their lives. The challenge is aptly put to each of us as well as we embark on any new Jewish year, each one a point on the ancient calendar marked by our small, widely disbursed and often beleaguered tribe. We mark the year's beginning in rituals and traditions designed to instill in us a mood of sober celebration, joy that emerges from a serious ten-day process of self-reflection, self-criticism, and, we hope, spiritual growth.

But why partake in so much seriousness? Why subject ourselves to ancient rituals together in packed spaces? Why take up a book of prayers with which many of us have grown unfamiliar? Why continue to attach ourselves to a mixed tribal multitude engaged in a religious culture that runs counter to the mainstream? What meaning do we attach to our own Jewishness? Or, acknowledging a further sociological complexity, for those of us who live in Jewish families but without a personal Jewish identity, what meaning do we attach to the Jewishness of those in our family who do affirm "I am

Jewish"? Not even Daniel Pearl's parents can know with certainty what he meant to communicate in the calm and defiant dignity of that utterance. But no matter his intention, we do well to honor his memory by posing the question to ourselves: what do we mean when we say those three words?

The book *I Am Jewish* presents over 140 distinctly different ways to reflect on the meaning of the words. I offer my own response as a sample and as encouragement for each of us to compose our own. Were I invited to contribute to a second edition of the book, I might begin as follows: "I love being Jewish, and, seeing it as a choice, I choose to be Jewish, but that was not always the case. Three qualities lie at the heart of the Judaism that continues to claim my adherence and to entice me even as Judaism both delimits my humanity and permits it to express itself."

First, the Judaism that lays claim to my soul is a religion profoundly based on questioning. In *Genesis 3:9*, God puts the question to Adam, "*Ayeka*—Where are you?" God does not seek information here, does not expect a reply like, "Over here, God, here in the garden, next to the large beech tree." Rather, the question means to inspire Adam to consider his spiritual location, to become introspective, to pose questions of his own, such as: "Where am I in my life? What am I doing with my life? How ought I relate to my loved ones, other people, the earth, the One who put me here, my enemies, the impoverished? Where am I in my spiritual journey, and where should I be?"

I recently heard a curious statistic. Just a few years ago, when determining the nature of Jewish self-identification in America, a discouragingly high percentage identified as "secular" or "somewhat secular." However, among the self-identifying secular and somewhat secular Jews, a high percentage said that they believed in God, and a high percentage of those who said they believe in God believe that God hears their prayers and even performs miracles. Now, conventional wisdom is that secular people do not believe in God. Of course, surveys like this one do not uncover the emotional realities beneath the statistical data, but I would offer this speculation: some Jews identify themselves as secular, despite beliefs that most would call religious, when they do not choose to associate, for a whole host of possible reasons, with the institutions of Jewish religion. In any case, it would appear that among the many who self-identify as secular, the yearning for the holy, the desire for a spiritually rich life, yet abides.

In the words of Ronald Rolheiser: "We do not wake up in this world calm and serene, having the luxury of choosing to act or not act. We wake up crying, on fire with desire, with madness. What we do with that madness is our spirituality" (*Holy Longing*, p. 6). Rolheiser, a Christian, formulates well the assumption about human nature at the heart of Jewish spiritual teaching: we humans enter the world with an unquenchable thirst, a drive to grasp more than what is apparent, with questioning minds and questing souls.

My personal spiritual biography, by way of illustration, included an adolescent rejection of the Judaism I knew growing up as a child. As a spiritually seeking teen, like Garrison Keillor's character Guy Noir, I yearned for "the answers to life's persistent questions." For me, the persistent questions included: Why am I alive? Why do people die? Is there some master plan? If so, could I please have a peek at it? Is there a Master behind the plan? and the like. By contrast, the Judaism of my youth, and as I had come to disparage it in my adolescence, seemed unconcerned with substantial issues of the spirit, as it favored show and nostalgia. As a child, I made fun of the pompous robes of the clergy and the fancy hats the women wore on Friday nights at the suburban synagogue attended by my family. I do recall with great fondness, even now, the chocolate-y brownies at the Friday onegs and the sherbet punch prepared by the Sisterhood, but these did not serve as adequate spiritual nourishment. As my yearning for meaning grew in my late adolescence, the chasm between that yearning and what seemed to me superficial, even hypocritical Judaism, the only kind I knew, stretched to the point of breaking . . . well, nearly.

As I entered college, Eastern religions, with their emphasis on contemplative detachment, seemed to hold far greater promise for a rich inner life, and I turned to them until one day I picked up a copy of the college daily and noticed a free university course being offered on Jewish mysticism, a term that struck me as oddly oxymoronic. How could fancy hats and the rest of the superficial nonsense that I knew to be Judaism have anything to do with anything spiritually meaningful, much less mystical, a realm of thought and practice I then associated with Buddhism or Hinduism? Curiosity brought me to the class, in which I discovered that Jewish mysticism occupied one corner of an exceedingly large room, metaphorically speaking. And the room, it turns out, is one of many that together house the religious culture of our people. In those inexhaustibly ample rooms, human guides encourage one to seek, to question, and to explore. In each of the rooms of the Jewish house, one finds numerous companions, some contemporary and some ancestral, fellow seekers after a richer spiritual life. Thus did I enter the Jewish house for its promise of an immensely stable architecture, a firm platform upon which to engage in the search for meaning, a structure that could contain a growing spirit.

The second quality at my Jewish core: the Judaism that lays claim to my soul does not only sustain my personal yearning for spiritual deepening and purposeful living. Judaism does not serve as the basis for a private or monastic spirituality. Though we Jews trace our heritage to the singular Jewish couple Abraham and Sarah, the Jewish story begins as a whole people that is redeemed from slavery, covenanted at Sinai, and brought to the land of promise. That is, our primary birth myth is collective. The collectivity that lies at the mythic origins of our people renders inauthentic all efforts at a Judaism lived in isolation.

This past summer, Dela and I made a pilgrimage to eastern and central Europe, including the cities of Budapest, Kracow, Warsaw, and Prague. Though we certainly enjoyed ourselves at times, much of the trip met the intentionally dark purpose of allowing us to encounter places where Jewish ghosts haunt the streets of once vibrant communities. On the final Shabbat of our visit, we attended the Altneue Shul of Prague, known for its historical association with Rabbi Yehudah Loew, an important rabbinic scholar of the seventeenth century, but more famous in folk legend as the creator of the Golem. Before the trip, Rabbi Tom Gutherz had alerted me to the Hebrew inscriptions on the back wall of the sanctuary, including the acronym for the Talmudic teaching, "The one who says 'amen' is greater than the one who blesses."

My on-site contemplation of that teaching yielded the question: why would congregants select this phrase to decorate a synagogue wall? Two lines of response occurred to me, one trivial, one not. I suspect that from time immemorial Jews who care about synagogue decorum have conjured up techniques designed to keep congregants attentive to the task of prayer. If your "amen" counts so much more than the originally uttered blessing, then you must listen attentively in order to get credit. Attentive listening would reduce chatter, producing an uncommon decorum. The comparable teaching today might be: "The one who turns off his or her electronic device is greater than the ones you will disturb if you do not."

But the teaching on the rear wall of the shul embeds a deeper lesson. To say "amen" is to affirm the prayer of the other and also the one who prays. If I refuse or neglect to say "amen" to your *bracha*, my omission constitutes a denial of the legitimacy of your prayerful yearning. Not only do I deny or ignore your prayerful utterance, but my omission implies that you are not a part of the community I recognize as mine. By contrast, when I say "amen" to your *bracha*, I include you in my community and I affirm your aspirations. Regarded this way, saying "amen" is far from a trivial matter of adhering to the quaint ritual of appropriate formulaic response. It comprises a verbal building block of communal connectivity.

Prague was the last stop on our summer's journey. The week before we had stood at Jewish ground zero, Aushwitz-Birkenau, about which everything has surely been said. Having stood so recently in that place of the darkest manifestation of human evil, a place so disorienting and so shattering of hope, I would only offer: if Jewish identity does not motivate us to assent "amen" to our fellow Jews, to say "amen" to their *brachot*, to become builders of vibrant Jewish communities, do we not dishonor those who perished? However, if we can overcome the cultural forces of narcissistic absorption with the self, obsession with material acquisition, if we can pry ourselves away from our remote control devices and heed the voices that obligate us to move from self to community, then we will honor the memory of those who perished merely because they were Jews.

The Judaism I love obligates me to say "amen" to your *bracha* whether or not I share your prayerful aspiration, because I must affirm it at the very least as your prayer and because we Jews are obligated to build community together. "*Al Tifrosh Min Ha Tzibbur*—Do not separate yourself from the community," says Rabbi Hillel. The Judaism I love and the institutions that give it sustenance are not like Target stores where one shops when a desire to consume arises and otherwise stays home. The Judaism I love obligates us to lean into and overcome the culture of *Bowling Alone* (Robert Putnam's seminal study, published in 2000, that portrays American society as one in which its citizens live lives of increasing isolation from one another). The Judaism I love insists, *Kol Yisrael Aravin Zeh Bazeh*—we Jews, whether secular or religious, Reform or Orthodox, Conservative or Reconstructionist, nondenominational or postdenominational, Sephardic or Ashkenazic, by choice or by birth, rationalist or mystic, Yiddishist or Hebraist, or just plain Jewish, we are all bound up together, responsible for one another. We are wrapped together by bonds of familial interconnectivity that transcend ideological difference. Because we are fated to be in the same boat together, we would do well to choose a way to row in some semblance of harmony.

The Judaism I love calls its house of worship *Beit Knesset*, a house of gathering, a place of assembly. At a stage of history when communal structures have receded in strength, we do well proudly to regard our synagogues as centers of community formation, places to establish connection, vehicles for overcoming the loneliness and despair that characterize much of contemporary society.

The Judaism I affirm nurtures the spiritual quest, obligates me to participate in a community of amen-sayers ... and one more thing. Judaism does not permit Jewish insularity ... and never did. One could go back to Abraham, the first Jew. His very first act after formalizing his Jewish identification by performing a *brit milah* on himself (do not, I repeat, do not try that at home!) was to scamper off his porch so that he and Sarah could provide hospitality to the non-Jewish strangers passing by. Jewish tradition accords that seemly trivial mitzvah with high significance, regarding it as a paradigm of *Hakhnasat Orchim*, the obligation to practice hospitality to others. But *Hakhnasat Orchim* is not merely about good manners. *Hakhnasat Orchim* is the having one's antennae raised, the disposition of watchful peering outside of one's home and one's primary community of identification. As I read it, *Hakhnasat Orchim* means that although Judaism frames the spiritual life of a Jew with particularly Jewish coloration, some of which distinguishes us as unique and separate from our non-Jewish neighbors, still, we may not forget or ignore our membership in the human family. We may not forget that all humans, not only the Jewish variety, were created *B'tzelem Elohim*, in God's image and likeness. We may not ignore our Jewish obligation to concern ourselves with the welfare of all others.

When we first coalesced as a people privileged and obligated by the covenant of Torah, we began to hear the refrain, over and over again, thirty-six times in the Torah, "you were strangers in the land of Egypt" not as reason to frame our identities as still enslaved victims but so that we would pay attention to others still residing on the margins of society: the poor, the uneducated, the handicapped, the foreign, the abused, the disenfranchised, and the persecuted. The Judaism that I love reminds me of our collective history of enslavement, a history that obligates us to empathize with those who suffer in our midst.

On Rosh Hashanah, we Jews take up the shofar and hear the primitive instrumental jolt to our complacent tendencies. As has been noted, the shofar that goads us to self-critique produces its insistent drone only when we blow from the narrow end. It only works in that direction, from small to large. From the particular we go to the universal. Thus does my Jewish particularism insist that all who draw breath on this planet are my brothers and sisters. Thus does it insist that we, members of this particular Jewish congregation, join together with members of area churches as one larger faith community seeking social justice in our region. That is, working for systemic social change toward a more just society, acting in concert with members of other faith communities, is a Jewish imperative. Thus does my Jewish particularism insist that as a congregation we continue to seek contributions for our Tzedakah Fund that supports many local projects that improve the lives of others, that we participate in IMPACT and PACEM and AIM and Habitat for Humanity and support the Emergency Food Bank, among the worthy ways in which we members of CBI properly express our Jewish concern for the welfare of others in our region, not to mention a host of crucial, more global causes. Our collective Jewish memory of enslavement obligates us to overcome the instinct for insularity.

Do you know that, according to custom, Jewish places of prayer must have windows? Why? Because, although we Jews proudly establish and maintain institutions devoted to nurturing unique and precious Jewish traditions, these institutions must be open to the outside. Our prayers must begin with ourselves, must extend to a community of primary identification, and then must stretch out beyond.

The Judaism that I love recognizes that humans at their core are embodied spirits with a constant yearning, a perpetual need to ask, "Where am I?" The Judaism that I love provides a complex and multifaceted framework for Jews to grow our spirits in a community of amen-sayers. The Judaism that I love instills in us the obligation to concern ourselves with issues of social justice in society at large. That is why I am proudly Jewish.

In the new year now under way, may we reflect well on the ways that Jewish identification can frame our spiritual journeys: as individuals, in Jewish community, and through the call to social justice. May our reflections, our commitments, and our deeds bring honor to those who proudly affirm "I am Jewish." In gratitude may we all affirm: *Baruch Attah Adonai Elohenu Melekh Ha-olam Sh'asani Yisrael*—Blessed are You Lord our God, Sovereign of the universe, who has made me a Jew, as you say: "amen!"

ON JEWISH TIME:
A VISION FOR A NEW YEAR
Rosh Hashanah 5753/1992

Rosh Hashanah is late this year. Last year it was early. Is it ever on time?

Not too profound in and of itself. But it got me to thinking about time and how time structures our lives, or rather, how the way we conceive of time pertains to how we structure our lives and affects the way we see ourselves in relation to others and the world.

Consider the digital watch with its numerical display and its precursor, the analog watch with its round face surrounded by twelve numbers and hands for hours, minutes, and sometimes for seconds. They both tell time, but not in the some way, not in the same context. The digital watch presents only the moment: forty-five minutes and eight seconds after eight o'clock p.m. The time is now. The analog watch lets us see the present time in relation to the rest of the day. The time is now, but it is also two hours after dinnertime, three hours before bedtime. Both watches tell time equally well, but they structure its passage differently.

Rosh Hashanah is actually on time this year, as it was last year and the year before. It always falls on the new moon, the first day of the month of Tishrei, on a calendar that at best supplements the one we use most often. What might it mean to live primarily on Jewish time, according to the Jewish calendar, to keep time by a Jewishly informed clock?

The Jewish clock, it would appear, combines features of both digital and analog. As on the analog display, the Jewish clock always presents time in relation to past and future: it includes faces for the day, for the week, for the season, for the year, for one's lifetime, for all the events of Jewish history as well as Jewish mythic history, and for eternity; it is not made by Casio and cannot be purchased at Wal-Mart. On the Jewish clock, it could be an hour past *shachrit*, morning prayer, five hours before *minchah*, afternoon prayer; it might be the second day after Shabbat, a certain number of days before Shabbat Shuvah or before Sukkot; it may be a precise number of months before your daughter becomes Bat Mitzvah. It is 5,700-some years since the creation of the universe according to the reckoning of our tradition (Happy Birthday, universe!) and 1,900-some years since the Romans destroyed Jerusalem and burned the Temple that had been the focal point for the religion of our ancestors. The Messiah, at last notice, has yet to come, but is expected soon, at least by some of our coreligionists.

A story: four Jewish men lay bedbound in a hospital room. Their disabilities did not permit them to leave the room, and, with one exception, they were not even able to leave their beds. The man whose bed stood farthest from the door and nearest to the outside wall of the hospital was Moshe. And every day, about an hour after breakfast, Moshe would, with difficulty, sit himself up in bed, lean over toward the wall, and with his arms slowly and painfully pull himself up the wall, huffing and puffing, until he reached a ledge. He would then pull himself up to the ledge, part the curtain, and look out the window, too high up for the others to view.

As he looked out the window, Moshe would describe what he saw to the other patients. There was a park across the street from the hospital. On some winter days, he reported seeing the snow-covered ground and a man bundled up in a heavy coat, wearing boots, walking his dog. During the days of spring, he depicted the trees becoming green and flowers blooming, a woman briskly striding through puddles on a rainy day, her umbrella blown by the wind. In the summer, he mentioned the children he regarded playing with Frisbees and the elderly people he saw feeding the ducks in the pond. And in the fall, he would see the vibrantly changing colors, and occasionally, families or couples picnicking on blankets in the grass.

Each and every day, Moshe would, with difficulty, pull himself up to the window ledge, would look out, and would describe what he saw on the outside to his companions inside the hospital room. This went on for many months. And the men looked forward to the ritual of the window, to Moshe's descriptions. These narrated scenes produced the only variety in their daily routine; they molded a sense of connection to the outside world; they reminded the patients that there was a world outside of their hospital room, a world with variety, possibility, yearning, and hope.

One day, as the men awoke, the three became aware that Moshe was not in his bed. He had, it turned out, died during the night, and his bed was now occupied by another patient by the name of Shmuel. Of course, the men were grieved by the death of their companion and also by the loss of their daily ritual. They told Shmuel about their former companion and the ritual of the window, and they asked whether he might perform the same role. Shmuel agreed to try to do what Moshe had done. He wasn't sure he could manage it physically, but he would try. So, later that morning, Shmuel sat himself up in his bed and began, with great difficulty and considerable pain, to inch his way up the wall. He made it up to the ledge, parted the curtains, and peered out, but did not speak. He lingered at the ledge for several minutes, then let himself down the wall, and lay back on his bed; he said nothing. Of course, the other patients were eager to hear Shmuel's report, but they figured he must be exhausted from the exertion, so they were quiet for quite some time until they noticed that Shmuel had tears in his eyes. "Shmuel," one of them asked, "what is the matter? Tell us what you saw." "I cannot tell you what I saw," said Shmuel, "because there is no window. There is only a wall."

All human beings seek vision; we all seek windows that allow us to see beyond the confines of our rooms, that permit us to transcend the certainties that come to us through our physical senses. Human beings crave vision that outstrips the scientifically verifiable, vision that pertains to meaning of the deepest kind, meaning that sustains us in the awareness of our own mortality.

Can Judaism serve as a source of vision, a window to the outside, a means for perceiving what lies outside the four visible walls, a vehicle for connection to that which is beyond ourselves? If we could strap on the watch that displays Jewish time, would we see our lives more meaningfully situated than otherwise? Does Judaism, can Judaism provide the framework, the means for seeking that vision? Can it do so for us?

Indisputably, the Jewish religion has served Jews of the past as a vehicle for framing a life of meaning. Moreover, the distinct clock of our religious tradition plays a large part in that framing role. And, it seems to me, the fact that we gather here and now, indicates that we too believe, or at least hope, that we too can partake; that when we hear and utter ancient words, sometimes in a language that we do not understand well but that we retain because it connects us to our ancestors and to fellow Jews all over the world, the fact that we gather on these Days of Awe, on Rosh Hashanah and Yom Kippur, and on holidays, and on Shabbat, the fact that we make *motzi* over bread and marry under a *chuppah* and enter our children into the *brit*, the covenant of Mother Sarah and Father Abraham means that we too desire at least a glimpse of the Jewish vision that situates our lives in that larger context of purpose.

There are many rubrics within the concept of the Jewish time by which we might keep time this New Year.

For example, we learn in *Pirkei Avot* that three things sustain the whole world: Torah, prayer, and *gemilut hasadim*, deeds of simple kindness. Each of the three might well be regarded as faces on our Jewish timepiece. How so?

Torah: "Torah" here refers to the broadest sense, the entire tradition of sacred literature, written or Biblical, and oral or rabbinic. It means the Talmud, the Halachah and the Aggadah, the law and the legend; it refers to the Bible and the commentaries on it and the midrash that grows out of it. When, in the famous encounter, the sage Hillel tells the prospective proselyte that the essence of Torah is "what is hateful to you do not do to another. The rest is commentary. Go and study," his answer is less of a complete answer than it is guidance, a map for finding the way. "The rest is commentary. Go and study" means: "I really cannot fully and precisely satisfy this request for reducing Judaism to its essence while standing on one foot, but if you immerse yourself in the study of Torah, worlds will open up for you, you will become transformed in unexpected and worthwhile ways, you will acquire the tools to cope with life's puzzles and challenges. If you are willing to strap the Jewish watch to your wrist, you will find your hours, days, and weeks suddenly organized by a structure that can frame your life with value."

Tefillah—Prayer: The most common form of Jewish prayer is the *bracha*. A bracha is simply a prayer whose first or last line begins "Baruch atah Adonai," usually translated "Blessed or Praised are You Lord." But "blessed" does not convey what *Baruch* conveys. Baruch makes me think of Berech or Birkiyim, the knee or knees that are bent figuratively or actually whenever one acknowledges the existence of the Supreme Being, whenever one takes to heart the concept that I am not the center of the universe, that I am not ultimately in charge even of my own life, much less of others. "Baruch" also makes me think of *beraichah*, the pool, the wellspring of all life that is also the fountain of nourishment for body and soul, the paramount source for that which cools, calms, and comforts.

And *atah: alef, tav, hay*. The first two are the first and last letters of the Hebrew alphabet, suggesting the entirety of creation; a midrash has it that God spoke creation into being by pronouncing the letters of the alef-bet, from *aleph* to *tav*. The first two letters also spell the word et, which has no meaning but indicates the direct object, the thingness of a thing; it points us to the universe of cold objects, of disconnected parts and pieces ... until one adds the *hay*, the letter that indicates God's name and presence, producing the word "you." God's presence transforms objects into persons, into you, as in the "you and I" of relationship.

According to the relational philosophy of Martin Buber, God's presence dwells in I-you relationships, where people are present for one another.

So when our weeks and days are permeated by prayer, when we invoke *Baruch Atah* at regular intervals or when the occasion warrants, we acknowledge God's presence, we connect our smallness with His vastness, we join our voice to the echoing sounds that began when God first fashioned letters into sounds and sounds into forms.

Gemilut Hasadim: The third pillar of the universe is *gemilut hasadim*, deeds of simple kindness. Unlike Torah, which ideally one would study at set times each week, and unlike prayer moments, which occur usually in response to specific awareness, deeds of kindness occur as opportunities often and unpredictably during each and every day.

Rabbi Israel Salanter, the prominent rabbi of nineteenth-century Lithuania, was once asked to set up criteria for the kashrut of matzah being baked for the coming Passover holiday. He replied that if the women doing the baking were well paid and if their supervisors spoke respectfully to them, then the matzah was kosher.

It is also said about the same Rabbi Salanter that one year, as the time of Kol Nidre approached, he failed to appear at the synagogue. Where could he be at this most solemn day of the year? The people waited until they could wait no more; the service began without him. When he did finally arrive he explained what had happened. He left his home in good time, but as he passed by an alley, he heard the sound of a baby crying. He found the baby and comforted it until its mother returned.

Opportunities for *gemilut hasadim* present themselves often, and not just in stories about famous rabbis. If I ever felt despair about human nature, all I would need to do would be to think of the many congregants I know who organize much of their lives to maximize the comfort, support, and kindness they offer others. I do not know any saints, but I know of many, many saintly acts going on in our midst every single day.

On Rosh Hashanah, right on schedule, we begin a new Jewish year.

With God's help, may it be a year of windows and vision,
a year devoted to Jewish study,
a year full of hope and prayer,
a year full of kind deeds,
a year organized according to the Jewish timepiece that enables us to live with great purpose, with optimism, and with spiritual depth.

SEARCHING FOR WHOLENESS
Kol Nidre 5754/1993

If the religious quest is a quest for personal wholeness, for ever greater spiritual integrity, for fullness, for wisdom, for purpose, then the path toward personal wholeness is the one upon which we would walk this day. Yet the search for wholeness is an elusive search, fraught with problems, among them that the search itself may be wearying, may frustrate or break us. The search itself may leave us ever farther from the goal.

In the Talmud, one finds an enigmatic story that illustrates the potential perils entailed by the religious quest. Four men enter the garden, namely, Ben Azzai, Ben Zoma, Aher, and Rabbi Akiva. Rabbi Akiva says to them, "When you arrive at the slabs of pure transparent marble, do not say: 'Water, Water!' For it is said, 'He who speaks falsehood shall not be established before My eyes' (*Psalms 101:7*)." Ben Azzai casts a look and dies ... Ben Zoma looks and becomes demented.... Aher mutilates the shoots [i.e., he becomes a heretic]. Only Rabbi Akiva departs unhurt, whole (*Hagigah 14b*).

In my interpretive reading of the Talmudic parable, the four sages, Palestinian rabbis of the second century, enter the garden of enticements and challenges, the garden each and every human being enters by simply growing out of infancy. As we enter that garden in its contemporary version, it confronts us with a vast and often confusing array of inducements, with alluring promises of painless gain, with temptations of pleasure and freedom, and then with the disappointing gap between fantasies and realities, letdowns, and unanticipated sorrows. Set loose from the security of parental care enjoyed by most of us, we set out, like the four rabbis, to explore the garden, more or less equipped to successfully navigate the journey but never entirely prepared for the thorns and thickets, the complex and numerous obstacles, never entirely certain how to choose among alternative paths, never quite sure which voices to trust, which truths to affirm.

We hope to emerge from the experience enriched, ennobled, deepened, and whole. However, as the parable warns us, the garden is a place of challenge and dangers that prove overwhelming for many. Only one of the four great sages, only Rabbi Akiva, emerges unharmed.

Ben Azzai dies. I imagine his contemporary counterpart as my high school friend Bob. Bob's home, like too many in our society, was particularly devoid of love: affection took the form of monetary gifts from Dad but rarely hugs or heart-to-heart talks. Bob left home and went off to study at a prestigious university. There, Bob entered a garden of delights, a university with academic offerings galore in a city full of cultural stimulation, but he entered that garden with no limits, no personal boundaries, no ability to make distinctions between the professor and the street-corner preacher, between the pleasure of art and the drug-induced stupor, between values honed by generations of disciplined living and thinking and those spun out to sell the latest perfume or beer. Feeling unhinged and unloved, unworthy and confused, Bob became depressed. When depression turned into despair and despair persisted, Bob chose suicide, a shock to those who saw his as a life of privilege and opportunity.

Ben Zoma becomes demented, touched, I imagine, by narrow-minded obsession. Unable to handle the multiplicity of stimuli of contemporary society—who can?—he narrows his world to an absurd degree. Unable to cope with the bewildering array of choices, he cloisters himself in a self-imposed ghetto, perhaps one with cult-like trappings. He seats himself before a guru who provides seemingly clear and simple answers to life's dilemmas, who directs, guides, and, perhaps, controls his steps. Or maybe our contemporary Ben Zoma does not opt for the life of the religious cult, but rather one of addictive materialism, where the acquisition of wealth for its own sake becomes the single-minded obsession, family, friendship, and all other values to the side. Or his addictive behavior could direct itself at food or drink or drugs or sex.

And what about Aher? He is one of the most fascinating figures of rabbinic lore. Elisha ben Abuyah becomes known as Aher, meaning "the other," after a distinguished career as rabbi and teacher of rabbis, among them Rabbi Akiva and Rabbi Meir. He comes to be called Aher after famously losing his faith, rejecting the basis of Judaism. The circumstances of his apostasy become the subject of much speculation and several legends, but it boils down to this: the garden he has entered opens his eyes to realities that profoundly disturb him, that force him to face the presence of radical evil in the world, the fact that horribly awful things happen to decent, innocent, and righteous people. This awareness leads to his rejection of the faith of his ancestors. His experience and his honesty drive him to the decisive pronouncement: there is no Judgment, and there is no Judge!

It is a tricky business, entering the garden of delights and enticements that is the garden of life. We want to enter and emerge whole, but, if you are like me, you find wholeness not only elusive but, at times, a receding goal, ever more so with increasingly numerous and complex demands on our energies and time and with an increasingly vast array of voices haranguing us about a confusing multiplicity of contradictory values and truths.

What, for example, is a reasonable sexual ethic for a young adult today? AIDS has taught us that free love is, in fact, not free. From one side, a young person hears, "condoms, condoms!" From another, "abstinence, abstinence!" From yet another, the pervasive world of TV, film, and popular music, the implicit or explicit message is unlimited indulgence, the consequences of which are rarely depicted. Which voice is one to believe? It is confusing out there in the garden. It is not easy to pass through intact, much less whole.

Judaism, particularly at this season, has something distinct to say to those of us who feel more broken than whole, to those of us who feel more scarred this year than last year, to those of us who aspire for wholeness, but for whom that very aspiration brings into sharp focus our faults and imperfections, our inconsistencies and shortcomings. Judaism has something distinct to say to those of us who would like to avoid the despair of Ben Azzai, the obsessions of Ben Zoma, and the cynicism of Aher.

One central Jewish teaching on seeking wholeness when it appears to be absent comes from the mouth of a thirty-two-year-old Episcopal priest who, while dying of AIDS, asked to speak with Rabbi Harold Kushner. Rabbi Kushner asked the priest if he felt that God had abandoned him or was punishing him, issues often confronted by religious AIDS patients.

> "No," answered the priest who went on to say, "I think I misused my sexuality, as a lot of people do in different ways, and I'm paying a high price for it. But I don't feel I'm dying without God. The only good thing about my illness is that I learned something which I could only have hoped was true: God loves and forgives people no matter how much they've messed up their lives. My main source of comfort is that God has not turned away from me.... [And] I hope my congregation won't reject me ... for I have one more sermon to preach ... that God

knows how flawed and imperfect we are, and loves us anyway." (Feinstein, "Almost Perfect")

God knows how flawed and imperfect we are and loves us anyway. The priest's words reflect a central Jewish teaching, one we would do well to take to heart. For do we not often hold ourselves to a standard so high that not only must we fail but we imagine that no one can possibly have any regard for us for having failed, that no one, and certainly not God, could forgive us for our many shortcomings? I do not think this is only a problem for priests and rabbis. I am amazed at how frequently I meet people with significant accomplishments and successes, who regard their shortcomings as unforgivable and themselves as essentially unfulfilled, inadequate, and unlovable.

The theme of the ten Days of Awe, the theme of renewal, *teshuvah*, turning, repentance, has two facets, of which we often emphasize but one. True, we are bidden at this season to be self-critical, to strive for serious improvement, to make amends, and to change. However, we are also bidden to know that our sincere efforts to improve, our honest attempts to do *teshuvah*, no matter how inadequate, will be accepted. Our tradition sees God as receptive to human effort, allowing the divine quality of mercy to overtake the attribute of severe and harsh judgment.

The notion of God's receptivity to our efforts at seeking forgiveness goes quite far. In a collection of *midrashim* on the theme of *teshuvah*, the rabbis pose the question: What about some of the great sinners of all time, the archetypical sinners? If they do *teshuvah*, does God forgive even them? What about Cain, the first murderer? Yes, says the midrash, even Cain is forgiven, even his *teshuvah* is accepted by the Holy One. Therefore, one infers, ours can be accepted too.

What about Manasheh, who as King of Judah in the seventh century BCE sets up idols in the Holy Temple in Jerusalem, and who thus not only commits idolatry, one of the three gigantic sins in classical Judaism, but leads the entire nation into habitual sinful practice? As punishment for behavior displeasing to God, Manasheh is captured by Assyrian forces and exiled to Babylonia. Noting Manasheh's subsequent return from captivity, the midrash asks whether some kind of reconciliation with God has occurred. Has he repented, and has the repentance of this horrible idolater been accepted? As midrashically imagined, here is the scene:

After Manasheh is dragged off to Babylonia in chains, his captors toss him into a copper cauldron shaped like a jackass, under which a slow fire burns. In desperation, Manasheh begins to petition all the idols of which he has knowledge, one by one, pleading, "Idol So-and-So, please rescue me!" Only after exhausting the list does he recall in a dim corner of memory a bit of Torah verse, taught to him by his father, King Hezekiah: "In your distress, when all these things are come upon you, in the end of days, return to the Lord your God, and hearken to His voice; for the Lord your God will not fail you, nor destroy you" (*Deuteronomy 4:30, 31*).

So Manasheh says to himself, "I will call upon God. If He answers me, fine. If not I will know that all deities are similarly worthless." At that moment the ministering angels, not particularly impressed with the quality or sincerity of Manasheh's repentance, begin to close the windows of Heaven in an effort to prevent Manasheh's prayer from reaching God. Meanwhile, they put the question to God: "May a man who set up an idol in the Temple be accepted in repentance?" The Holy One replies: "If I do not accept his repentance, I shall be barring the door to all who would repent." What does the Holy One proceed to do? He fashions a trap door under His very own throne, where the angels cannot interfere, an opening through which Manasheh's supplications ascend. (*Jerusalem Talmud Sanhedrin 28c*)

Thus, in this midrashic understanding, God extends Himself greatly to a human, even a wicked human of inadequate sincerity, but a human in need of forgiveness.

Perhaps one might surmise from the Manasheh story that tradition dismisses the necessity of sincerity. Not so. As the Mishnah teaches us, one who plans to transgress over and over again, thinking that Yom Kippur is coming and will atone for his transgression, forget it! For such a person Yom Kippur effects no atonement. And furthermore, says the Mishnah, Yom Kippur atones only for sins between humans and God. For transgressions among humans, the offended party must first be appeased before Yom Kippur will effect atonement.

Does the teaching about divine receptivity to imperfect human efforts at turning have an analog in the human realm? Does the divine readiness to forgive translate to the sphere of human interrelationships? It does.

The paragraph immediately preceding Kol Nidre reads: "By the authority of the Heavenly court and by the authority of the earthly court, with the consent of the Omnipresent One and with the consent of this congregation, we declare it permissible to pray with sinners." Who are these sinners? They are us. We may aspire to the purity symbolized by the white garments worn by many on this Day of Atonement. We may seek wholeness of spirit. But we are not a congregation of wholly perfect individuals. Rather, we are sinners praying among sinners.

In this regard, Rabbi Richard Levy's creative elaboration of that same paragraph captures that sense of ourselves as the sinners whose presence we permit. His version:

> By the authority of the heavenly court,
> And by authority of the earthly court,
> With the permission of God the Ever-Present,
> And with the permission of this congregation,
> We who have ourselves transgressed
> Declare it lawful to pray with others
> Who have wronged either God or human beings:
> The keeper of Shabbat who, by her silence,
> Allowed crime to flourish among her associates
> Consents to pray with the supporter of the oppressed
> Who disdained to put on tefillin.
> The one who gave tzeddakah but cheated on [taxes]
> Consents to pray with the one who worked hard for Israel
> But exploited his friend.
> Joined in the recognition of our own failings,
> We pledge to pray both for ourselves and for
> The others around us who have fallen short. (*On Wings of Awe*, p. 245)

That is to say, not only would we come here this day trusting in divine receptivity of our imperfect human efforts to repent and return, but we would, as well, take on a more forgiving and open posture toward other members of our worshipping community of imperfect beings.

In our quest for wholeness along the pathways in our gardens full of challenge and delight, we do well to consider one of the prominent symbols of these holy days, the primitive horn known as the shofar. The shofar serves well as the vehicle for and symbol of our longing for wholeness.

Its primal blasts come in sequences beginning with a whole sound, *tekiah*, followed by a tripartite *shevarim*, whose very name means broken, and then the even more fragmented *teruah* followed again by a whole *tekiah* and finally by *tekiah gedolah*, a long solid sound. Our wordless shofar prayer says, "We begin life whole, but life's experiences break us and smash us to pieces. We are bruised and wounded, but we shall continue to yearn for wholeness and will, with Your help, become whole again."

Are repentance and forgiveness always possible? One intuits that there must be limits. Perhaps, but Jewish tradition waxes hyperbolic in asserting that whereas "the Gates of Prayer are sometimes open and sometime closed, the Gates of Forgiveness, the Gates of *Teshuvah*, are always open."

> We gather this Day of Atonement, yearning for wholeness.
>
> Like the four sages, we have entered the gardens of our lives, seeking spiritual integrity and inner peace, striving for improvement of character.
>
> As we gather this evening of Yom Kippur, fractured and broken,
>
> May we be strengthened in our resolve to accept one another, in all our faults, with all our shortcomings.
>
> May we come to trust that the supplications of our hearts, directed heavenward, will find an approving and forgiving ear on the throne of divine glory.
>
> And may we come to feel, this day and all our days, essentially loved, forgiven, and accepted, by our fellow humans and by the Holy One.

THE TORAH OF BEING WHERE WE ARE
Rosh Hashanah 5756/1995

As Moses climbed up Mount Sinai to receive the covenant, God spoke to him, saying, "Come up to Me on the mountain—*veheyei sham*—and be there" (*Exodus 24:12*). Our rabbinic ancestors, close readers of the text always and never doubting for a second that every word of every verse of Torah is deliberately and purposefully included, wonder, "Why does the Torah say, 'Come up to the mountain and be there'?" If Moses comes up to the mountain, where else could he possibly be? Sipping a Heineken Light in downtown Jerusalem, perhaps?

As the Hasidic Rebbe Menachem Mendel of Kotzk puts it, "If Moses had come up to the mountain, why did God also have to tell him to be *there*? Because," the rebbe replied, "it is possible to expend great effort in climbing the mountain, but still not be *there*." Not everyone who is there is *there*. Sometimes they are somewhere else.

How to be where one is precisely what that wound-up scroll of parchment and what all the traditions that have developed around it are all about. In my view, we of the Western world, living in the so-called postmodern age, have less certainty about how to be where we are than ever before.

During my family's travels this past summer, I noticed a curious and distressing pattern, especially when we toured in Spain and were on the move most days, rarely staying in the same town or city more than two nights. In minute and larger matters, Dela and I often found ourselves so concerned with the upcoming phase of our travels that we did not entirely attend to what we were doing or seeing at the moment. We were not always where we were. Imagine yourself in the Prado, one of the world's great museums of art, standing in front of some magnificent work by El Greco or Goya, while dividing one's attention between the piece of great art and thoughts about the next activity of the day. With the masterpiece in view, we would begin to wonder aloud, "Should we go to another museum perhaps or on a walking tour or visit some plaza or cathedral or monastery or botanical garden or return to the hotel for a rest?" Or, a particularly favorite topic of mine, "Where will we eat lunch?" For heaven's sake, when one is in the Prado, shouldn't one be entirely in the Prado?

My illustration is not perfect. When traveling, sometimes one must play both tourist and tour guide. A dual role splits the attention. But often the issue is not merely one of a necessarily dual role. Too often, while engaged in a conversation, I'm thinking about my next sermon. While writing the sermon, I'm pondering the most recent family feud (not the TV show). While attending a concert, I'm contemplating the next family vacation or worrying about an ill congregant or a troubled acquaintance or a phone call not yet returned or some other unfinished business. Even in the midst of prayer, a flood of extraneous notions, from the trivial to the momentous, distracts me from what I presumably intend for that span of time. Being where I am, fully and completely, is an art I too rarely master. Like the tourist trying to take in so many sites that he fails to see any of them well, my attention can flit about, even as my body occupies one place.

Now that I have shared this personal failing with you all, trusting that I do not stand entirely alone in these matters, the challenge deepens. In an important sense, I believe, an ability to be where one is correlates to an ability to be who one is.

At bottom, the inability to be where one is may belie a more serious discontent. Perhaps we often are unable to be where we are because we are not certain we want to be there. And perhaps we are not entirely happy with where we are because we are not entirely happy with who we are. We may suspect that life has more to offer us but are unsure of what. We may fantasize about our own future accomplishments, but reality falls short. And every day, it seems, the sands shift yet again and the rules change: is there a young woman or man today who has clarity about what it means to be a woman or man, how to relate to others of the same or the other gender or gender orientation, which career aspirations to consider, which values to affirm, whether to aspire to political correctness or dismiss it as a passing fad?

The vast array of available and stridently expressed views do not make for clarity. Rather, they overload our children and us with conflicting claims based on a confusing multiplicity of perspectives and points of view. No wonder both young and old these days have trouble defining the boundaries of their own identities, no wonder folks have trouble maintaining focus, sticking to one career, one marriage. No wonder the fundamentalists are uptight. Some of us nonfundamentalists are a bit uptight ourselves. No wonder so many of us find it so difficult to be where we are.

Which brings me to Smoke, a film released earlier this year that wafted through theaters, mostly unseen and unnoticed; perhaps it did not cost enough money, contain enough sex, violence, or special effects to garner attention. However, it does present, in my view, a lovely metaphor for the challenge of getting a grip on reality in a postmodern age. And in a gentle and subtle way it embodies a central theme of Torah teaching, a response to the concern about just how one might begin to be where one is in our time.

Much of the simple story of this film involving three main characters revolves around a tobacco shop on a corner in Brooklyn. Let me recall just two scenes from the film. Near the beginning, the owner of the shop, Audie (played by Harvey Keitel) and a couple of his customers are schmoozing as they are wont to do. The subject becomes the nature of smoke itself and whether one can measure it, to ascertain its substance, its reality. After all, smoke floats ghostlike; smoke occupies the air, but it is not the air; it drifts along, appears momentarily to have definite form, but the form folds into itself and off of itself, moving slowly but constantly until it disbands into no perceptible thing.

Like all of reality to postmoderns, smoke is difficult to grasp. But Audie, the tobacconist, insists that one can ascertain for a certainty the reality of smoke and that one can measure it, albeit only indirectly and only by attending with great care to details. With a very sensitive scale, Audie claims, one can weigh the cigar before lighting up and can then weigh all the ashes afterwards, noting the difference. Smoke may be ephemeral, but it has weight and substance and is real.

A little ways into the film, we are introduced to one of the other characters, an author (played by William Hurt) who regularly patronizes Audie's shop, as he lives in a nearby apartment. The author has suffered from an extreme case of writer's block ever since the accident in which his pregnant wife was killed, some three years earlier. On this particular evening, when the perpetually depressed author discovers Audie's hobby of photography, Audie urges him to come and view his collection of pictures.

Invitation reluctantly accepted, the two pore over the collection. The author quickly realizes the collection has an unusual quality. He begins to flip through the pictures more quickly. It must be some kind of a joke. All the pictures are numbered and dated, and they each present the same black-and-white view of

Audie's tobacco shop. It turns out Audie has taken each photograph of the tobacco shop from exactly the same spot, catty-corner from his store, across the intersection, at 8:00 a.m. of each and every day since he acquired the camera. His albums contain over eight thousand pictures.

The author laughs a nervous and uncertain laugh. The pictures are all the same. The audience laughs. The pictures are all the same. Simultaneously, the author and the movie viewer begin to wonder what manner of obsession prompts such an odd hobby. But Audie grows insistent and a bit testy. "Don't flip through so quickly. Don't you get it? This is not a joke. This is my life's work. Don't you understand? Each of these photographs are unique. Each tells a story. Each recalls a distinct day. Together, they describe a flow of seasons and events and people and change."

Not entirely convinced, the author begins to turn the pages of the album more slowly, to look a little more carefully. He sees that the same camera mounted on the tripod pointed at the same scene shot from the same place and angle at the same time every day does indeed produce a unique picture each time. The lighting varies as does the weather and the cars and the clothing and the pedestrians, among the details captured and frozen by the camera's eye.

The author continues to flip the pages until he comes to a picture taken some three years ago. Same tobacco shop, same everything, but this time he gasps as he recognizes his wife; this picture was taken on the day she was killed; she had intended to pick up some cigars for him. In that gasp of recognition, past joins present, awful, painful moments come alive, deeply submerged grief rises to the surface and flows forth.

One picture, just like all the others, but not really the same at all. This one picture trips an invisible switch that, in turn, sparks an internal transformation, a realignment of perspective, a new beginning. The past is not erased; the sadness is not gone, but the author can now begin to acknowledge the sadness and the loss and do the grieving necessary so that his life can go on, so that he can become creative once more. He does not suddenly write the great American novel. However, for him, that photograph becomes the catalyst for *teshuvah*, not in the narrow sense of repentance, but in the fuller sense of turning within and returning to his life's path. The picture becomes such a catalyst for *teshuvah*, but only when the author slows down and generates enough patience to look closely and carefully, with concentration, with what our tradition calls *kavvanah*.

Only in such a state of concentration, only by attending fully to the uniqueness of each recorded moment, only then does the uniqueness make a difference. Only then can the author become fully present in a still smoky but substance-filled reality.

Rabbi Lawrence Kushner tells about the Hasidic rebbe who walks through his village accompanied by some of his students. As they walk, they come to a crowd of people, all of whom are gazing upward at a man who has stretched a tightrope across the central plaza of the town, between its only two tall buildings. The man is slowly walking the tightrope.

> There is no net to catch the acrobat should he fall, God forbid. There is, however, a hat to pass around for donations. But, for now, no one notices the hat. All eyes look upward. Of course, the Hasidim have more important things on their minds than high-wire tightrope walkers. And so after pausing only briefly, they proceed on their way, until the students realize that the rebbe has not kept up with them. Where could he be?
>
> The students return to where they saw the crowd and the tightrope walker. Sure enough, there is the rebbe staring intently upward, just like all of the ordinary townsfolk.
>
> "Strange," think the students. "It is so unlike the rebbe to dwell on something so trivial as this carnival act." After a few minutes, one of the students asks, "Rebbe, are you feeling okay?"
>
> For a few more silent instants the rebbe continues to stare. Then he speaks quietly, so as to disturb none of the onlookers: "Do you realize that that man cannot be thinking about what he will be eating for dinner this evening?" "Yes, rebbe, I suppose that is so."
>
> "Because," continued the rebbe, "if he were thinking about tonight's dinner, he could not maintain his balance. . . . And do you realize that that man cannot be thinking about the money he will be paid for his performance? Because if he were thinking about the money he will be paid, he would fall. . . . And do you realize that that man must not be thinking about how dangerous a position he is in? Because if he were thinking about the danger, that would be the end. . . . And do you realize, that that man cannot be thinking about what he is doing at all? If he were thinking about it he would tumble to his death immediately. That man is totally and completely where he is." (oral presentation, Congregation Beth El, Sudbury, MA, Spring 1998)

It isn't easy. However, we humans are capable of being where we are, and that is exactly what the Torah would have us strive to do, all the time in every conceivable way. That is why it enumerates 613 different mitzvot, categories of religious obligation (some not applicable in our time, but many that are) and their numerous subcategories as well. That is why these mitzvot pertain to all areas of interpersonal conduct, as well as to obligations strictly between an individual and the Almighty; they apply to business and to leisure, to private and public matters, to how we discipline our speech and our eating and what clothes we wear, to how we organize time into days and weeks, months and years, spiced with Shabbat and holidays, each with its own flavor and function and manner of observance, to times of work and times of refreshment and rest, to deeds of kindness, charity, and righteousness, to the attitude and demeanor that we bear in the performance of all these mitzvot, to obligations and responsibilities that make wonderful sense, to those whose rationales remain, for now, inscrutable.

It may seem that Jewish tradition intends to erect a burdensome system of endlessly obligating mitzvot, a system constructed for our guaranteed failure. Not so. Concerning this system of mitzvot, the Torah teaches us that we are to "live by them and not die by them." They are intended to enhance our lives, not weigh us down. The mitzvot of our tradition stand as opportunities for endowing moments with purpose, with godly intention. For Jews, for us, they constitute the best opportunity for being where we are.

Sometimes we experience our lives as smoke, drifting formlessly and without the substance we crave. Yet if we pause, listen, and attend to one another and ourselves, if we learn to regard each scene in the drama of our lives as a potential trigger for renewal, if, in fully being where we are, we come to treat each moment as a sacred opportunity to perform yet another mitzvah, then we may indeed begin to transform the otherwise undifferentiated pages of our hours, days, and years into lives full of holy purpose.

ON BEING CALLED TO THE RABBINATE
Shabbat Vayikra 5764/2004

Vayikra El Moshe Vayidabber Elav Me-Ohel Moed Lamor—The Lord called to Moses and spoke to him from the tent of meeting (*Leviticus 1:1*). God calls Moses, the one later referred to as Moshe Rabbenu, Moses our rabbi, the first rabbi, the one who introduces Torah to the world, the one who first presents the concept of a covenant in the form of a system of sacred obligations, mitzvot, by which we Jews uniquely identify ourselves and by means of which we seek meaning and holiness. God calls Moses, the paradigm for all future Jewish professionals who would choose or be chosen for careers of service to the Jewish community, rabbis among them. Following Moses, subsequent generations of rabbis typically see themselves as links in that chain of rabbinic tradition, a tradition populated by those who receive and teach Torah to a community at times willing and receptive of their efforts and at other times recalcitrant and disengaged.

One word—*Vayikra*—He (the Lord) called—arrests my attention. Why did God call Moses? Why does or does not God call us? What constitutes a call from God? The first word of the third book of the Torah impels such questions in me, especially while still feeling the glow from the recent ceremony in New York City where my Hebrew Union College–Jewish Institute of Religion (HUC–JIR) classmates and I received the degree of Doctor of Divinity, an honorary degree that is awarded to rabbis twenty-five years following ordination.

And why does God call [*Vayikra*] Moses this time when so often God simply speaks [*Vayomer* or *Vay'dabber*]? That is, does the specific choice of verb suggest a direction for consideration? Nachmanides, a thirteenth-century Spanish commentator, stipulates that Moses had been afraid to enter the *Ohel Moed*, the tent of meeting, a place of elevated holiness and danger. Thus, God needed to arouse and fortify Moses with an insistent "call." To personalize this notion, one might ask: does God sometimes calls us to do that which our fear would prevent? I had not always thought of my choice of rabbinic career as a calling in the way many Christians describe similar decisions, but I have come to see it exactly thus. Gazing back on my twenty-four-year-old self (then in my first year of marriage) from the vantage point of greater age and experience, I can now identify the considerable fear and anxiety that animated my decisions at that time. The array of career possibilities seemed bewildering; any choosing seemed so momentous, so definitive, so impossibly irrevocable; no choice seemed obviously the right one. Like Moses, to draw an inapt comparison, I had much to fear in approaching the tent where rabbis-in-training gather together.

As for the appearance of the word, one notes the scribal tradition of writing *Vayikra* with a small aleph, a tradition that naturally has evoked comment. The rabbinic sages say that the small aleph reflects the humility for which Moses was known. They imagine that Moses wished to omit the letter entirely. Had he done so, the word would have read *Vayikar*, suggesting an appearance of God by luck or by chance, a verb found in conjunction with the appearance to Balaam, the pagan prophet. Here, say these commentators, God insists on the aleph of *Vayikra* in order to demonstrate His deliberate favor and love of Moses. Hence, the scribal tradition preserves a kind of compromise between Moses and the Holy One. In this way, the small aleph suggests that in the mysterious realm of divine calling one never can distinguish between an encounter resulting from chance and one resulting out of divine favor.

Not being a prophet or the son of a prophet, I have no certainty about what events might have constituted a calling in my life. The topic reminds me of the oft-told story about the man of faith who finds himself in the torrential rain. As the water level rises above the first floor of his house, and rain keeps falling, the man moves to the second floor. When a neighbor rows by in a small boat and offers help, the man shouts that he has faith in God and that God will help him. When the water continues to rise, the man is forced to climb onto the roof of his house. When a coast guard cutter arrives and offers assistance the man again declares his faith in God and that he is sure God will help. As the water level rises some more, forcing the man of faith to perch himself on the crest of the roof, a police helicopter appears and drops a rescue line. But again, the man insists that he has faith that God will rescue him. However, the water continues to rise, causing the man to drown. When he arrives in heaven, the man immediately approaches God and testily demands: "God, I trusted in you. I had faith in you. Why did you let me drown?" God replies, "What are you talking about? I sent you a rowboat, a coast guard cutter, and a helicopter!"

It is hard to know from our human vantage point when God calls or how to recognize the signals. Regarding my rabbinic calling I think I can discern three biographical moments that might constitute my rowboat, coast guard cutter, and helicopter, signals I decided to heed, invitations I determined to accept.

On one sunny day during my junior year at Rutgers University in 1970, during the period when "relevance" and "counterculture" and most anything noninstitutional reigned supreme, I picked up a student newspaper and perused the listings of Free University courses. In those days, students like me were far more likely to devote time and effort to these not-for-credit but highly "relevant" offerings than to the institutionally mandated classes required for graduation. Indeed, my GPA reflected accurately this weighting of my priorities. I had to that point and for several years nurtured a kind of adolescent rebellion that included a rejection of the suburban Reform Judaism I had experienced as a child, replacing it with some dabbling in Eastern religious thought as filtered by Alan Watts and D. T. Suzuki and in a sprinkling of existentialist philosophy.

None of it was consistently or well-worked out on that sunny day when I spotted the stunning newspaper listing. That afternoon in the student center, a rabbi named Steve Shaw would offer the first session of a Free University class in something called Jewish mysticism. Here is the thing: to me, the term "Jewish mysticism" was oxymoronic, an extreme contradiction in terms. The Judaism I knew consisted of organs and hidden choirs and women in fancy hats and rabbis and cantors wearing silly-looking academic robes, and, on the positive side, brownies and punch at the *oneg*. "Mysticism" meant Hinduism or Buddhism and ashrams and Zen koans and meditation on a sound or on no-thing. How and where, I wondered, could the sound of one hand clapping possibly meet the fancy hats of suburban Judaism?

What became pivotal for me was not so much the content of that course or anything about Jewish mysticism per se but rather the meeting with Rabbi Steve Shaw. Rabbi Shaw opened the door for me to a vast Jewish room, a rich and varied space, one more than ample for my spiritual seeking both at that time and since. *Vayikra*—and God called. The rowboat.

The coast guard cutter followed. After Dela and I married in 1973, we went to live in Los Angeles, where she began her graduate studies in social work while I worked as a laboratory technician at UCLA Hospital. I also spent much time at UCLA Hillel, taking courses and becoming a regular at the Westwood Free Minyan, a wonderful traditional-egalitarian setting that embodied the values of the do-it-yourself Judaism that I came to embrace. As the months in Los Angeles wore on, I began to get restless with work as a lab tech and eager for some positive career move. But what? Too many possibilities presented themselves, but none stood out as the obvious choice. I began to talk to folks I looked up to, elders with some life experience and with whom I could test ideas. I went to one of these elders, the UCLA Hillel director, Rabbi Richard Levy, to get his feedback on the possibility of pursuing graduate work in Jewish Studies. He shared his notions about Jewish Studies and then asked: "Have you ever considered becoming a rabbi?" *Vayikra*—and God called. The coast guard cutter had arrived and transported me to the threshold of the world of rabbinic studies, a world from which I have no desire to depart, and to a career that has been and continues to be deeply satisfying.

The helicopter: after ordination in 1979, I considered both Hillel positions and congregations. It happened that the two openings for rabbis in Charlottesville, Virginia, both attracted me. I recall well the formal interview with the search committee of Congregation Beth Israel at the home of my hosts. One crusty elder put the question: "What do you think of organ music?" He meant organ music in Jewish worship. I replied quickly, honestly, and without suspecting the bushwhacking under way: "I like organs for Bach but not much for Jewish prayer." The elder then responded that he and his wife had donated the organ to the synagogue. I knew at that moment my rabbinic career would begin as a Hillel director. *Vayikra*—and God called. The helicopter had dropped its rescue line.

Since that series of callings, twenty-five years have passed since ordination, thirty years since setting out with fifty-nine classmates in Jerusalem on the unique career and life path of the rabbi. As I reflect on that passage of time, I acknowledge a strong sense of amazement, a sense of unreality in the awareness that so much time passed. But, since it has, do I regard the passage of time with sadness over youth lost? I do. Regret over accomplishments not achieved? Admittedly, yes. However, to receive an honorary degree to mark the passage of time suggests reason to celebrate, a moment for taking a modest bow, for smelling both the pleasant fragrance that lingers from those years and the roses of the present reality of an ongoing rabbinic career in a supportive community.

And yet for years I have been dimly aware that the D.D., the Doctor of Divinity—also known in the field as the doctor of durability (or duration) or sometimes the "didn't die yet" degree—would someday be handed to me. To a certain extent, I never had much regard for the concept of an honorary degree that would obtain by virtue of mere endurance. My dismissive attitude played a minor part in motivating me to acquire the academically earned Doctor of Ministry a couple of years ago, as I told myself: "I prefer to earn one before they give me one for free."

On the other hand, some have argued: It's about time! Rabbinic ordination at HUC–JIR requires a prior undergraduate degree, then a master's degree in Hebrew Letters, usually obtained in three years, and finally two additional years of graduate study including a thesis involving work in primary texts. Some have maintained that such work merits some kind of doctoral degree at the point of ordination.

I do not know how to assess what degrees should be conferred for what academic work, but I am glad I went back to school to work on and earn the D.Min. not because I got the extra paper, but because the actual study has truly been its own reward. And I am glad that HUC maintains a tradition of recognizing its graduate rabbis, cantors, educators, and communal service professionals in a way that marks twenty-five years of experience, a good time to take stock and to appreciate the good fortune that comes with the opportunity to make a contribution through one's lifework on behalf of the continuity of Jewish community and in service to the divine name.

Vayikra—and God called. In another interpretation (*Etz Hayyim*, p. 586) of God's call, Moses, by this time, was feeling pretty good about his career. How many leaders get to confront and overcome the world's most powerful ruler, take their enslaved people to freedom, help them constitute a new national life under a constitutional covenant received at Mount Sinai, supervise the construction of the Tabernacle, and then bring their people to the threshold of their promised homeland? After filling up such an impressive resume, Moses could well feel satisfied that he had completed his mission, received high marks for job performance, and could now retire in comfort. Thus, God had to call Moses to jolt him from his complacent mood, to remind him that, despite all his accomplishments, while he has life, his work was not finished. So too, while we have life, our work is not finished. God calls us still.

THE IMAGE OF THE RESTING CLOUD
Shabbat Pekudei 5768/2008

The very last passage of the *Book of Exodus* contains an evocative and mysterious image, one with embedded spiritual meaning:

> When Moses had finished the work [of constructing the tabernacle and all its contents], the cloud covered the Tent of Meeting [*Ohel Moed*], and the Presence of the Lord filled the tabernacle [*Mishkan*]. Moses could not enter the Tent of Meeting because the cloud had settled upon it and the Presence of the Lord filled the Tabernacle. When the cloud lifted from the Tabernacle, the Israelites would set out on their various journeys; but if the cloud did not lift, they would not set out until such time as it did lift. For over the Tabernacle a cloud of the Lord rested by day and fire would appear in it by night, in the view of all the house of Israel throughout their journeys.

What is this about? What are we to make of a cloud so dense that it prevents entry into a tent? And not only dense but, like a traffic arm at a railroad crossing, this cloud signals when to go and went to stay. I'm not sure whether this is exceedingly cool or scary—or both. As a kind of postscript, God also provides a big night¬-light, fiery assurance that God does not disappear with the fading sunlight; that though the day may cycle through phases, God's Presence abides. What does the Torah mean to teach us here? Along what avenues for spiritual growth does it take us?

One teaching that emerges from this image:

> "For over the Tabernacle a cloud of the Lord rested by day and fire would appear in it by night, in the view of all the house of Israel throughout their journeys." Clouds and fog generally obscure one's vision, so that one is unable to see. Fire is the exact opposite— it shines and allows one to see things better. The Jews need both of these quali-

ties "throughout their journeys." (Arno Shel Yosef, found in the collection *Torah Gems*, p. 239)

The Hasidic commentary goes on to make a point of prosaic and unappealingly provincial pietism, likening the obscuring cloud to hedonism, which ought to be seen as ephemeral, and the light of fire to Torah, whose commandments bring light to the world. However, I prefer to stop at the suggestive notion that we Jews need both an obscuring cloud and a brightening fire on our spiritual journeys. It is probably not difficult to recall an incident when the bright light of clear insight or sharp discernment helped you on your journey. However, when or how has an obscuring cloud aided your spiritual growth? When has not seeing been helpful?

Christian mystics speak of the "dark night of the soul," a concept referring to the periods of spiritual aridity experienced by otherwise genuinely pious individuals. The notion of spiritual aridity is also well documented in the biographies of Hasidic masters, such as Nachman of Bratslav and Menachem Mendel of Kotzk. It is often the case for these spiritual masters that periods of intense doubt, opaqueness of vision, and inability to sense the divine presence incubate the most fertile periods of subsequent spiritual growth. One specific challenge for me is the cultivation of sufficient patience to permit the generation of faith during such periods. Sometimes it helps merely to know that brightness and vision often follow the darkest moments.

A second possibility: regarding the phrase "throughout their journeys" Rashi says: "The place where they camped was also known as a journey." Rashi highlights what appears to be a reference to both periods of rest and periods of wandering as "journeys," suggesting a direction not only for physical movement but also for spiritual guidance. Not all journeys are physical journeys. One might further add that not all journeys of deepening personal growth require physical movement. Some of us are of the generation who journeyed somewhere to "find ourselves," traveling as far as California, Colorado, India, or Israel. We travelers often found the searching no less and no more productive in those new environs. On the other hand and speaking as someone who has spent an entire rabbinic career in one community, one may experience a continuously dynamic, never static journey in one geographical place. I find that one of life's ongoing challenges is to remain alert to the potential directions for spiritual journeying at each and every stage and age.

Finally, we read: "Moses could not enter the Tent of Meeting because the cloud had settled upon it and the Presence of the Lord filled the Tabernacle." Continuing to read the text as a metaphor for personal growth, one might ask: When do you feel invited to assert your own leadership and when do you feel there is no place for you (as Moses felt there was no place for him in the cloud-filled tent)? I once received an odd but lovely compliment from a former teacher, a revered professor of liturgy, after leading worship at a regional biennial conference. He said, "Thank you for not getting in the way of my worship experience." Do you sometimes feel, as do I, in certain settings of worship that there is no space for your prayers? When God filled the tent, Moses could not enter; but when God vacated, as it were, Moses could enter.

The great mystic of sixteenth-century Tzefat, Rabbi Isaac Luria, built a theory of divine creation on the idea of the vacating of space. He proposed that creation itself had occurred by virtue of God vacating a corner of the universe into which all that is not God could enter. This divine contraction—*tzimtzum* in Hebrew—has also been applied by Rabbi Eugene Borowitz as a model for constructivist education. Borowitz says that the *tzimtzum* Luria proposes as the divine scheme in allowing creation to unfold also works for teachers who, rather than imparting knowledge to students as receptacles, instead provide the environment, the tools, and then the vacated space that students require to actively seek and satisfy their inborn desires to learn through discovery. The students become, in effect, their own teachers. ("Tzimtzum: A Mystical Model for Contemporary Leadership," pp. 320-331) One might even say that the teacher who applies *tzimtzum* as a teaching model will deliberately obscure the educational goal in the service of more impactful learning.

I have enjoyed seeing the tension between two models of education at work in real time in our preschool when, on a recent wintery day, a volunteer scurried around to gather the children's coats in order to effect an efficient dismissal. Seeing the gathered coats, Ellen Dietrick, preschool director and master of constructivist learning, quickly and firmly directed the volunteer to replace the coats so that the children could fetch them on their own. This way, the dismissal became less efficient but far more effective as an opportunity in furthering self-reliance.

Tzimtzum implies empowerment of students when applied to education. As one of Borowitz's disciples, I have consciously attempted to use this concept often by empowering lay leaders and congregants with the goal of promoting Jewish self-reliance, though I am sure, at times, to the detriment of short-term efficiency or even quality. For example, I continue to value highly the culture of lay leadership that characterizes our local Shabbat morning minyan. By virtue of that culture, we sometimes fall short on some scales of quality but we continue to offer the space into which seeking individuals may enter to grow in synagogue competency, comfort, and Jewish self-reliance.

May it continue to be so.

FALLING GRACEFULLY
Rosh Hashanah 5771/2010

Matthew Sanford teaches yoga, one among many instructors for the ever-larger number of Americans seeking new modes of integrating the physical and the inner dimensions of existence, the body with the mind and the spirit. In at least one respect, Matthew Sanford is unique among yoga instructors in that he has lived as a paraplegic, paralyzed from the waist down, since surviving an automobile accident at the age of thirteen some twenty-seven years ago. In his memoir, entitled *Waking*, Sanford describes his journey of self-discovery, of healing without curing, of reintegration of his mind with the changed body that would now encase him for life. Not surprisingly, he often attracts students who themselves struggle with severe physical limitations. His description of one such student struck me as a germane tale for High Holiday reflection:

> I have a student named Chris. He is now in his mid-twenties and lives with cerebral palsy. He gets around in an electric wheelchair but can stand on his feet briefly with help. His fingers do not follow his instructions very well; his hands cannot bring food to his mouth. His tongue and speech are slowed by his condition but not the glint in his eyes and never his laughter.
>
> He has come to my class nearly every week for eight years.... It is obvious that yoga and a deepened mind-body relationship will never reverse his condition. He will always live with cerebral palsy. But can he still actively heal, not just psychologically or spiritually, but in practical ways that include his mind and body? Of course he can.
>
> Not surprisingly, Chris needs help getting into the shower. It is a difficult transfer into a small space. Falling is not unheard of and is always quite painful. When Chris starts to fall, he startles. When he startles, his body spasms, adding awkwardness to the velocity of his descent. One such fall resulted in a broken tooth.

During a [recent] class, Chris told me about a fall in the shower he [had] experienced earlier in the week. Apparently this time, as he lost his balance and began his descent, he did not startle. He did not break into spasm but instead dropped ever so gracefully to the floor. He told me it was because of yoga that he did not startle, that he was able to reach the ground softly for the first time in his life. Chris's eyes caught mine, and we shared a realization of freedom—the freedom to fall gracefully. (pp. 220–221)

"The freedom to fall gracefully" may be the awareness we Jews seek at this season. In the words of Rabbi Lawrence Kushner: "The core teaching of yontif [these High Holidays] is pretty straightforward: We're all gonna die" (*"Death without Dying," Who by Fire, Who by Water*, p. 109). We do not know whether it will be by fire or by water, by sword or by beast, or by other means described in the *Unetaneh Tokef* prayer. We do not know the means or the precise timing, but we know our end will come. Lest we had forgotten or were intent on denial, these Days of Awe arrive to remind us.

However, the liturgy of these Days of Awe does not leave us to wallow in morbid depression; rather, it ushers us on to the threefold means by which we might temper the severity of the death decree. *Teshuva*, *tefillah*, and *tzedakah* will not produce immortality. But, according to the liturgical poet, they constitute the recipe for living well in our allotted time, for falling gracefully.

The choice of these three ingredients for averting the severity of the decree is not totally obvious. Many other candidates, other central Jewish values, suggest themselves. For example, Rabbi Akiba chose "love your neighbor as yourself" as the preeminent mitzvah. Speaking of mitzvot, how about the big ten? How about pursuit of peace? Or, since we are talking about averting death's decree, how about a low cholesterol diet or a routine of regular exercise or Tai Chi or daily stress-reducing meditation? What does the threefold formula have to commend it?

In contemplating the shared element of the three decree-averting activities, Kushner points out that *teshuvah*, *tefillah*, and *tzedakah* have in common a diminution of the self, a reduction of the ego, what is known in Kabbalistic thought as *Bittul Hayesh*. To elaborate, *teshuvah*, often translated as repentance, literally means returning to God. This process of return involves admitting our shortcomings, our failures, our excessive pride and self-righteousness. It involves redirecting ourselves from the pursuit of material or political cravings so we can turn to a different path. When we return to God, no matter how we understand that redirection of effort, we usually reduce the space we allocate to our egos, not down to nothing but down to size.

About *tefillah*, prayer, Rabbi Abraham Joshua Heschel said: "To worship God is to forget the self. . . . In prayer we shift the center of living from self-consciousness to self-surrender" (*Man's Quest for God*, p. 7). This may not be the only way to think about prayer, but in the sense in which Heschel defines it, the act of prayer constitutes giving oneself over to a larger force. Just before the Amidah, we offer a short prayer of petition, requesting God to "open up our lips" for us—*Adonai S'fatai Tiftach Tiftach Ufi Yagid T'hilatech*—because, at that moment, we become aware of our radical dependence on God, of the fact that we cannot even express ourselves on our own. As the Magid of Mezerich once put it, comparing us to the shofar, if God does not blow air through us, we will make no sound. The very act of prayer involves the consciousness of a reduced ego.

Giving righteously of money or time or attention or talent, all varieties of *tzedakah*, obviously involves a kind of diminution of substance, physical decrease accompanied almost invariably by spiritual increase.

Allow me to amplify on each of the three tools, beginning with a public confession: although I am more than 60 years old, long past my years of physical prime, I still harbor a blatantly out-of-date self-imagine. Perhaps I am not alone in accommodating such fantasies. In the outdated image of myself, I possess a full head of hair; I weigh thirty pounds less without restricting the quantity of my eating; I do not require glasses to read or to see congregants from the *bimah*; I can do twenty pull-ups, can run faster than most, and can climb a steep mountain trail without slowing down. I am, in this fine vision, twenty-four years old. Sometimes, when I dwell on this image, I still imagine for myself a realistic possibility of standing on an Olympic podium as "The Star-Spangled Banner" plays in honor of my gold-medal performance in the 400-meter race recently completed.

Returning to reality, and by contrast with the young man, Chris, I do not have cerebral palsy or any of the many, many seriously limiting conditions that afflict many in this congregation. However, I most certainly experienced a kind of falling sensation when, some months ago, I suffered a second and intense bout of sciatica. Even with a steady consumption of pain medications, I was unable to walk or stand or sit or sleep more than a couple of hours at a time. I had no choice but to rely on the help of others, my wife, my dad, my stepmom, my kids, good friends, and then the fine healing artistry of doctors, nurses, and medical technicians, not to mention the hidden Power of healing behind it all. Although I was determined to recover to whatever extent possible and by whatever means possible, I also had good amounts of time, six weeks or so, to contemplate "what if?" What if this is it? What if this will be my condition for the duration? What now, big-shot pretend Olympic champion!

That is to say, sciatica provided me with the gift of mindful awareness about the challenge of falling with grace. Since then I have learned a little more about the three-pronged approach offered by our tradition for achieving that skill.

Tzedakah: A few weeks ago, I met an older rabbinic colleague at a rabbinic retreat. I had never met him before and had never heard about him. All I knew at first is that he got around on a motorized wheelchair and required considerable help to get into and out of that chair. At one point during the retreat, I made the mistake of trying to help him by picking up some papers he had dropped. He indicated through slurred speech and hand gestures that, although it would have been easier for me, he wanted to do it himself. Later, speech still slurred but articulate nonetheless, he spoke about his condition in a way that went to the essential core of *tzedakah*.

Rabbi Leon Spots, by his own description, had been a strapping man, a football player in his youth. His current condition, a result of Parkinson's disease, renders him progressively weaker in his limbs, diminished of stamina, slurred of speech, but crystal clear of mind. He does not know how many months remain of his life, but he is determined to live them as fully as he can, to use the remaining strength he has, to render service to the community, teach, and offer pastoral counsel. He strives to serve as a role model so that people can learn to treat those with obvious disabilities as people with ability rather than as something lesser. Rabbi Spots, it seems to me, bears witness to one manner by which *tzedakah* indeed averts the severity of the decree: by employing one's gifts, no matter how limited or reduced, for godly purpose.

Tefillah: For those of us who rely primarily on the left side of our brains, the side that thinks rationally, chronologically, and abstractly, the essentially right-brained activity of prayer always poses challenges. The act of prayer, for many, may seem pointlessly absurd or impossibly inaccessible.

And yet, I have noticed over the years of my rabbinate a curious pattern. When a local congregant suffers the loss of a loved one, dies, I sometimes find myself in the position of trying to persuade the survivor to allow me to organize a *minyan* or two or more during the period of *Shiva*. Sometimes the reply is one of reluctance because, the relatives will say, "we live too far from town," or "we have only recently arrived and do not know anyone," or "we are not involved in the synagogue and don't know anyone," or the like. If and when the resistance is overcome, invariably the *minyan* is successfully organized and the mourner receives a real and symbolic sense of being surrounded by a community of caring. That is, it is less the prayers that are said than the feeling of comfort that comes when people have gathered to say them. Whatever the explanation, these gatherings in the homes of mourners in our community have illustrated one tangible way in which *tefilah* averts the severity of the decree.

Finally, a word of illustration about *teshuvah*: Every year, as the High Holidays approach, we are all aware of those among our friends who are no longer alive, whose memories may remain strong, whose influences stand firm, who may live on in many ways, but for whom we grieve.

The poet Yehuda Amichai writes:

Once I saw a violinist playing and I thought: Between
his right hand and his left—only the violin,
but what a between, what music! (*Open Closed Open*, p. 13)

On his deathbed, Rabbi Simcha Bunim of Przysucha said to his wife, "Why are you crying? My whole life was only that I might learn how to die." Rabbi Eliezer urges us to do *teshuvah* one day before our death (*Pirke Avot 2:10*). Given the impossibility of determining that day, the common understanding of the teaching is that we ought to do *teshuvah*, we ought to turn hard to the godly path, every day.

The message, then, of the Days of Awe becomes: turn from the trivial and toward the essential and the godly each and every day. With God's help and in the awareness of those who have modeled the role well, may we determine to live our lives engaged in *teshuvah*, *tefillah*, and *tzedakah*, and, when necessary, to fall with grace.

THE HEART II
Moral Virtues

THE VIRTUE OF TRUTH
Kol Nidre 5768/2007

There is a *Dilbert* comic strip in which the pointy-haired boss is conducting a meeting with some of his employees. In the first panel he says, "We can't compete on price." In the second he says, "We also can't compete on quality, features, or service." In the third and last panel he says, "That leaves fraud—which I'd like you to call marketing."

On Yom Kippur, more than any other time of the year, tradition urges us to get serious about our interior selves, to perform a *Cheshbon Nefesh*, an inventory of our souls, checking for qualities that might be missing or rusty or otherwise damaged and in need of repair. We do well, in my view, to concentrate some of that attention on the soul quality, the *middah*/virtue of truth, and its close cousins, truthfulness and truth-telling.

Do we even notice any more how much of the communication that reaches us reflects the marketing strategy of the *Dilbert* manager and does not have truthfulness as a guiding principle? No one expects an advertisement to say: "Our product is really no better than the one made by our competitor, but since we added some fake lemon odor, please buy it." Still, I find that the pervasive nature of communication designed to persuade masquerading as information corrodes the collective expectation that we can trust what we read and what we hear.

Continuing in the vein of Torah lessons from comics, a *Non Sequitur* strip illustrates a second feature of the contemporary cultural scene as it pertains to truth-telling. In it, the precocious Danae character has just received a disappointing report card from her school. Confronted with the untenable dilemma of how to share the bad news with her father, she decides to emulate communication patterns she has observed among some of the famously fallen. She holds a "press conference" for her father in which she "takes full responsibility" for all failures of her office. Her rhetorical "acceptance of responsibility" has the desired result of relieving her of all guilt or embarrassment. That is, by rhetorically "accepting full responsibility" she actually accepts none at all, a perfectly fine result as far as she is concerned.

Each year, we hear a string of new assaults on straightforward, honest speech, ever more creative ways to dissemble, empathy-inducing failures of memory ("I can't recall remembering if I recall") to vociferous assertions contesting charges that no one has made ("I am not a homosexual and never have been one") to pathetically blatant denials ("I am not a thief") or equally pathetic appeals to creative grammatical parsing ("Just what does 'is' mean, anyway?"). The prevailing lack of truthful speech among public officials has contributed to a widening pervasive cynicism that challenges our collective ability to trust one another.

Some have described our culture as "a culture of cheating," one in which the values of truthfulness, truth-telling, and integrity compete with getting ahead at all costs. Living in a culture that in many ways devalues truth-telling, though, does not let us off the hook; it does, however, suggest that the Jewish imperative to place truthfulness at the center of our character runs counter to prevailing culture. That Judaism affirms truth as one of its core teachings is beyond dispute. "Speak the truth in your heart!" implores Psalm 15. The Talmud tells us: "The Holy One of Blessing hates a person who says one thing with his mouth and another in his heart" (*Pesachim 113b*). The contemporary teacher of Mussar, Alan Morinis, says: "Emet—truth is the ground upon which all spiritual [growth] . . . rests." (unpublished material used with the permission of the author)

Thus, if we would heed the Torah's demand that we place truthfulness at the core of our personal system of values, then we find ourselves confronting many cultural hurdles. However, even beyond the cultural, this *middah*, this quality of soul, presents challenges to our inner human circuitry. A sober examination of our interior selves should help us explore the challenging nature of truth.

Every Shabbat and every holiday, we beseech God, "*V'taher Libeinu L'ovdecha B'emet*— Purify our hearts that we may serve You in truth." Thus, our prayers echo the Biblical and Talmudic emphasis on both the paramount importance and the difficulty of striving for truthfulness in our lives.

Consider two rabbinic passages, one suggestive of the relationship between this *middah* and human nature and the other about the way the call to be truthful may compete with other values or claims from our tradition. The first midrash depicts an imagined dispute among the angels in anticipation of the creation of humankind:

Rabbi Shimon said: When the Holy One was about to create Adam, the ministering angels formed themselves into groups and companies, some of them saying, "Let him be created," while others urged, "Let him not be created." Thus it is written, "Love and truth fought [usual translation: met] together, righteousness and peace combated [or "kissed"] each other." [*Psalm 85:11*] Love said, "Let him be created, because he will perform acts of love." Truth said, "Let him not be created because all of him will be falsehood." Righteousness said, "Let him be created, because he will do righteous deeds." Peace said, "Let him not be created, because he will be all strife."

What did the Holy One do? He took truth and cast it to the ground, as it is said, "You did cast down truth to the ground." [*Daniel 8:12*] The ministering angels dared to say to the Holy One, "Master of the Universe, why do You humiliate Your seal? Let truth arise from the earth." Hence it is written, "Let truth spring up from the earth." [*Psalm 85:12*] . . .

The elder Rabbi Huna of Tzippori said: While the ministering angels were parleying with one another and disputing with one another, the Holy One [went ahead and] created Adam and then said: What are you parleying about? Humankind is already made. (*Genesis Rabbah 8:5*)

I read the midrash as an expression of profound curiosity about the nature of our species. We might agree that there is something both awesome and odd in the idea that a Supreme and Perfect Being would think to create an inferior being like a human. It is also by no means clear what the purpose or the essence or the good of the inferior human being could possibly be. In the dispute over the wisdom of the concept of human creation among the four positive, angelic qualities, how are we to understand God's casting of truth from heaven in order to allow human creation to take place?

I understand the midrash to be asserting that the quality of truth, absolute truth as found in heaven, which the midrash reminds us is referred to as the divine seal, God's immutable mark of perfection, is in some essential way incompatible with human creation. Thus, truth in all its absoluteness and perfection must be cast out of heaven in order to permit the existence of the irredeemably untidy and imperfect human. Where humans dwell, this midrash intimates, there is freedom to choose either well or badly, a freedom that will render incompatible the kind of big-T Truth that is only possible in a place inhabited by angels. On the other hand, truth will spring up from the earth, from the abode of the inevitably flawed human. This is to say, whereas big-T Truth and human life may be incompatible, humans must strive to produce the kind of truthfulness of which they are capable. Moreover, though not an automatic impulse, only humans have this capacity to raise truth up from the ground where it has been cast. Thus, the incompatibility of human nature and big-T Truth does not relieve us of responsibility. Striving for truth is still included as a required element of the human curriculum this year and every year, and will be on the final exam.

A second midrash contrasts with the first and complicates the Jewish understanding of truth a bit further. I paraphrase a Talmudic passage that presents as a point of departure the Mosaic description for God as "Great, Mighty and Awesome [*Ha-El HaGadol, HaGibbor, V'Hanora*]" (*Yoma 69a*). It is taken as an assumption that a kind of sacred immutability attaches to the Mosaic formulation because it comes from God. However, despite this assumed immutability, it is pointed out in the Talmudic passage that in two Biblical cases, prophets arrive on the scene and alter this Mosaic formulation; each prophet comes along and uses a double rather than triple ascription for God and in doing so raises two questions: (1) Why do the prophets change the Mosaic formula? (2) What allows a later association, the so-called Men of the Great Assembly, to show up and restore the Mosaic formula back to its original three-part luster? The questions may be of little interest to us, but the answers reveal something important about how our tradition regards the quality of truth.

The Talmud says that the prophets Daniel and Jeremiah each omitted one of the qualities ascribed to God by Moses because, in their experience, the quality was absent. Jeremiah, who witnessed the destruction of Jerusalem, simply did not see how one could ascribe *awesomeness* to God, and so he omitted the word *Hanora*. Daniel, who experienced the enslavement of the people in Babylonia, did not see how one could call God who allowed such a travesty *mighty*, and so he omitted *Hagibbor*. The Men of the Great Assembly came along and reinterpreted the language with a sophistication that allowed for restoration of the original Mosaic formula. All well and good, but the passage won't let go, as if the experience of the prophets does not by itself fully justify their reluctance to give full throat to that original three-part cluster of attributes. So it asks again: what made them alter a Mosaic formula? "Because," says the Talmud, "*they knew that God insists on the truth.*" When confronted with the competing claims of allegiance to a demand of tradition and a demand to be truthful, they opted for truth as they saw it and, it would seem, merit praise for doing so.

God insists on the truth from us even when our wiring makes truth-telling exceedingly elusive. But what are the counterclaims recognized by Jewish teaching? What are the limits to my impulse to stand on the corner of the downtown mall and shout out the truth about my friends, my family members, my acquaintances, to report the truth about who is doing what to whom?

As one might expect, our tradition teaches several kinds of restraint. One large area of restraint, one that merits its own separate and fuller discussion, relates to the category of *Lashon Hara*, evil or hurtful speech, speech that our tradition deems as forbidden, even if truthful, when it could damage the reputation of another. Consider the recent, now discredited allegations against the lacrosse players at Duke University, where a rush to get to the supposed truth in an environment of political correctness has left a sticky residue of hurt feelings and damaged reputations. Not surprisingly, Jewish tradition counsels silence as the default position for one who would seek truth and at the same time avoid hurtful speech.

On the other hand, of course, there is a time to speak. Sometimes, one ought to speak truth to power, as it were, or must tell a friend an embarrassing truth for his own growth or to preserve the integrity of the relationship. I am sure that each of us could supply any number of real-life dilemmas where one must make the difficult choice whether to speak, what to say, and where truth rests. Says Alan Morinis: "Many people equate *emet*/truth, with speaking their minds. But speaking your mind may simply be articulating your opinion, and your opinion may have nothing to do with reality. It is very important that [one] ... be capable of discerning the difference between truth and reality, on the one hand, and ... opinion and deeply held convictions on the other." (unpublished material used with the permission of the author)

For many of us, an important area of potential improvement as it pertains to truth has to do with some subtle turns in how we communicate to others and to ourselves. Morinis describes a prosaic incident:

> I was walking the dog one day soon after a big windstorm. I met a neighbor and we stopped to chat. "You know," I said, "I saw two cars that had been smashed by trees." In truth, I had seen one car with its windshield shattered. The other car I had been told about. I caught myself,

and with tortured mental effort, I forced myself to utter, "Actually, I saw one and heard about the other." (*Climbing Jacob's Ladder*, p. 109)

I would guess that I am not the only one who can relate to the impulse to make the fish I caught a little bigger, the suffering I experienced a little more awful, or my role a little more important than it might really have been. No doubt a difficult standard, but "Speak the truth in your heart!" means that in giving in to the impulse to spin or extend or amplify the truth, we not only deceive others, but we run the risk of diminishing our capacity to remain honest to ourselves.

Yet another nuance pertaining to truth is revealed by the Biblical proverb that says: "Kindness and truth, do not forsake, tie them on your neck, write them on the tablet of your heart" (*Proverbs 3:3*). In my mind, the pairing of kindness and truth suggests the ideal of a balance between the claims of truth that may at times seem severe and those of kindness that cause one to pause and consider consequences. Laura Shipler Chico fleshed out this notion in a recent segment of NPR's *This I Believe*. Pregnant at the time of the broadcast, she reports contemplating the three qualities she and her husband hoped their first child would possess. The first quality that leapt to their minds was honesty/truthfulness. So did the second: caring for others/kindness. The third quality won in competition over a long list of traits, but finally they agreed on the ability to laugh at oneself. About honesty and truthfulness she said: "When you are honest you are less likely to end up in jail. And when you are honest you are probably willing to take the harder path sometimes. So you're always pushing yourself to grow. When you are honest people trust you and when people trust you, you begin to trust yourself. When you really trust yourself, I believe that is the foundation for all the rest."

About caring for others and kindness, Ms. Shipler Chico says: "Honesty can be a bit harsh. But when you care about other people that can be a powerful combination. When you care about other people you are also less likely to end up in jail."

Finally, about the lesson she attributes to her grandmother, that you should be able to laugh at yourself, she adds: "If you can laugh at yourself, it means you like yourself and you know you're no better and no worse than anybody else. You'll probably have more fun in life and be more likely to forgive yourself when you are not honest or not caring about others. Finally, if you do end up in jail, you can always laugh at your stupidity for getting caught" ("The Person I Want to Bring into This World," *This I Believe,* NPR, August 27, 2007, http://thisibelieve.org/essay/27267/).

I would add that the ability to laugh at oneself is a way to express kindness to oneself, to care for oneself. Thus Ms. Shipler Chico's contemporary formulation echoes the proverb: "Kindness and truth, do not forsake, tie them on your neck, write them on the tablet of your heart."

A final nuance on the quality of truth: "Rav Yehudah said in the name of Shmuel: In only these three matters is it the practice of rabbis to deviate in their speech from the truth: in regard to knowledge of a [Talmudic] tractate, in regard to matters of the bed, and in regard to hospitality." (*Bava Metzia 23b, 24a*) Regarding these permitted deviations from truthfulness, I surmise that "in regard to knowledge of a tractate" means that if one finds that a student or a teacher knows less than you, it is important to refrain from revealing this truth in order to avoid potential embarrassment or humiliation of the one less knowledgeable.

In regard to "matters of the bed" means that although partners to marriage ought to aspire to honesty in their relationships with one another, that honesty sometimes competes with the imperative to support and comfort and nurture one another, even when doing so could mean withholding some of what one regards as the truth. Rabbi David Ellenson often publically quotes his wife, Rabbi Jacqueline Ellenson, who in the midst of a spat will ask, "Do you want to be right or do you want to be married?" In a somewhat related teaching, the Talmud requires wedding guests to speak admiringly of the beauty of the bride, irrespective of her physical attributes objectively perceived.

And similarly "in regard to hospitality," the offering of which is a sacred obligation in our tradition: extending hospitality includes trying to make the guest feel welcome, even when doing so requires one to refrain from truthful appraisal of his table manners, fashion, intellect, and the like.

That is, the injunction to aspire to truthfulness is not absolute, but rather subject to context and counterclaims to exhibit kindness and to avoid unnecessarily hurtful speech. The difficult standard of truth claims us as do others with which we must wisely hold it in balance. Thus do we continue to pray: *V'taher Libeinu L'ovdecha B'emet*—Purify our hearts that we may serve You in truth.

FOR KINDNESS AND THE LOVE OF KINDNESS
Yom Kippur 5700/2009

There is the story and then there is the backstory. Here is the backstory as imagined in a midrash as told by Rabbi Ed Feinstein:

> In the beginning, God created all the animals—the fish, the birds, and the bugs. But when it came to the human being, God decided to proceed in a different manner. Unlike every other creature in the world, the human being would be given a special gift: the human being would be created in God's image.
>
> God revealed this plan to the angels. The angels were outraged. How can something as pure, as precious, and as powerful as God's own image be entrusted to a creature as evil, as deceitful, and as corrupt as the human being?
>
> If human beings possess God's image, the angels reasoned, they will think the way God thinks, feel what God feels, create as God creates. They will imagine that they are God and rule the world with tyranny and egotism. Human beings will demand that all creatures worship them. They will think it their right to impose their will on other human beings, and they will terrorize all of Creation. Human beings will most certainly destroy all that God has made and ruin all that God loves. "We cannot let that happen!"
>
> So they decided to save God from this folly. They stole God's image.
>
> However, once they possessed the holy image, they knew it had to be concealed somewhere, hidden in a place where humanity would never find it. But where?
>
> "Let us put it at the top of the highest mountain!" one angel suggested. "But no. One day they will learn to climb the mountain and find it."
>
> "Then let us put it at the bottom of the sea!" another offered.
>
> "But no, they will find a way to plumb those depths one day and they will find it there."

"Let it be hidden in the farthest reach of the most forbidding wilderness!" suggested another angel. "But no, one day they will traverse the wilderness and find it even there."

They all offered suggestions, but each was rejected. Then the cleverest and shrewdest of the angels stepped forward and said, "No, not at the top of the mountains, not at the bottom of the sea, not at the farthest reaches of the wilderness. Let us place it where human beings will never look for it. Let us place it deep within their hearts, deep in their souls. They will never look for it there."

So God allowed the angels to hide the precious image deep within the heart of the human being. And to this day it lies hidden in a place that is deeper and farther away than any place any one of us can find on our own. (*Capturing the Moon*, pp. 148–149 © Behrman House., Inc., www.behrmanhouse.com, reprinted with permission)

Yom Kippur, Shabbat Shabbaton, the Sabbath of Sabbaths, the twenty-five-hour culmination of the Days of Awe, bids the Jewish people to get in touch with the soulful core of being and the spiritual and moral implications that arise in the process.

About the essence of those implications, midrashic legend reports this ancient controversy among three rabbis of the early second century:

Rabbi Akiva said: "Love your neighbor as yourself (*Leviticus 19:18*) is the fundamental [ethical] principle of Torah." Ben Azzai retorted [with an alternate verse]: "This is the record of Adam's line. When God made the human, He made him in the likeness of God, male and female, God created them" (*Genesis 5:1*). *This* is the fundamental principle greater than *that* so that you might not say, 'since I am despised, let my neighbor also be despised with me, [or] since I have become corrupt, let my neighbor become corrupt.' [Then,] Rabbi Tanchuma piped in: "If you [ben Azzai] do that [i.e., apply the 'love your neighbor' concept to yield an undesired result], know Who it is Whom you despise for He made him in the likeness of God." (*Sifra Kedoshim 4:12*) (*Genesis Rabbah 24:7*)

As I read the midrash, one could go back and forth in debating the relative merits of the two views on whether "love your neighbor" or human creation in the divine image is a more foundational ethical principle.

Rabbi Tanchuma's contribution to the argument demonstrates the inextricable link between the two concepts. In his view, in order for self-love to provide an adequate basis for behaving well toward our neighbors, one requires an adequate sense of self-esteem or, if you prefer, an adequate sense of the esteem due to the other. Recalling human creation in the divine image yields both.

Consider this poetic fragment by Adrienne Rich:

In those years, people will say, we lost track
of the meaning of we, of you
we found ourselves
reduced to I
and the whole thing became
silly, ironic, terrible (cited in Morinis, *Everyday Holiness*, p. 196)

For all its focus on self-examination, on the individual getting on the right track with God, so many of the prayers and lessons of the Day of Atonement point us toward the realm of *Bein Adam Lachaveiro*, to the relationships among human beings, away from being "reduced to I." From the perspective of Mussar, the Jewish literature of improving character one virtue at a time, the injunction to love others, in linkage with the concept of creation in the divine image, becomes an invitation to cultivate of the soul trait of *chesed*, often translated as kindness or, as in *Gemilut Chasadim*, deeds of lovingkindness.

We read, for example, the famously hyperbolic statement in the Mishnah Avot: "The world stands on three things: Torah, worship, and deeds of loving-kindness," or as one could rephrase it, three human endeavors sustain civilization: continuous study of sacred lore [Torah], a spiritual discipline that raises to consciousness the constant presence of a benevolent deity, and acting with kindness to spread good and to improve the lot of others. In Psalms, we find even a simpler cosmic architecture: "The world is built on *chesed*/kindness." (*Psalms 89:2*)

Chesed, along with its partner qualities, mercy, and long-suffering patience, is also the quality of the Holy One of Blessing that we Jews repeatedly invoke throughout the Days of Awe in the humble awareness that humans depend on it for survival. The Talmudic sages pondered divine manifestations of undeserved kindness as they imagined a day in the life of God as follows:

Rabbi Judah said in the name of Rav: The day consists of twelve hours:

during the first three, the Holy One, blessed be He, sits and occupies Himself with Torah [though All-knowing in some ways, the revelation that unfolds from engaging in Torah study apparently can inspire even God!]; during the next three hours, God sits and issues judgments for the entire world. When He sees that the world is so guilty as to deserve extermination, He rises from the throne of judgment and sits down on the throne of compassion [and kindness]; [On that throne] for the next three hours, He sits and feeds the entire world, from the horned wild ox to lice. During the final three hours, He [unwinds/]sits and disports with [his pet,] the Leviathan, as is said, "There is Leviathan, whom You have formed to sport therewith." (*Psalms 104:26*) (*Avodah Zarah 3b*)

As rabbinically imagined, then, the work part of the divine day consists of the rendering of judgment first from the perspective of strict justice but always proceeding to the perspective of compassion and kindness. Only from that second perspective do we humans "merit" the sustenance God provides. That is, as the rabbis have it, we are sustained only because God refrains from judging according to strict justice but rather exhibits *chesed* on our behalf. Therefore, are we humans are enjoined to do the same, to imitate God, in our dealings with one another.

"That cannot be right!" you might say. "How," you might ask, "can one be expected to imitate a quality of God?" Created in the divine image or not, God is God, Eternal, mighty, All-seeing, basically all-everything, while we humans are mortal, limited of sight and physical capacity, not even all-regional. Here is how: noting the Biblical passage "Walk after the eternal your God" (*Deuteronomy 13:5*), the Talmudic sage Rabbi Hama bar Rabbi Hanina responds to the same question:

Is it possible for a human to walk right behind the Presence? Has it not already been said, "The Lord your God is a devouring fire" (*Deuteronomy 4:24*)? Yes, but what the verse means is that you are to follow the ways of the Holy One. [Just as] God clothed the naked—"The Lord God made for Adam and for his wife garments of skin, and clothed them" (*Genesis 3:21*)—so should you clothe the naked. [Just as] the Holy One visited the sick—"The Lord appeared unto him (Abraham) in the terebinths of Mamre" (*Genesis 18:1*)—so should you visit the sick. [Just as] the Holy One buried the dead—"He buried [Moses] in the valley" (*Deuteronomy 34:6*) —so should you bury the dead. [And just as] the Holy One comforted mourners—"and it came to pass after the death of Abraham that God bestowed blessing upon Isaac his son" (*Genesis 25:11*)—so should you comfort mourners. (*Sotah 14a*)

That is to say, according to Rabbi Hama bar Hanina, imitating God in performing acts of *chesed* means performing as obligations a few eminently doable but often inconvenient tasks that do not result in any apparent reward. Deirdre Sullivan, an attorney from Brooklyn, writes in an essay penned in 2005 about examples of divine expression of *chesed* calling for our imitation. In describing a lesson taught her by her father, she probes the nature of deeds of kindness, illustrating the importance of both "comforting the bereaved" and "burying the dead," as follows:

I believe in always going to the funeral. My father taught me that.
The first time he said it directly to me, I was sixteen and trying to get out of going to calling hours for Miss Emerson, my old fifth-grade math teacher. I did not want to go. My father was unequivocal. "Dee," he said, "you're going. Always go to the funeral. Do it for the family."
. . . Sounds simple — when someone dies, get in your car and go to calling hours or the funeral. That, I can do. But I think a personal philosophy of going to funerals means more than that.
"Always go to the funeral" means that I have to do the right thing when I really, really don't feel like it. . . . I'm talking about those things that represent only inconvenience to me, but the world to the other guy. . . . In my humdrum life, *the daily battle hasn't been good versus evil. It's hardly so epic. Most days, my real battle is doing good versus doing nothing.* In going to funerals, I've come to believe that while I wait to make a grand heroic gesture, I should just stick to the small inconveniences that let me share in life's inevitable, occasional calamity.

Ms. Sullivan concludes her essay:

On a cold April night three years ago, my father died a quiet death from cancer. His funeral was on a Wednesday, middle of the workweek. I had been numb for days when, for some reason, during the funeral, I turned and looked back at the folks in the church. The memory of it still takes my breath away.

> The most human, powerful and humbling thing I've ever seen was a church at 3:00 on a Wednesday full of inconvenienced people who believe in going to the funeral. ("Always Go to the Funeral," *This I Believe*, NPR, August 8, 2005, http://www.npr.org/templates/story/story.php?storyId=4785079)

Surely, deeds of *chesed* do not always come around with so much poetic symmetry as they did for Deirdre Sullivan, but they do, I believe, invariably contribute to the cultivation of a culture less given to the narcissistic "reduction to I," and they do partake in the expansion of the individual heart ever more disposed to the habit of kindness.

With regard to cultivating the heart more disposed to kindness, the Prophet Micah famously epitomized Torah-based ethics, saying: "Do justly, love *chesed*, and walk humbly with God!" Not satisfied with our deeds of kindness alone, the prophet implores us to implant them in our loving hearts.

On cultivating the heart for *chesed*, a story:

> One day Rabbi Israel Salanter, one of the most famous of rabbis in Lithuania in the early decades of the nineteenth century, boarded a train bound for Vilna. Next to him sat a young man who did not recognize the famous rabbi. After a few minutes the rabbi lit a cigarette. However, the young man complained curtly and disrespectfully, so the rabbi extinguished the cigarette. A little later, as the compartment was stuffy, the rabbi opened a window. Again the young man complained in a manner bordering on abusive and the rabbi quickly closed the window. As the train proceeded along, everything the rabbi did received an abrupt and disrespectful complaint from the young man followed by a compliant response from Rabbi Salanter.
>
> Finally, the train reached its destination and the young man was shocked to see a large and joyous reception awaiting his travel companion. Only then did he learn that he had been riding with a famous sage. That awareness caused him suddenly to feel shame at his rude behavior. He then determined to offer an apology and seek forgiveness as soon as possible. So the next day he did just that. As the young man gained entry to the rabbi's home, he immediately launched into a cascading apology, "I am soooo sorry. I did not know who you were. Please forgive me. I was in a grumpy mood . . ." and on and on until Rabbi Salanter interrupted with assurances that he forgave him and that no further apology was necessary.
>
> However, instead of leaving it at that, Rabbi Salanter proceeded to

question the young man about his reasons for coming to Vilna. When the young man informed the rabbi that he had come in order to train to become a *shochet*, a ritual slaughterer, the rabbi responded: "You know what? I happen to have a son-in-law who is *shochet* and I believe he can help you." And so, that very day, Rabbi Salanter introduced the young man to his son-in-law and made arrangements for him to receive the instruction he required to train for and pass his *shochet* exams. In time, Rabbi Salanter even helped the young man find a job not far from Vilna.

When the day arrived for the young man to leave Vilna for his new post, he paid Rabbi Salanter a visit to thank him for his kindnesses and to ask this question: "When I asked you for your forgiveness for my behavior on the train, you forgave me. That I understand. In retrospect I realize that that is what one is supposed to do when somebody asks for forgiveness. But after all that I had done to you, after the way I behaved so disrespectfully toward you, I do not understand why you didn't just leave it at that. I do not understand why you went out of your way to help me."

"Now that is a good question," responded Rabbi Salanter. "Here's why I did what I did. You see, when you asked me for forgiveness, I really forgave you. I had no hesitation. However, human nature, being what it is, when somebody wrongs you, there is usually a residue of ill feeling in the heart. Something remains, and that something is not healthy. It is not good to have such feelings. And I know that the only way in which I could rid myself of the residue of ill will was by doing something good for you. So I resolved that if there were any way I could help you, I would help myself as well through the process. You see? Helping you helped me rid my heart of any residue of ill feelings that I had." (modified from "Forgiveness," as told by Reuven Bulka in *Three Times Chai*, pp. 85–86 © Behrman House., Inc., www.behrmanhouse.com, reprinted with permission)

An appreciative member of the synagogue I serve as rabbi recently found herself in the position to receive some concrete expressions of kindnesses. She remarked to me: "What I really love about Judaism is that the feelings of sympathy are expressed in actions."

On the sacred Day of Atonement and all days, may we find ourselves ever more energized by the knowledge that the divine image abides both in ourselves and in the other and that it is activated when we exhibit kindness. May this be God's will.

LEADERSHIP AND THE QUALITY OF PATIENCE
Shabbat Nitzavim Vayeilech 5769/2009

What is the single most important quality of personality required by a lay leader of a synagogue?

Most would agree that to be chosen to take on such a role is to be honored, as fellow congregants entrust such leaders with decision-making authority in the confident hope that they will employ careful discernment in rendering wise decisions, decisions rooted in Jewish values with the constant goal of sustaining and improving the Jewish community.

On the other hand, to be chosen to serve as a leader in the community also constitutes something of a burden. Even though board members are unpaid volunteers who give generously of their time, talent, and energy, and even though some congregants will express appreciation for the generosity of that gift, as leaders, those individuals inevitably bear a variety of burdens. In lieu of appreciation, too many will employ the "no good deed goes unpunished" philosophy and will treat the volunteer leaders as serf labor, where the accountability is great and the authority nil. They will reserve the right to second-guess every decision while expecting much to be done on their behalf.

Many will forget that all synagogue members have implicit responsibilities. Some will fail to distinguish their synagogue membership from that of a country club or an athletic club where one pays a fee for various amenities and services. Synagogue membership, by contrast, properly comes with the expectation that every member will engage in and take responsibility for the communal life of the synagogue in some way, through prayer, study, social action, planning, baking hamantaschen, serving at a homeless shelter, attending an event for social action, or by writing a generous check.

Given that the role of leader, whether in a professional or volunteer capacity, carries both honorific and burdensome aspects, one rightly asks, returning to the opening question: what are the qualities of personality a lay leader of a synagogue would do well to cultivate? From my perspective as a rabbi with more than three decades of experience, a few ideas have taken shape on this subject. One Jewish way to begin a thoughtful reflection on the preferred ingredients of leadership would be to consider those individuals, mythic or historic, held up as paradigms of leadership by our tradition. If we were to turn to the heroes of the Bible, who emerges as the most prominent leader of all? Most would say Moses. However, it could be said that Moses stands out as so unusual that ordinary folks could not learn anything from him—in the way my tennis game is not helped by watching Roger Federer play. In this regard, toward the end of *Deuteronomy*, immediately following the death of Moses, we read these words of testimonial:

> Moses was 120 years old when he died; his eyes were undimmed and his vigor unabated.... Never again did there arise in Israel a prophet like Moses whom the Lord knew, face to face, for various signs and portents that the Lord sent him to display in the land of Egypt, against Pharaoh and all his courtiers and his whole country, and for all the great and awesome power that Moses displayed before all Israel. (*Deuteronomy 34:7, 10–12*)

When I hear that, at 120, Moses had undimmed eyes and undiminished vigor, I am thinking that, by contrast, I need to renew the prescription on my eyeglasses and that my new "friend," my sciatica, puts a big crimp in the already greatly diminished vigor that I once enjoyed. What could one of us learn from this supercharged guy?

From another angle, though, and one I find appealing, Moses emerges as an excellent paradigm for real-life leaders because of some very un-Federer-like qualities and experiences. Although the Torah, as well as later Jewish tradition, ascribes many superlatives to Moses even as it enumerates his extraordinary accomplishments as a lawgiver, teacher, poet, judge, community organizer, redeemer, warrior, and religious innovator, at the same time it reveals him to possess many human foibles and flaws. For example, Moses, as depicted in the Torah, was plagued by self-doubt. He made some poor decisions and suffered the consequences thereby. He struggled to balance the demands of his role as a leader with those of his family. He often experienced conflict at the hands of the very people he had rescued and strove to guide. He even suffered the disapproving eye of the divine Boss who had called him to serve in the first place. Thus, the Torah portrays Moses, the superhero, as flawed and, therefore, useful as an exemplary leader from whom we ordinary mortals might learn.

How, then, might we apply the example of Moses to the question, what is the single most important quality of personality required by a lay leader of a synagogue? In the collection of whimsical contemporary midrashim called *Does God Have a Big Toe?* Rabbi Marc Gellman responds to this question in his retelling of the burning bush story. In Gellman's version of the story, God had not selected Moses until first deciding that the paramount quality for the one He would choose to lead the Israelites out of Egypt was *patience*. As Gellman puts it, "God wanted somebody who would not give up, no matter how bad things looked, no matter how much people complained, no matter how long it took to get to the land of Israel" (p. 69). In Gellman's midrash, God places the burning bush in a spot where many might see it and where some actually walk right by it without even pausing. However, only Moses actually notices that the bush is burning, that it is not getting burned up, and that the fire is not going out. Only Moses has the patience to savor the miraculous in the ordinary.

Whether or not one feels drawn by the notion of the burning bush as a test of patience, the notion that patience might be the paramount quality for a leader bears reflection. What is patience? The Mussar teacher Alan Morinis defines patience by reference to the Hebrew term *savlanut*. *Savlanut* comes from the root *saval*, to bear, as in to bear a burden. A *sablan* is a porter. Thus, one might think of patience as the quality that enables a person to bear a burden until it becomes appropriate to set it aside.

With whom might a synagogue president, for example, seek to cultivate a capacity to bear a burden? Who can count the ways? For now, consider four categories of relational interaction that could call for this quality.

First: fellow board members and other lay leaders. All presidents work with the synagogue board and relate to the chairs of committees. These others, lay leaders in their own right, often bring their own agendas. Some may want the board or the synagogue as a whole to focus more attention on the needs of a particular cohort in our community (ambidextrous gays in interfaith marriages where the Jewish partner is a Reconstructionist, for example). Others may feel that the synagogue requires structural reorganization. Some may feel that if the board fails to address a particular issue in the next six months it will have been derelict in its duties. Others may regard any time spent on that particular issue as an utter waste of time.

Board members also bring their own personal styles and tendencies. Some tend to speak with great force and at considerable length, possibly without full information on the subject at hand. Others almost never say a word, irrespective of who has a good insight. A notion I learned long ago in a course on group work: in any group, some have a knack for raising the level of tension, turning almost any discussion into a heated exchange, while others have a knack for lowering the tension, the ability to channel even issues over which people hold passionate and differing views into calm and respectful discussion. Given the variety of individuals with whom a president must work to provide oversight for the synagogue, then, he or she would do well to cultivate the quality of patience.

Second: not only will the president need patience in solidifying constructive relationships with other members of the board but with congregants in general. In part this is so because congregants often turn to the president (as well as to other board members, the rabbi, and other staff)—and properly so—in order to express their desires and concerns about the synagogue. These expressions will come in many flavors, some as tasty words of appreciation for the welcoming and caring community or for the touching or transformative moments that occur in and around a congregation. However, unless the Messiah has arrived unannounced, other expressions will undoubtedly have a more sour taste, possibly tinged with disappointment or even anger at one thing or another, at some act of commission or omission, at any number of issues, both perceived and real. Thus, every president is challenged first to cultivate an ability to listen, to receive especially the sour-tasting expressions with patience and without judging, and then to bear the burden—and it is a burden—of the sour taste until such time that it may be set aside. Often the president must make the effort to learn the greater context into which these expressions fit; the harder task will be to realize that although sometimes there will be a resolution, at other times there will not. Sometimes patience requires one to take to heart the obvious but difficult truth that one person and one synagogue cannot possibly please all Jews all the time.

Third: early on, every president of every synagogue will require a patient disposition in dealing with the rabbi. Speaking generically, every synagogue president from time to time will come to wonder how the rabbi could possibly be so obtuse in failing to see things as clearly as he or she sees them, in failing to see an opportunity for communal enhancement, for membership growth, for a terrific program, for raising funds, or for reviving some moribund activity. All new presidents seeking to establish good working relationships with experienced rabbis come up against the rabbi's priorities established over many years as well as his or her sense of the community and its needs as perceived from the unique and privileged rabbinic angle. While the president may have had years to witness, usually at a distance, some manifestations of both the weaknesses and strengths of a particular rabbi, and some of the outcomes of that rabbi's efforts, his or her patience could well be tried in new and surprising ways as president and rabbi seek to work together in the vineyard of Torah on behalf of the congregation they both serve.

Fourth: finally, presidents require patience with themselves. Most presidents agree to serve in this capacity out of a love of Judaism and a love of the Jewish community. But sooner or later, a synagogue president must come to the realization that not only can he or she not be all things to all people, not only can he or she not provide the magic solution to resolve every issue or problem that every congregant perceives, not only do many issues have large and complex social and cultural dimensions that resist resolution, but the president himself or herself has personal limitations (of available time and skills, among others.) That does not mean the president or the rabbi or synagogue as a whole should ignore such matters. It does mean that one does well to adopt a healthy measure of some humility about the capacity to resolve them and some patience about the process of resolution.

There is a folk tale about a peddler who returns home every day after a long, tiring, and stressful day of work. Just before he enters his home he removes the bundle of wares that he carries upon his back and affixes them to the tree in his front yard. As he ties up his bundle, he imagines that the worries, concerns, and burdens he has accumulated during the day are inside it. As he hangs the bundle on the tree, he feels unburdened not only of the pack but also of the accumulated burdens of his travels. That way, he can freely enter his home and greet his wife and children with lightness and joy.

In the same way, our volunteer leaders must feel free to relieve themselves of their burdens, particularly when they enter our synagogue to worship. No president and no board member should ever feel that their service to the synagogue has become a burden that is too much to bear. Patience with oneself dictates the necessity to go off duty, to retain private time, family time, and even synagogue time that is personally meaningful and free of synagogue business.

May all who take on the mantle of synagogue leadership feel that the efforts put forth and the time put in toward the enhancement of the Jewish community are appreciated by fellow congregants who respond with support and engagement. And may they be blessed with the quality of patience in the measure with which they require it.

REGARDING THE SPIES THROUGH THE LENS OF HUMILITY
Shabbat Sh'lach L'cha 5769/2009

Consider the *middah*, the trait of personality, of *anavah*/humilty as found in some of the literature of Mussar. Mussar is the Jewish approach to personal growth that would have one cultivate the *middot* on a certain list, one at a time. Although many such lists exist in the literature of Mussar, I have never seen one that did not include *anavah* and did not regard it as a foundational trait upon which the others depend.

One fruitful way to study Torah as a means for personal growth is by reading it through the lens of a *middah* such as that of *anavah*. Or, conversely, one might reflect on a *middah* such as *anavah* through the lens of a particular *Parasha*, the text of Torah read on a given Shabbat. For example, take the story of the spies (*Numbers 13*). The Torah portion Shelach Lecha features an account of the twelve spies Moses sends to scout out the land of Canaan prior to its conquest. Ten of the twelve spies return with a report that strongly discourages the adventure, while Joshua and Caleb, alone among the twelve, assume a cautiously optimistic disposition regarding the land as a potential home. In the report of the ten, one verse jumps out at me as it regards *anavah*. The ten spies report, "We saw the *Nephilim* there—the *Anakim* [giants] are part of the *Nephilim*—and we looked like grasshoppers to ourselves, and also to them."

First, one might raise the issue, as many commentators do, of how the spies could have known how they appeared to the *Nephilim*. Do any of us really know how we appear to others? Do I appear tall, short, overweight, pleasant, unhappy, or happy to you? I do not know. Some commentators take the spies to task over just this matter, that, in a report meant to be limited to facts and personal experience, they indulge in a kind of speculative subjectivity that undermines the report's factual credibility.

Be that as it may, the speculation about relative size pertains to the *middah* of *anavah*/humilty. From the perspective of Mussar, one exhibits *anavah* by occupying the right amount of space, not too much and not too little. When I am consciously working on the trait of humility, I make an effort to notice, for example, how much I speak in a meeting. In the quantity of my speech, do I occupy sufficient space but not too much? In one of the recent campaigns for the Democratic nominee for governor of Virginia, I heard folks say that when candidate Terry McAuliffe would walk into a room, he would "fill it up." All eyes would shift toward him. By contrast, when Creigh Deeds, another candidate, would do the same, people sometimes seemed not to notice. People can occupy different amounts of space in the sense of drawing differing amounts of attention to themselves by their behavior, manner, quantity and style of speech, dress, and designated role.

As for the ten spies, their comments bolster the view that the Israelites are puny by comparison to the big, strong, and presumably unfriendly and unwelcoming current occupants of the land designated for conquest. But maybe their sense of appropriate space is at issue. Maybe their esteem requires building. If the *anavah* scale extends from the extreme of self-abnegation on one end to the extreme of self-absorption or arrogance on the other, I would say I tend to encounter more people who reside too close to the first extreme. In my experience, many people seem bruised and could benefit more from building up their self-esteem than from limiting any tendencies to exhibit arrogance.

If, in the Hasidic teaching, we all require two pockets, one for the phrase "I am but dust and ashes" and the other for the phrase "for my sake was the world created," then I meet more people who seem to require the latter phrase more than the former. And I meet more than a few who seem to require each, depending on the setting or our disposition at the moment. Maybe those ten spies needed a note in their pockets saying, "You are a giant and not a grasshopper." More to the point, when we, like the spies, are overly fearful about an uncertain adventure, overly resistant to accepting a responsibility rightfully ours, when we lack faith in ourselves or in others upon whom we have good reason to depend, or upon the Holy One of Blessing, maybe we also need to be reminded that we are not grasshoppers.

Still applying the lens of Mussar, we turn more briefly to the conclusion of the Torah portion, which contains a brief and odd report about a specific Shabbat violation, odd because it has no context and odd because a seemingly minor infraction, gathering wood on Shabbat, receives the harsh punishment of death by stoning. It should be said that Jewish tradition has variously understood this passage but always as an oddity and never as a paradigm for communal norms by which Shabbat violators are punished. So rabbis may often urge their congregants to avoid shopping in the mall on Shabbat but have never, to my knowledge, suggested treating the Shabbat shoppers as deserving of capital punishment.

However, taken as a curious and hyperbolic description about Shabbat violation, the passage does raise a question or two about the way Shabbat may have greater importance in establishing balance in one's life than one might imagine and about the way in which failing to cultivate a habit of Shabbat observance could result in a kind of death. Speaking personally, I know I require Shabbat observance. I know that my spiritual health requires a disciplined weekly respite, a pattern of suspending the rush of the week, a period when I shut down my computer, resist answering the phone, turn off the cell phone, breathe with a little awareness, take a walk, have a relaxed conversation with someone I love, visit a friend, read a book, take a nap.

If Shabbat is, as Rabbi Abraham Joshua Heschel describes it, a cathedral in time (*The Sabbath*), a period set aside, of refraining from acting on the earth, of letting go of our ego-driven needs to achieve and create, then Shabbat comprises the weekly nutrient we must absorb in order to restore spatial balance and reestablish a properly situated place somewhere on the scale between the extremes of arrogance and self denial.

Finally, the portion concludes with the injunction to tie fringes on the corners of our garments as a reminder of the entirety of the *mitzvot*, lest we forget them and instead follow the lustful urges of our hearts. This section of Torah has entered the liturgy as the third paragraph of the Shema, meaning long ago, the rabbis who organized our prayers deemed it of great importance. This idea, that the fringes are a necessary reminder that God expects us to refrain from behaving as our baser instincts sometimes direct us, assumes that humans have both good and not-so-good impulses, that at times we require disciplines imposed on us from the outside and tangible signs to goad us toward becoming our better selves in the way speed limit signs remind us to drive more safely than some of us otherwise would. Sometimes our inner drives and passions direct us to noble action or high achievement but, uncontrolled, they also may lead us astray.

How could fringes on a garment remind us to love our neighbors, avoid hurtful speech, take care of one another and the earth, teach Torah, act kindly, judge fairly, improve the social conditions of society, and, more generally, live humbly? Tongue-in-cheek, the Talmud tells the story of a pious Jewish man who had some lustful urges that he mostly suppressed until he could not. He had heard of a famous and high-priced courtesan who lived in a distant city, and he went to visit her, paying her high price up front. As they were preparing for their intimate encounter, he came upon the fringes he wore on his undergarment. Abruptly, his shame overwhelmed him and he scampered from the bedchamber. Meanwhile, the courtesan was so impressed by his restraint that she later sought out the pious man who informed her that his fringes had reminded him of the behavioral boundary he was about to transgress; they shamed him into exhibiting self-control. This explanation increased the courtesan's interest in a tradition that could cultivate consciousness about behavioral boundaries. Thus did she become, in succession, a student of Torah, a pious proselyte, and, eventually, the wife of the pious man.

Another story about inhibiting impulses involves the Chafetz Chaim, the famous nineteenth-century rabbi, Yisrael Meir Kagan, known as a master teacher and practitioner of Mussar. Besides teaching Torah, the Chafetz Chaim owned and ran a shop. It is said that in a particular day, as soon as he had sold enough to support his family that day, he would close his shop in order to allow his competitors to get the business that he felt he no longer required. Materially speaking, he had acquired enough. And enough is enough.

I would not say that *tzitzit* always have the desirable effect of restraining one from following lustful urges—whether they be sexual, material, or otherwise—but clearly, by instructing us to make for ourselves visible and tangible reminders of its values, the Torah bids us to become self-aware, to strive for balance in our dispositions, to cultivate habits of humility in our deeds, and to inhibit our destructive and self-destructive tendencies while we nurture our capacities for decency.

May this day be for us all one of heightened awareness about the desirability of occupying no more and no less than the right amount of space.

ENGAGING THE DAY WITH ZEAL
Rosh Hashanah 5770/2009

When the Hasidic Master Israel of Rizhyn began his rabbinic career, he had high aspirations. He felt that if he were to exert great energy, he could transform the entire world. He felt that if he were to apply himself with sufficient enthusiasm, he could inspire a generation to achieve holiness. However, after a few months into his job, that goal began to appear somewhat beyond his capacity, so he decided he would narrow his focus to his nation alone. But when it appeared that he had had little impact on the nation, he decided to concentrate on transforming only the Jews. As more time passed and as few Jews transformed themselves into holy women and men, the rabbi of Rizhyn decided to focus his attention mainly on the Jews of his town and, later still, primarily on those of his congregation. After the passage of more time, however, even that goal began to seem unrealistically difficult, so the rabbi of Rizhyn decided to work on his family. But in time, he became aware of how resistant the members of his family were to all his best efforts to effect their transformation into holy exemplars. Only then did Israel of Rizhyn realize that his work of transformation had to begin with himself.

Jewish tradition designates the *Yamim Noraim*, the ten Days of Awe, from Rosh Hashanah through Yom Kippur, for the work of transforming our characters. Character transformation is what is meant by engaging in the process called *teshuvah*, in the sense of turning toward one's core values, returning to the divine, soulful center of the self. True *teshuvah* is not a vague or abstract idea but entails a careful process of serious self-reflection that Jewish tradition designates as *Cheshbon Hanefesh*, literally an audit of the soul. Although in an ideal world, Torah teaching would have us engage in such an audit in an ongoing fashion, throughout the year, we are especially bidden not to evade the Torah's system of accountability during this sober season, as we bid farewell to one year's journey and embark upon a new one.

For what are we to be held accountable? All of us are enrolled in the same course: Life 101. And all of us have received the same course text—we Jews call it *Torah*. And each of us, if we have taken the course goals to heart, know that we will be graded according to the extent to which we observe but one injunction found near the center of that text: "*T'hyu Kedoshim*—Be holy!" However, the instructions for how to move toward holiness are extensive and vary in their details from individual to individual. That is to say, we each receive our own individualized educational plan, our own curriculum custom tailored to the spiritual growth we each require at this stage.

If one makes concrete the interior work that constitutes *teshuvah* by segmenting it into specific qualities of soul or character, those that enhance the quality of holiness and those that inhibit it, then the Jewish literature of Mussar speaks directly to the task at hand. Mussar provides individualized guidance as one turns to audit the soul; Mussar aids one in the discovery of his or her individualized spiritual curriculum. On that curriculum, some will find the need to work on generosity. Others will need to work on being more kind with words. Some could grow in the capacity to speak less and be quiet more. Perhaps some ought to overcome the tendency to be overly meek and withdrawn while others could do well to suppress an overgrown sense of self-importance. And on and on.

In the *Mishnah Avot*, we read: "Be daring as the leopard, light as the eagle, fast as the deer, and powerful as the lion, to fulfill the will of your Father in Heaven." Thus does the Torah present one supporting text for the *middah*, the virtue or soul-trait, of *zerizut*, call it enthusiasm, alacrity, or zeal. Although most sages would not list it as the first or most primary of *middot*, it does support the others and, in my view, commends itself for special attention in this particular season. An old midrash from Yemen speaks to this contention:

> They say to a certain man: "Go to a certain town and learn Torah there." But the man replies: "I am afraid of the lions that I will encounter on the way." So they say, "You can go and learn in another town that is closer." But the man replies, "I am afraid of the thieves there." So they suggest, "There is a sage in your own city. Go and learn from him." But the man replies, "I am afraid that people may harm me on the way." So they say, "There is a teacher in your own house. Go and learn from him." But the man replies, "What if I find the door locked and I have to return to where I am?" So they say, "There is a teacher sitting right here in the chair next to you." But the man replies, "You know

what? What I really want to do is go back to sleep." (Yalkut Midreshei Teiman, *Yom Kippur Readings*, p. 259)

While Jewish tradition instructs us to make like a leopard, an eagle, a lion, and a deer and the like in performing mitzvot, to engage the world with gusto, strength, and speed in the service of the divine will, it recognizes at the same time the all-too-prevalent human tendency to resist adopting an enthusiastic posture, but rather to indulge in all manner of rationalization for remaining curled up in bed.

A contemporary version of the midrash appeared recently in the comic strip *Doonesbury*. In it, an elderly mother, her son with graying temples and reading glasses perched on his nose, and the daughter-in-law are seated at the kitchen table. Mom brings up the topic of "the elephant in the room."

"What elephant is that?" asks her son.

Mom replies: "The grandchildren that are not sitting around this table," to which daughter-in-law replies: "That's still under discussion."

"I don't get it—what's to discuss?" mom wants to know.

The son: "There's my age to consider—there are certain medical risks and actuarial risks—I want to be around!"

On the next panel, he adds: "Then there's the economy—what if our business tanks? And what about child care? Or schooling? Or college? What about our retirement?"

The daughter-in-law then pipes in: "Don't forget terrorism."

Addressing the latter, mom then suggests: "You could raise them in Canada. They'd be safe there."

To which son replies: "We certainly can't raise them here—Mom's in the only spare room we have."

Mom now offers: "Don't blame me—I'm fixing to die."

Son, looking shocked, murmurs: "What?"

Finally, daughter-in-law concludes the conversation with: "Okay, it'd be great if you both could get a grip."

When you wake up and consider what life has in store for you on a particular day, do you not sometimes feel challenged to "get a grip"? Do you not sometimes just feel like going back to sleep? Maybe you are among the lucky ones who typically regard the world through a lens of optimism and joy, a lens where aggravations are minimized and blessings magnified, where one sees the wonders of the world and appreciates the goodness of life even amid struggles, where telemarketers who call at dinner receive gentle replies, where signs of aging become motivation for living well in the moment, where the glass is always half full. But even a joyful optimist might find reason to cower under the bed covers from time to time. Even the perennially upbeat among us must at times grow weary from the sadness of the world. Even one who is essentially happy must at times feel weighted down by the sorrows close to home.

Who can help but feel weighted down, knowing that we live in a world full of pain and woe; that even among us are those who have lost jobs recently and, despite persistent effort, have found only inadequate replacement work or no work at all; that many have watched retirement funds dwindle over the past eighteen months and with them the fading of long-held plans for the future? Some who are retired have found themselves in genuine crisis; others are suffering from addiction to drugs or alcohol or food or unhealthy behavior; more than a few are lonely or depressed or chronically anxious or sleep deprived; some find themselves tending to parents or a loved one in extreme physical or mental decline, trying to negotiate changed expectations for interacting respectfully and lovingly; others now live with the gaping hole left by having lost a parent or a spouse or a child or a friend—and the pain of that loss. And of course, young men and women, in far-off places, are engaged in fighting our battles, undergoing the multiple traumas of a sort known only to them. Look at the faces of fallen American men and women in the wars of Iraq and Afghanistan—as one does at the conclusion of the PBS *NewsHour*—and you will see a cross section of America, each face a reminder of the emotional and spiritual cost of war.

Life weighs us down. Moses Chaim Luzzatto, in the chapter on the trait of zeal in his seventeenth-century work *The Path of the Upright*, describes the weightiness of life as something built into the very physicality of human existence:

> A person's nature exercises a strong downward pull upon him. This is so because the grossness which characterizes the substance of earthiness keeps a person from desiring exertion and labor. One who wishes, therefore, to merit to serve the Creator, may His name be blessed, must strengthen his nature and be zealous. If he leaves himself in the hands of his downward-pulling nature, there is no question that he will not succeed. (*Path of the Upright*, p. 98–99)

The image of our earthy, downward-pulling nature, a nature that hinders exertion and enthusiasm, became personally meaningful to me some months ago as a bulging lumbar disc produced symptoms of sciatica, the pain spiking down my leg and sharply reducing my ability to engage in productive activity. Given this or any particular aggravation or the more constant one that accompanies life's inherent physicality, what would it take for us to serve the will of the Creator with zeal, with alacrity, with enthusiasm? Despite the gravitational pull of life, despite the particular issues of the day that cause us grief, and despite the physical, emotional, and spiritual pain that we each suffer, Judaism calls us to resist, to seek life over death, to find joy, to engage in the holy deeds required of us for spiritual improvement, to strive to serve a higher purpose—and to do so with energy and enthusiasm.

This is not rocket science. The quality of zeal is cultivated when you meet a day, a week, or a new year with a simple question: what noble task calls you? What simple good deed that you have been putting off claims your attention? Is there a friend you have been meaning to call, a relative you have been meaning to visit, a child who could use some of your attention, a book you have been meaning to read, a charity to which you have been meaning to donate, a cause on behalf of which you have been meaning to volunteer some time, a bit of Torah you have been meaning to study, a prayer you have been meaning to offer, an appreciation you have been meaning to express, a concrete bit of work you have been meaning to complete?

Of course, not all zeal is good or healthy. Zeal, by its nature, requires proper channeling. One could exhibit great zeal for a bad cause. One must harness zeal, then, to a well-functioning moral compass in order to apply it with appropriate discernment of direction. The contemporary sage Yogi Berra once said: "We are lost but making good time." Making good time in the service of the wrong direction is no virtue.

The theme of misdirected zeal pervades a book by John Krakauer and a film by Sean Penn, both entitled *Into the Wild*. *Into the Wild* documents the adventures of Chris McCandless, a young man who, in 1992 after his graduation from college, severed his relations with his family. With no money—he burned or gave away what he had—and with only the possessions he could wear or carry in a backpack, he made his way to the Alaska wilderness, there to live a life of simplicity. Unschooled in the ways of wilderness survival, after about nine or ten weeks he starved to death. Whereas his early journal entries include glowingly effervescent odes to the grandeur and beauty of nature and the joy of living, the last entries read: "Lonely, scared," and "Happiness is only real when shared." At the end, but too late, Chris McCandless acquired his moral compass.

Most of us, I suspect, do not risk the kind of unbridled exuberance that will have us heading off into unchartered territory alone and without proper provisions. However, I would venture to say that many of us could stand to pause a moment to consider the implications of what we are about to say or do or assume about someone else—before charging ahead with an erroneous assumption, a hurtful word, or an unjust or unkind charge. Zeal requires temperance.

The contemporary Mussar teacher Alan Morinis identifies two primary barriers to living with a proper amount of zeal: (1) The incapacity to feel and express appreciation and (2) the well-honed capacity to rationalize our lack of zeal for doing good.

It may not be obvious how the capacity to express appreciation relates to well-channeled zeal. Consider: almost every day I wake up dry because the roof above me has protected me from the rain. I am unharmed and not bitten up because the walls of my home have kept out the insects, the beasts, and the bad guys. I am not too cold and not too hot because I have blankets. Probably there is food in the refrigerator and, thank God, there is a refrigerator and electricity to power it, and indoor plumbing. And for another day the sun continues to freely shower the earth with life-sustaining photons, and on and on and on. There is so much goodness in my world, so much to appreciate, so much about which I ought to feel exceedingly thankful all the time. But you know what? I confess that I do not always notice any of the things I mentioned. Often what draws my attention are my aches and pains or the aches and pains of others or some aggravation or other or a worry about a family member or a community member or a matter of local or national or international politics or the latest failure of the Giants.

When the Torah enjoins us to choose life and not death, it has no simplistic notions about determining one's fate. Rather, the Torah seeks to push us to determine the attitude we bring to life. An attitude of appreciation becomes a platform for a life lived with enthusiasm and force. An attitude of worry and woe stifles life. The sages of the Talmud instruct us to say at least one hundred *brachot*/blessings every day, each blessing an articulation of appreciation, each one a foundation block supporting a life yearning for full engagement.

As for the second barrier, the ability to rationalize, the reasons one can muster to avoid the performance of *mitzvot* are many. I will tell you why

I cannot call my friend or make a sick visit or speak gently to my mate or respond positively to a request for my time or my money or why I miss an opportunity to greet a stranger or give to a cause I believe in or offer a prayer. I am too busy. I am stressed. I am tired. It is too cold. It is too hot. It might rain or snow or there could be a hurricane or a lion. Or, for that matter, there could be terrorists. I have at least ten fine reasons to curl up and go back to bed when there is a mitzvah calling my name. Or, to put it differently, if you prefer, the *Yetzer Ra*, that wily, ever-present Evil Inclination about which our sages warn, is very clever and knows exactly what to whisper in my ear in order to block the path of my spiritual growth, to prevent me from achieving my better self.

In one sense, the quality of *zerizut* is about Jewish time. Jewish time is the opposite of what some might think. "*Vayashkem Avraham*—Abraham arose early." Three times Abraham modeled Jewish time by eagerly arising to respond to a calling. Or, as the Talmudic sages instruct us: "Run to do a minor (or less weighty) mitzvah just as much as much as a major (or more important) one because *mitzvah goreret mitzvah*, one mitzvah generates another." The performance of mitzvot, even easy ones, even simple ones, generate others as they cultivate a culture characterized by mitzvah consciousness and mitzvah performance. And one more thing: the act of running to do a mitzvah lifts the weight of life from one's shoulders; it literally lightens the load; it replaces sorrow and worry with joy. I cannot prove this assertion logically, but I know that we experience its truth.

A final point on meeting the world with zeal by way of conclusion, again from *The Path of the Upright*:

> The angels are extolled for their zeal, as it is said in *Psalms 103:20*: "Mighty in power, they [angels] do God's word, to listen to the voice of God's word,"... A man is a man and not an angel, and it therefore impossible for him to attain to the strength of an angel, but he should surely strive to come as close to that level as his nature allows. (pp. 108–109)

We are not angels, and so there is no expectation that we will exhibit perfection of zeal or of any other quality. Our challenge is simply to appreciate the blessings that surround us, to resist the rationalizing tendencies that block our paths to our better selves, and to get out of bed and meet the day with the enthusiasm of which we are capable. May it be so.

A MORAL VIRTUE FOR A NEW YEAR
Rosh Hashanah 5761/2000

"Suppose there is a heaven. When you arrive, what would you like to hear God say to you?" That is the hypothetical question with which Professor James Lipton concludes every interview with actors, directors, and performers on the television program *Inside the Actors Studio*. With greater immediacy, the Hasidic Master Reb Zusya of Hanipol contemplated a similar question shortly before his actual death. As he tearfully told his disciples, "When I appear before the *Kadosh Baruch Hu*, the Holy One of Blessing, I will not be asked why I was not Abraham. And I will not be asked why I was not Moses. But I will be asked why I was not Zusya."

On Rosh Hashanah, neither the scene nor the question is hypothetical for us Jews. For this is *Yom Ha-Din*, the Day of Judgment, the day when we contemplate our lives in the light of our deaths, when we readjust our vision, when we redirect our paths, when we consider and contemplate whom we have become. On this day, we approach the Holy One, each of us imagining: What reception will I receive? Will it be the one I desire or the one I deserve? Why, indeed, am I not the person, the me, I ought to be? What changes, what *teshuvah*, what returning to the path, do I want to make in the days ahead so that I encounter the heavenly reception for which I yearn?

Usually, when we Jews think about the development of moral character, we think behavioristically; we emphasize the performance of mitzvot. We deem mitzvot not only desirable but also sacred and obligatory; while some mitzvot seem to be purely ritual (like inaugurating holidays with the lighting of candles), and a few seem completely inexplicable (not mixing wool and flax in a single garment), many mitzvot have moral dimensions: refraining from the shedding of blood, avoiding gossip or other hurtful speech, returning lost property, not stealing, giving *tzedakah*, visiting the sick, respecting the elderly, and many more whose performance we regard as solid responsibilities, irrespective of whim or wish. With all due respect to the cogency and value of an ethical system built on mitzvot, I would propose for consideration at this auspicious season another, equally Jewish model. I would propose for our consideration an approach to moral formation exceedingly well suited to a sober beginning of a new year. I refer to the model propounded by Mussar, a movement inaugurated by several yeshivahs in nineteenth-century Lithuania, a movement focused on the teaching of *Middot*, the ethics of Jewish virtues.

Virtue ethics assumes that just as people develop physically and intellectually, they also develop morally. If so, and if we care about moral development, our own and that of others, then one would agree that we ought to nurture within ourselves the moral qualities we desire with as much intentionality as we do the physical or the intellectual. This approach to moral formation, the development of desired moral qualities over the course of a person's lifetime, thus begins not with mitzvot but with virtues essential for the formation of moral character. Obviously, we want both virtuous character and moral behavior, but here the idea is that moral behavior will necessarily follow virtuous character. If we wish to utilize this approach, the question then becomes: Where should we begin? With which virtue should we begin to construct our moral selves? I was hoping you would ask.

There are many virtues. Classical Christian texts speak of four cardinal virtues (Prudence, Temperance, Justice, and Fortitude), all of which have fine, Jewish equivalents, but none of which strikes me as the core virtue for a Jewish system. In a welcome recent addition to the field of Jewish ethics, in a book entitled *The Jewish Moral Virtues*, Eugene Borowitz and Francine Schwartz highlight twenty-four moral virtues with which they would construct a program of Jewish moral formation. Their selection of virtues is based on the work of a thirteenth-century Roman Jew, Yechiel ben Yekutiel HaRofeh. After carefully considering their compilation, I would like to propose, at this time of beginnings, that we begin with what I regard as the first and primary Jewish virtue, the one without which the others will not stand, namely *Yirat Shamayim* (or *Yirat Ha-El*).

Yirat Shamayim, in its most blunt translation, fear of heaven, is the rabbinic term for the attitude that acknowledges the greatness of God and the relative smallness of humans. I select it despite the awareness that many of us recoil from the language of "fear"—and for good reason. Fear implies a childlike impotence and dependency before a towering, authoritarian, parental God. It means that our obedience is chosen only to the extent that the godfather's "choice you cannot refuse" is chosen. Yet the term *Yirat Shamayim* has richer dimensions. It also connotes "awe," an awe that encompasses a sense of wonder and respect.

The eminent Rabbi Louis Jacobs relates *Yirat Shamayim*—in its purest form—to a sense of the numinous, in Rudolf Otto's usage. Here, it is not fear of punishment for sin that operates but a sense of inexpressible awe before the Holy One. In a state of such awe, one avoids sin not out of self-interest (before the supreme godfather) but out of the shame that would accompany sin and a simple, powerful desire to do what is right before the Awesome, Holy One. A sense of awe yields an awareness of moral order and a desire to participate in and not violate it.

To illustrate with a personal anecdote: at a recent retreat of the synagogue board, the facilitator asked the participants to recall the first and then the most impactful spiritual experience of our lives. The first I could recall were memories of lying in the grass as a seven- or eight-year-old child at our Westfield, New Jersey, home with the sun gently warming my back. I would lean on my elbows and stare into the thick world below the grass tops. The scene struck me then as now as profoundly amazing: that tiny, jungle-like world of plants and animals, usually ignored by those of us living several feet above ground level and on a larger scale. As I lay without moving on my front lawn, my youthful reveries inspired a sense that the natural contained sublime intricacies, supremely beautiful and reflective of marvelous design. Thus, the awareness of that complex world, always present but just out of our usual consciousness, filled me with a sense of wonder about other worlds of possibility, worlds both larger and smaller than those I typically perceived, and about the Grand Architect of all worlds.

In response to the second question, I recalled my first conscious awareness of personal mortality. It occurred some weeks after my Bar Mitzvah. On successive nights, as I lay in bed unable to sleep, I was filled with a sense of what I could later label "existential dread," the acute pang of horror at the contemplation of personal non-being. What triggered these fearful nights I do not recall. But I do remember the days following those nights, days spent in the classes and hallways of Thomas Edison Junior High School, watching as if detached as other students walked nonchalantly to and from class, sometimes joking or teasing or fighting about this or that, seemingly unaware of and uncaring about the "big problem" that then preoccupied me. Looking back on those nights of youthful, existential angst, I now regard them as key to my ongoing insistence that the religious world I inhabit speak to the big human concerns and that it provide language and ritual and narrative forms with sufficient capacity to carry our deepest longings.

What makes an experience spiritual, then, is that it directs one outside of oneself, that it heighten one's awareness of the divine reality of which one is a part, that it inspire a sense of amazement and awe, that it evoke the disposition of *Yirat Shamayim*. I am convinced that we all have such experiences and can all draw on them to map out our spiritual realities and, in particular, can allow them to nurture our own sense of awe before heaven. However, on a matter of such ultimacy, one would do well to supplement personal experience with external sources of wisdom. Hence, the question: beyond personal experience, what paradigms of *Yirat Shamayim* does the Torah offer?

In one of the most poignant portrayals of *teshuvah*, character transformation involving the acquisition of the virtue *Yirat Shamayim*, the Torah depicts the conflicted character of Jacob, the father of the Jewish people. Jacob has received his brother's birthright by stealth and deception; now he must flee for his life into the dry and barren Judean hills. At the moment, his future seems uncertain, without direction; if anything, Jacob seems to be escaping from any possibility of covenantal continuity with his grandfather Abraham and his father Isaac. As night falls, the pampered Jacob places a rock under his head. He dreams a dream about a ladder connecting heaven and earth with angels ascending and descending. He senses God's presence and evokes the renewal of the covenant first struck with his father and grandfather. Filled with awe and wonder, Jacob awakes and says: "Surely God is in this place and I [*Anochi*] did not know" (*Genesis 28:16*).

David Elcott, a contemporary Jewish teacher, points out two divergent Hasidic understandings of the verse, two attempts to imagine what Jacob did not know, from which we can learn something crucial about the nature of *Yirat Shamayim* and the *teshuvah* required to attain it. According to the first understanding, the fleeing Jacob is consumed by the emotions associated with his conflicted past; he is overwrought by fear and anger; he is plagued by his own deceit and consequent shame. In short, Jacob's ego is battered; he is weak at the core, lacking security about his own worth. When he says, "*Anochi*—I did not know my 'I,'" he means that, until that moment, he had not appreciated his own worth; until the dream, he had not realized the divinity lodged within him; he had not recognized that the place of God is within the human soul, including his own. With Jacob's newfound sense of self-worth came the concomitant ability to experience the divine presence.

The second, divergent, understanding (suggested by Tiferet Shlomo) is as follows: just when Jacob becomes aware of God's immanent presence, he says, "*Anochi*—I do not know," meaning that for God to be present I must not be consumed with myself, with my ego. Only by diminishing the ego and the corresponding, self-serving tendencies and excuse-making in which we are all so skilled, and by confining one's sense of self-importance, can one allow God-consciousness to enter the heart.

The two contrary understandings yield a harmonious truth about what it takes to acquire the virtue of *Yirat Shamayim*. One leads a person to a sufficient sense of self-worth even to imagine the capacity to attain this disposition. The other would have a person cultivate the ability and volition to reduce one's sense of self, to admit dependence, insufficiency, and relative impotence.

Thus, it would appear that in order to acquire the disposition of awe before heaven, one must achieve a balanced sense of self: one must possess a measure of modesty and humility, on the one side, and a sense of importance, on the other. In the famous image of Rabbi Simcha Bunim, every person should have two pockets so he or she can reach into one or the other according to need. In the right pocket are to be the words: "For my sake was the world created," and in the left: "I am but earth and ashes."

For some of us, the greater challenge is to overcome a low sense of self; others face the challenge of achieving an adequate dose of humility. More than a few of us, I imagine, face both challenges alternately. When I feel insecure, inadequate, or unimportant, I reread the first chapter of *Genesis*. *Genesis* reveals nothing about the scientific origins of the universe; it tells us nothing about the biological, geological, or historical beginnings of the world. However, it does speak in deep, resonant tones about the value of human life. It teaches us that—from the view of Torah—human beings were created with the endowed purpose of carrying on the work of a deliberately incomplete creation, each according to her or his capacity. And, lest one bemoan the smallness of one's own capacity with respect to that of others, *Genesis* asserts, in narrative simplicity, that no human can claim superior origins to those of any other. There is no divinely ordained human hierarchy of worth. We all descend, as the Torah has it, from the same original human progenitor.

As for the issue of insufficient humility or modesty, consider a rather different description of human origins by the eleventh-century Spanish moralist, Bachya Ibn Pakuda:

We must recall our humble origins. As the Talmud asks, "why did God wait so long, not creating humankind until the sixth day of creation? So that if people became puffed up, they could be quickly deflated by pointing out, 'The gnat was created before you.'" (*Sanhedrin 38a*)

Or in the words of the Psalmist: "Lord, what are we that You bother with us, human beings that You involve Yourself with us?" Were it not that God's involvement in our lives gives them considerable significance, we would be very insignificant. Such perspectives lend themselves to the cultivation of a quality of humility sufficient that in turn could serve to modulate the grandiosity of one's self-image even as it would permit the possibility of a disposition of awe before heaven.

Perhaps the virtue of *Yirat Shamayim* is not such a hard sell at the time of sober beginnings that is the Jewish New Year. And yet, at the same time, I admit that I do not easily hold this virtue in my heart as constantly as I might desire. I suspect others have the same problem, and that is why above the arks housing the Torah scrolls in many synagogues, including the ark in our small sanctuary, are the Talmudic words *Know before Whom You Stand*. At bottom, *Yirat Shamayim* is the moral virtue by means of which one achieves that knowledge and senses that abiding, divine presence.

As a practical matter, whether or not those words grace the space in which I pray, I often imagine them there. I imagine them there especially when I find myself obsessing about the choreography of our public worship instead of my own need and requirement to pray. I imagine them there when, during silent and supposedly heartfelt prayer, I cannot focus on anything but the most recent aggravation. I imagine them there in my study or in the mall or whenever I forget that I am not the final arbiter of truth. *Yirat Shamayim* is the solid foundation upon which a well-constructed system of Jewish ethics should be built. One ought to strive to acquire and maintain it as the primary Jewish virtue of one's character.

A story by way of conclusion:

Reb Naftali, the Rebbe of Ropshitz, was taking an unaccustomed way home when he came across a magnificent estate. He approached the man he saw patrolling the grounds, and asked him for whom he worked. The guard mentioned the name of one of the great men of the city and said he was employed to protect the estate. He then asked Reb Naftali,

"And for whom do you work?" That question hit the Ropshitzer so hard that he said to the man, "Will you come work for me?" The man replied, "And what would be my duties?" Answered the Reb Naftali, "To remind me." (Buber, *Hasidic Tales: Later Masters*, p. 193)

Because we do not always possess *Yirat Shamayim*, we require such reminders to move us from where we are to where we want to be. Because we do not always sense the reality that there is a magnificent presence in the universe before whom we stand, we require inspiration to help us get in touch with and maintain a sense of awe before heaven. In that spirit do we Jews assemble as we do in congregational communities. In that hope do we pick up books with timeworn prayers, evocations of spiritual encounters from the distant past. If we allow, these become the means for us to know before whom we stand, for whom we work, and from whom we derive the deepest and most abiding meaning our lives can have. These reminders can help us attain a sense of awe before heaven, the foundational virtue for becoming the people we wish to become and, ultimately, for receiving the heavenly reception we desire.

THE HAND
Deeds of Kindness & Virtue

WHAT IS BLESSING?
Kol Nidre 5762/2001

On the fifth day of creation, the Ribbono Shel Olam, the Master of the Universe, turned to the fishes and the birds and the swarming and creeping things that had just been created, and He blessed them. On the sixth day of creation, the Ribbono Shel Olam, the Master of the Universe, turned to the first human being and blessed them. On the seventh day, the Ribbono Shel Olam, the Master of the Universe, blessed the seventh day and declared it holy. When the Torah begins its final section, the narration opens: "And this is the blessing which Moses, the man of God, bade the children of Israel before he died." At the center of the Torah, when the Tabernacle of the covenant is dedicated, Moses and Aaron bless the people. Thus, one might well regard the blessing, the *bracha*, as *a* central motif, if not *the* central motif, of the Torah. People, creatures, place, and time all come under the rubric of God's blessing. One might well say that Judaism seeks as its central mission to cultivate a culture of blessing.

If so, then we must ask: how might we contribute to that culture of blessing?

One might begin an exploration of a Jewish approach to the idea of blessing with the observation that the traditions of Judaism prescribe verbal responses for many of the circumstances in our lives. In response to what we eat or see or acquire or do, our tradition would have us pronounce a formula of blessing, a *bracha*, whereby we invoke God's name in conjunction with the object or action over which the *bracha* is spoken. Thus, the tractate of the Mishnah that primarily addresses the subject of prayer, the tractate Brachot, lists short prayers, verbal reactions to the experience of shooting stars, earthquakes, thunder or lightning, mountains or hills, seas, rivers, deserts, trees, rainbows, the Mediterranean Sea, rain, the construction of a new house, the acquisition of a new possession, the eating of various foods, or the imbibing of various drinks. As far as I know, there is no *bracha* to be recited upon meeting a Hollywood celebrity or a famous athlete; however, there is one for seeing a great Torah scholar or someone of great secular wisdom or a national ruler or someone with a physical deformity, and on and on.

Life is full of a dazzling array of occasions for uttering *brachot*, and one achieves merit, our tradition tells us, by taking advantage of these opportunities. Perhaps the most curious and troubling of all the Mishnaic injunctions to utter blessing has a particularly chilling resonance these days: for rain and for good tidings, one says, "Blessed be the One who is good and bestows good." For evil tidings (in particular the news of a death), one says, "Blessed be the True Judge." And lest one think the idea of pronouncing a blessing over bad tidings got into the text by mistake, a kind of weird and unusually egregious scribal error, the Mishnah goes on to say: "Over evil, a blessing is said similar to that over good and over good a blessing is said similar to that over evil." In other words, we heard correctly the first time. Over bad or evil news, we offer blessing as we do over good news.

How counterintuitive! How curious! How eerie to contemplate the many recent unanticipated occasions for such a strange blessing! How it makes me realize how little I understand the nature of blessing in the first place.

Baruch Attah Adonai—Blessed are You, God. We chant or recite or whisper these words so often that they become like the air we breathe and whose presence we take for granted. So let us pay attention and ask: What is a *bracha*? What does it mean to bless God? What does it mean to receive blessing? What does it mean for one human being to bless another?

Professor Ellen Davis, a Bible professor at Duke Divinity School, defines blessing as follows: "A blessing is the experience of entering, through prayer and openness to God, into a mode of existence where the paramount realities are God's goodness and God's power for making or doing good" (conference presentation, Wildacres Interfaith Institute, Summer 2001). Blessing, according to Davis, is not merely or simply a verbal formula, a certain type of prayer with the introductory words *Baruch Atah Adonai*; rather, a blessing is an experience.

Furthermore, says Davis, humans are not the only blessing producers, maybe not even the most adept blessing makers. According to many of the psalms, mountains, hills, thunder, ocean waves, the creatures of the land, sea, and sky all proclaim blessing, all enter into that godly mode of existence, more gracefully and naturally than do humans. It is said that the famous composer Arturo Toscanini once visited the Grand Canyon. He walked to the canyon's edge and stood silently for several moments. He then began to clap and to shout, "Bravo! Bravo!" We have all experienced similar moments where nature proclaims divine awesomeness in ways no human could. To Davis, then, there is an "ecology of blessing," a web of connections in which the entire divinely created world takes part. So how may we humans, in our less instinctive way, perhaps take part in the ecology of blessing?

According to Rabbi Nehemiah Pollen, the Biblical concept of blessing aggregates around three ideas: first, fruitfulness ("Your progeny will be as numerous as the stars of the heavens!"); second, bestowal of a gift or power ("You shall inherit the land!"); and third, a cluster of meanings, by far the most suggestive, that may undergird the rest: a blessing may simply be a greeting, nothing more or less (conference presentation, Wildacres, Summer 2001). In First Samuel 13:10, we read: "He [King Saul] had just finished presenting the burnt offering and Saul went out to meet him [the Prophet Samuel] and welcome him [*Likrato L'varacho*, literally, to meet him to bless him]." Saul went out to meet and bless/greet the advisor for whose arrival he had so expectantly awaited. Saul's blessing of Samuel consisted of nothing more or less than his greeting, his recognition of the prophet. At its root, a blessing involves recognition.

In this regard, there was a key moment in the life of the United States when, a few days after July 4, 1776, a U.S. warship sailed into the well-fortified harbor of the Island of St. Eustatius. To date, no state had recognized the newly self-declared nation. It was an anxious moment until the guns of St. Eustacious fired the hoped-for military salute proffered to the ship of a nation it recognized as sovereign. That military salute was a *bracha* of this root kind in the form of recognition, an affirmation of the identity of the other. Psychologically and symbolically, no small matter that *bracha* of greeting.

Contemplating the idea of blessing as simple greeting, as a salute in affirmation of the identity of the other, reminds me of the following, a true story. It takes place on a wintery Tuesday morning. I am sitting in my study going through the mail and thinking about the tasks of the day and the week: a sermon that needs writing, a couple of classes that entail preparation, a talk to a local church group I still must write, four or five Bar and Bat Mitzvah students to tutor, some counseling, some hospital patients to see, a couple of evening committee meetings to attend, a few one-on-one meetings with congregants to discuss this and that, and there is mail to review and phone messages to answer. In other words, it is a typical day in a typical week with me feeling just a little short of the time essential to do everything well.

Then, the phone rings. It is a staff nurse from a nursing home in Culpepper; they have a resident who is quite sick and declining and who would like a visit from a rabbi. I would like to say that, filled with an abiding generosity of spirit and a longing to leap at every opportunity to perform a mitzvah, I immediately hopped into my car and drove to Culpepper. However, I will tell the truth instead. I remember thinking at the time: Culpepper is forty miles away. That's fifty minutes each way, and then maybe thirty minutes at the facility. We're talking two and a half or three hours out of a day to visit a woman who has absolutely no connection to me or to our synagogue. After determining that the woman—her name was Alice Walker—had been a member of a synagogue in Northern Virginia, I suggest to the staff nurse that, although I am willing to make the visit, it would be more appropriate if one of the rabbis from her own synagogue would drop in. I tell them that I would appreciate it if they would attempt to follow that route, but add that if necessary they should call me back. That afternoon, the staff nurse does call back. No other rabbis are available. Would I please come out? I had said I would, and so, the next day, I drive to Culpepper.

As I pull into the parking lot of the nursing home, my feelings of being put upon begin to dissipate as the more powerful emotions that always accompany a visit to a nursing home or a hospital arise, emotions related to the function of the facility, to illness and decline and the circumscribed lives of those of us who reside in such places, and, I suppose, my own sense of mortal impermanence. When I enter Alice Walker's room, I find myself in the presence of a frail woman with a thin but luminous face. She is seated upright in her bed, her sparse hair neatly combed. She is breathing oxygen in shallow breaths.

I introduce myself as Rabbi Alexander from Charlottesville and stick out my hand. She grasps my hand gently but firmly and holds onto it for what seems a very long time, as if she might not let go at all. She smiles and thanks me for coming. I no longer recall the details of our conversation. Probably we talked about her life and my life, where we have lived, our families. After twenty minutes or so, she begins to tire visibly, so I know my visit cannot last much longer. My initial feelings have given way completely to those of awe, wonder, and curiosity. I wonder: has the reason for her request for a rabbi's presence been fulfilled? How might I know?

Before leaving Mrs. Walker, I tell her that I need to return to Charlottesville, but before I do, would she like a prayer? Without hesitation she replies yes. She would like a prayer. She then closes her eyes and extends both her hands for me to grasp. I take hold of her hands and offer a version of the final *Viddui*, the confession that Jewish tradition has us say before we die or has another say on our behalf. It asks for health if that is God's will and, if not, that our death be counted as expiation for our transgressions. To the words of the Shema with which I conclude, Alice Walker moves her lips. There are tears on her face and on mine as well.

Three days later, I received a letter from the nursing home. Alice Walker had died the day following my visit. I learned that the staff had been more assertive than they might have been in seeking a rabbi for her because they were especially fond of her. Ever since she had moved into the home, she had noticeably brightened the place by her presence. She was in the habit of thanking the staff for their attentions and care and often spent time engaging the other residents in conversation or just sitting with them. Both residents and staff alike had come to value her kindness and her small affirmations, hence the eagerness of the staff for a rabbinic visit and, after the fact, their appreciation. They all signed the card.

As for me, Alice demonstrated how, even when a life becomes confined by reasons of ill health, even when the canvass upon which we paint becomes tiny, we still have the ability to produce a good miniature. She also taught me about the reciprocal nature of the blessings humans may impart to one another. The process of blessing can be (and often is) mutual, according to Professor Davis. Like a telephone wire, the line of transmission for blessing carries the signals in both directions. Similarly, it may also be the case that a *bracha* can never be self-reflexive. One can no more bless oneself than tickle oneself. Rather, people need other people in the economy of blessing. Alice wished to receive a blessing so that she could depart life as she had begun, as a Jew. In serving as a conduit for that blessing and through the touch of her frail fingers, I know I felt blessed to have been in her bright presence.

The opportunities for blessing abound in the planned and unplanned human encounters of each day. Often, if we take those opportunities, we become vehicles for blessing even without knowing it. The author Rachel Naomi Remen recounts one of the first pastoral encounters of a Father

Patrick O'Shea, who as a newly ordained priest with a ministry of hospital chaplaincy was called by a woman facing major surgery the next day:

> He had no sooner pulled up a chair when she told him, "Father, I feel certain that I am going to die tomorrow."
>
> Nothing in his training had prepared him for this and he just sat there with no idea of how to respond. To cover his confusion he had reached out and taken her hand. She had begun to talk then. Still holding her hand and barely listening, he had reached back in his mind for some of the great words of comfort from his tradition, the words of Merton, of Teresa of D'Avila, of Jesus. He had them all with him when he entered the room but somehow now they were all gone.
>
> They continued to talk and even cry a little, and his heart went out to her in her fear. At last she closed her eyes, and he had taken the opportunity to ask God for help, for the words that he needed. But he had found no words at all. Eventually she had simply fallen asleep and he had left, vanquished, convinced that he was not cut out to be a priest. He had spent the rest of the day and most of the night in an agonized assessment of his shortcomings and his calling. He had been too ashamed to visit her again.
>
> But a few weeks later he had received a note from her, thanking him for all he had done for her during his visit, and most especially for all the wonderful things he had told her, the words of comfort and wisdom. She would never forget them. And then she quoted some of what she had heard him say, at length.
>
> [Father O'Shea concluded:] "Over the years I have learned that when I pray to be of service to someone, sometimes God says 'yes' and sometimes God says 'no,' but quite often God says, 'Step aside, Patrick. I'll do it myself.'" (*My Grandfather's Blessings*, pp. 331–332)

In the words of Professor Davis, "Blessings on the horizontal, earthly plane ultimately flow to and from the ultimate source of all blessing." An awareness of that ultimate source of blessing should do two things: it should make us humble about our own control over the capacity to bless, and it should empower us to become highly available as vehicles of divine blessing in the human encounter.

There is an economy of blessing whereby the blessing of one human being by another becomes reciprocal, and there is a sense in which all blessing flows from the ultimate source of blessing. Furthermore, some simple acts of blessing can send out ripples that last for years. Shlomo Carlebach used to tell of a certain man he knew in New York City. Some people find New Yorkers to be brusque, even abrasive, but this man always exuded warmth and kindness. So Shlomo once asked him how he had become like that. In reply, the man told the following story:

> When I was a boy, my family lived in small shtetl in Poland; we were very poor, but when my father died, things got even worse for my mother and six brothers and sisters, three older and three younger than I; most of the time I felt pretty unhappy and ignored; everyone was just so busy trying to survive that no one paid much attention to me; once, my mother took me to a nearby town where a famous rabbi had a Beit Midrash. We arrived late at night and, there being no other sleeping accommodations, I ended up spending the night on the floor in the rabbi's cold, unheated study. At some point during the night, the door to the study opened and in walked the rabbi. I pretended to be asleep as the rabbi tip-toed into his study. When he approached me, he said softly, "such a sweet boy lying here with no blanket to keep out the cold." With that the rabbi removed his coat and spread it over me. It has been more than 60 years since the rabbi covered me with his coat and it keeps me warm to this day.

Sometimes even the distant memory of a simple act of kindness can ripple across the years. In his book *The Tipping Point*, Malcolm Gladwell points out that small changes, if positioned in a certain way, can have a big impact; a one-degree change in temperature cannot normally be detected, but if the temperature were to drop from 33 to 32 degrees, a rainy landscape could be transformed into a winter wonderland. Who knows when a simple deed of kindness, a small blessing of affirmation may tip the balance between one who grows up to hate and one who becomes another link in the great chain of blessing-creation?

Rachel Remen remembers an incident from her childhood that goes to the heart of the notion of blessing as affirmation:

> A child somewhere in the Midwest fell down an abandoned well and for a week rescue teams worked to bring her out. This was the time

before television, and radios were playing everywhere—in the stores, in the buses, even at school. Strangers met in the street and asked each other, "Any news?" People of all religions prayed together.

As the rescue effort went on, no one asked if she was the child of a professor or a cleaning woman, the child of a wealthy family. Was the child black, white, or yellow? Was the child good or naughty, smart or slow? In that week everyone knew these things did not matter at all. That the importance of the child's life had nothing to do with these things. (*My Grandfather's Blessings*, p. 64)

The practice of blessing as greeting, as affirmation of the essential worth of the other, promotes a culture in which all human life is assumed to be sacred and of equal value. According to midrash, God created only one human being in the beginning rather than many in order to teach us a lesson. That way, no one could claim an ancestry superior to that of another. And everyone can claim creation in the divine image. In this manner, the rabbis teach: whoever destroys a life destroys an entire world, while whoever saves a life saves an entire world. There is no scale of value to human life; every human life has infinite value; that is why, barely two weeks after 9/11, there is no container large enough to accommodate our grief.

Which brings us full circle to the blessing said over evil tidings. How can one bless God in the face of sorrowful news? If to bless means only to thank or to praise, then to insist on offering blessing for bad news is to demand too much. Perhaps one might affirm, on the occasion of a death, despite all contrary sentiment, a belief in an ultimate goodness that will subsume sorrow and an ultimate truth that will encompass evil. Perhaps, but to praise or to thank God for the evil itself is to deny one's honest response. On the other hand, if to bless is to meet or to affirm, then our blessing of God may position us to receive exactly what God can provide and exactly what we need in our moment of sorrow.

One night a man had a dream. He dreamed that he was walking along the beach with the Ribbono Shel Olam, the Master of the Universe, at his side. Across the sky flashed scenes from his life. For each scene he noticed two sets of footprints in the sand on the beach. One belonged to him and the other to the Almighty. When the last scene flashed before him, he looked back at all the footprints and noticed that many times along the path there was only one set of footprints in the sand. He also noticed that this happened during the lowest and saddest times in his life. This really bothered him and he turned to question the Holy One. "Ribbono Shel Olam, you said that once I decided to walk with you, that you would walk with me. But I noticed that during the most troublesome times of my life, there was only one set of footprints. When I needed you the most, you deserted me. I don't understand why!"

The Master of the Universe replied, "My precious, precious child, I love you and I would never leave you. During your times of trial and suffering, when you saw only one set of footprints, it was then that I carried you." (based on Stevenson "Footprints in the Sand")

In blessing the Holy One of Blessing when the news is most grave, we place ourselves in hands that can provide the comfort we seek, the strength we require, and, when necessary, that can carry us when we are weary.

In the days and years of our lives, may we too experience the blessings we require and those we desire from God, from our neighbors and from those we love most. And may we choose to enter actively into the ecology of blessing.

RITE VERSUS RIGHT:
ISAIAH MEETS AZAZEL
Yom Kippur 5758/1997

Remember the Hokey Pokey? "You put your left foot in; you take your left foot out; you put your left foot in and you shake it all about." Other body parts ensue, and then "you put your whole self in; you take your whole self out; you put your whole self in and you shake it all about. You do the Hokey Pokey and you turn yourself around, and that what it's all about. Hey!" On Yom Kippur, we Jews put our whole selves into a day of prayer and study and fasting and, we hope, the self-reflective process of *teshuvah*, repentance, called for during this holiday season. But what's it all about? Both the Torah portion of Yom Kippur and the accompanying Haftarah provide us with guidance in this regard.

The Torah portion (from *Leviticus 16*) and the accompanying Haftarah (from *Chapters 58 and 59 of Isaiah*) offer sharply contrasting themes. *Leviticus 16* describes the ancient Yom Kippur ritual of Temple times whereby the High Priest, the *Kohen Gadol*, cleanses the community of its sins by placing those sins on the head of a goat designated "for *Azazel*." The original scapegoat is sent out into the wilderness, carrying away all the sins of the community in the process. Meanwhile, a second goat designated "for God" is offered as a sacrifice. In contradistinction, Isaiah issues a stinging condemnation of insular and empty ritual, especially the ritual of Yom Kippur fasting, when it fails to inspire a consciousness of concern for the needy: the hungry, the homeless, the poor, the marginal members of society. The Torah thus describes and defines ritual required by the community. By contrast, the Haftarah criticizes ritual and emphasizes the crucial importance of social justice. One might see the contrast as one of rite versus right.

I would suggest further that Isaiah's stirring words imply a deeper critique of ritual in general, one shared by many today. The critique implies that ritual inherently tends to blunt or sidetrack the ethical impulse. That is, one who holds this view would regard the time spent on prayer as time no longer available to help out in the local soup kitchen. Such a view impels the question: should I attend Kabbalat Shabbat service on Friday night or should I attend the meeting in support of the battered women's shelter or the AIDS Service Group or the Red Cross? Moreover, the utterance of pious prayer may dupe us into thinking that the prayer or ritual alone somehow suffices. Having prayerfully said that I will be just or kind or caring may actually obviate the urge to act accordingly. And in our own historical phase, when "spirituality" has become such a buzzword, one might add the concern that much of what now passes for spiritual activity, including some novel or modified forms of ritual, is, at least according to critics, nothing more than the latest version of the self-indulgent, narcissistic ego gratification so characteristic of the generation of baby boomers.

Returning to the two passages, one a prescription for an elaborate ritual and one a critique of the evolved version of the selfsame ritual, it would seem that our tradition directs us toward a careful balance of rite and right, ritual and ethical action, each in awareness of and reinforcement of the other.

I suspect that the ritual of the scapegoat strikes the modern ear as strange, disturbingly primitive, and even theologically offensive. The idea that we or our ancestors could imagine that one might rid oneself of sin by hocus pocus, by attaching it to some poor animal, may seem alternatively laughable or embarrassing. Certainly, the passage bothered many of our rabbinic ancestors, who felt strongly compelled to come to terms with a ritual seemingly grounded in problematic theology. Repentance, they believed, is not about attaching one's sins to a goat with the accompanying sacrifice. Rather, true repentance begins with inner transformation and a serious resolution to change.

Accordingly, the Mishnah reports that the ritual of the scapegoat had in latter days become a source of ridicule, that people would stand in the path of the goat marked "for Azazel" upon which the *Kohen Gadol* had confessed Israel's sins and mockingly remark, "Such a tiny goat for such a huge load of sins!"

Many commentators seek to downplay the magical assumptions underlying the ritual by proposing alternative, more rational interpretations. In this vein, Maimonides says that the scapegoat ceremony is "an active allegory, meant to impress the mind of the sinner that his sins must lead him to a wasteland." Witnessing the ceremony (or reading about it) will impel those who have strayed from the way of Torah to "break with their sins ... distance themselves from them, and turn back to God in sincere repentance" (*Guide for the Perplexed 3:46*).

Furthermore, Maimonides teaches that true repentance involves more than verbal or prayerful commitments. It requires an inner alteration of mind and spirit, a true breaking away from the desire to "go astray." The test of sincere and complete repentance, says Maimonides, comes in real time. If the repentant one still has the capacity to commit the same sinful offense and an actual opportunity arises but he refrains, voila!

Moreover, much is made by rabbinic commentators of the two goats involved in the ceremony, one marked "for God" that is sacrificed and the other "for Azazel" that is sent out to the wilderness. Abarbanel compares the identical goats to the identical twins Jacob and Esau. One of Esau's names, Seir, also means goat. According to Abarbanel, when the High Priest casts lots over which goat would be "for God" and which "for Azazel," the people were reminded of the significant choice always before them: one could live a life, like Jacob, devoted to God, or one could follow in the ways of Esau. Thus, to Abarbanel, the account of ritual reminds us of the choices always before us.

In addition, one notes the Talmudic specification that the two goats must be identical in size, appearance, and value. The goats symbolize, in this view, what we are willing to give for our own pleasure and what we are willing to give for the welfare and security of others. All we devote to personal pleasure and self-aggrandizement goes "into the wilderness," unless we also sacrifice for the Lord and "make atonement." Seen in this way, the ritual of the two goats by itself promotes a balance between the desires of the self and the needs of others.

Whether one leans toward the views of Maimonides, Abarbanel, Silverman, or none of the above, the point is that these and other interpreters of Jewish tradition felt compelled to find symbolic meaning for the Azazel ritual, meaning that placed the burden of responsibility for repentance back on the shoulders of the humans and off of the poor goat.

As to Isaiah's prophetic corrective to insincere ritual, one might find that it reinforces the central notion of balance as derived from a deep understanding of the Shema. Every Jew knows how to say the first line of the Shema in Hebrew and their native tongue and knows that when we say it in the evening or in the morning, when we lie down and when we arise, we affirm our faith that there is a unity principle governing creation. At the least, in reciting these words, we indicate our connection to a people that has asserted that unity principle from time immemorial. Those of us who have read the Shema in the Torah also know that by ancient scribal tradition it is written in an unusual way, with two oversized letters, the last letter of the first word, Shema, hear, and the last letter of the last word, *echad*, one. Since the two oversized letters, *ayin* and *dalet*, stand out, they call for interpretation. As the two letters spell a word in their own right, *eyd*, witness, one might well say that whenever we recite the Shema we serve as witnesses to God's presence in the world. Furthermore, the words of the Shema themselves call us to bear witness to that presence by acting in accordance with their meaning. That is, we truly hear and know God's oneness when we act as if it were so.

In this light, we might consider the blunt and radical words of the midrashic commentator on *Isaiah 43:13*, "Therefore you are My witnesses, said the Lord, and I am God." The commentator reads the conjunction as causative. Thus, the verse means that "when you people are My witnesses, then, I am God, but when you are not My witnesses, I am not God." That is, God is God only when we fulfill our proper role as God's witnesses.

God's "Godness," as it were, requires human witness in the form of godly behavior. That witness, returning to the message of the Haftarah, includes both ethically responsible action and rituals such as Shabbat observance and effective communal prayer, rituals that raise human social conscience. Thus, Isaiah too, on a closer, interpretive reading, does not denigrate ritual. Rather, he decries false and insincere ritual while seeking to restore balance between rite and right.

A postscript regarding Jewish prayer in general and specifically the public or communal prayer expected of every adult Jew. Jews instinctively know that to be Jewish means to pray together with other Jews. Presumably that is partly why so many Jews do gather during the High Holidays and during the holidays of Sukkot and Simchat Torah and on every Shabbat in synagogues all over the world, in spite of the fact that those who come to pray together may not agree about why we pray or to Whom we pray, and in spite of the fact that our sophisticated, rationally trained intellects often tend toward skepticism about prayer and ritual altogether.

About the underlying compulsion to gather for the ritual of public prayer, two observations are in order:

(1) Prayer is primarily a right-brain phenomenon. Scientists have

discovered that one can distinguish right- and left-brain functions. We think and analyze on the left side, but we free associate and intuit on the right side. A physical therapist once reported her observations about a certain patient, an observant Jewish man who had davvened in shul almost every day for his entire adult life. The man then suffered a stroke on the left hemisphere of his brain such that he could not remember his name or identify people he knew intimately. However, he could still pray the complete *Shemona Esrai* by heart. That is, for this man, and one surmises for many others, prayer is primarily a right-brain phenomenon.

That means that we do not have to reach rational agreement on what the words mean or even necessarily understand them in order to pray or pray together. I have heard Rabbi Lawrence Kushner suggest that the words of prayer may be there in part to satisfy or preoccupy the left side of our brains so that the right side can soar above and beyond those words.

(2) Harry Golden used to tell a story about his father. His father was an atheist, but the kind of Jewish atheist who attended the Mincha/Maariv davenning at shul every day. Once, Harry said to his dad, "Dad, I don't get it. You say you're an atheist. Atheists don't believe in God. So why do you go to shul every day?" His father's famous answer: "Harry, you know my friend, Garfinkle? He goes to shul to talk to God. I go to shul to talk to Garfinkle."

The flip answer has a deeper aspect. The rituals of public prayer are about community as much or more than they are about God. A Jew cannot be a Jew alone because Jewishness is not essentially about attaining some proper religious disposition or right attitude. It is, on the other hand, about getting right with God and that means participating in a community of people who, by davvening together, encourage one another and empower one another to feel God's presence in ways that otherwise we would not. That sense of God's presence, in turn, if it is heartfelt and sustained, will translate into a revitalized ethical stance in the world. It is not that prayer in and of itself dispels sin, or heals, or feeds the hungry; rather, a sense of God's presence in a community of davveners creates a certain mood, an air of communal responsibility and ethical compulsion.

Finally, one might well wonder about God and all this prayer ritual. As one Mendel the tailor once put it to his rabbi, "Wouldn't it be sufficient to praise God just once in a while, say once a month or every year? Why does our tradition mandate thrice daily prayer and extra on Shabbat and holidays? I after all am a tailor. If someone praises my work or thanks me for it, I feel great. One compliment can carry me for at least a week. But if people constantly praise me, 'Mendel, thank you, Mendel, you're wonderful, Mendel, you're the best tailor in the whole city,' it would make me nauseated; I would find it so annoying. Doesn't God get sick of all the blessings directed God's way?" Said the rabbi: "Mendel, you are absolutely correct. It is extremely difficult for God to hear all those prayers, all the thanks, and praise and blessing, but God manages to persist because God knows we need to continue to pray."

It is not that God needs our prayers of thanks or praise or blessing or anger or sorrow or repentance, but we certainly need to offer them, because by doing so we become more human than we otherwise would be. We become part of a community who, by its rituals of prayer, feels itself to be in God's presence and thereby called to become God's witness. As the Torah and Haftarah portion, taken together, teach, rituals ideally lead the way to community, to a sense of standing before the Holy One of Blessing, to ethical action, and to a fuller *menschlichkeit*.

And that's what it's all about.

FOR THE SIN
OF ENVIRONMENTAL ABUSE
Yom Kippur 5750/1989

Al Cheyt Sh'Chatanu L'fanecha, for the sin that we have committed before You by spilling tons and tons of oil into the coastal waters off of Alaska, Rhode Island, Massachusetts, and elsewhere, and by otherwise abusing the environment, the specific examples of which are too numerous to mention.

On this Day of Atonement (1989), I am concerned greatly about our need to address this category of misdeed, so graphically brought to our attention by the recent disastrous oil spill of the supertanker the Exxon Valdez. Of course, that spill was not the first; nor is it the only type of environmental abuse in which we humans currently indulge, in this age of high technology. As we approach the final decade of the millennium, we are guilty of environmental abuse when we pollute the air, the land, or the water with radiation, with toxic chemicals, with heavy metals or with nonbiodegradable garbage. We abuse the environment when we deplete our forests faster than we replant them, when we emit fumes from our factories and our cars that choke us and that produce the acid rain that threatens the habitats of freshwater fish and other wildlife, and when we punch holes in the earth's ozone shield by using chlorofluorocarbons.

Big sins to be sure. But what do they have to do with us on this Yom Kippur? What do they have to do with Judaism?

Yom Kippur is not merely about an abstract state of mind; it is not about the attainment of a nirvana-like oneness with the Almighty. For all its emphasis on accomplishments of the spirit, Yom Kippur also urges us to put forth a pragmatic agenda of behavioral change.

In the liturgical pinnacle of these High Holy Days, the *Unetaneh Tokef* prayer, we assert that *teshuvah*/repentence, *tefillah*/prayer, and *tzedakah*/charity will temper judgment's severe decree. However, as we know, *tzedakah* means more than charity. It comes from the word *tzedek*, meaning just or right behavior, as in "*tzedek, tzedek tirdof*—justice, justice, shall you pursue." That is, our right and righteous deeds will resound in heaven on our behalf. And *teshuvah* does not mean merely to be sorry for our sins, whether they be ones of commission or omission. Yom Kippur urges us to undergo radical self-improvement reflected by substantial changes in our attitudes and in our actions, wherever called for.

When we read on the morning of Yom Kippur from the Prophet Isaiah, we are stirred, even disturbed, as Isaiah warns us against being satisfied with the Yom Kippur rituals alone—which would then be empty rituals. He forces us to translate our accomplishments of the spirit into a program of concrete social action.

Moreover, Judaism does indeed have something to teach about the disposition of human beings toward the natural environment. That disposition will not solve the complex mess on the plate of environmental problems, but, if taken to heart, it would put us in a clearer frame of mind by which to proceed. And that by itself would be no small thing. Judaism, as I see it, directs us to a philosophy of environmental responsibility.

In 1973, I was fortunate to have heard one of the few public lectures delivered by the spiritual leader of Modern Orthodoxy, Rabbi Joseph Soloveitchik. Soloveitchik presented the Biblical roots of Jewish moral philosophy in a manner that pertains expressly to environmental responsibility. To begin with, Soloveitchik derives the concept of a bipolar system of Jewish morality from the two Biblical accounts of creation, the one found in *Genesis Chapter 1*, and the one found in *Genesis Chapter 2*.

In the first account of human creation, God blesses the first man and woman and tells them: "Be fertile and increase, fill the earth and master it; and rule the fish of the sea, the birds of the sky, and all the living things that creep on earth." God continues: "Every seed-bearing plant that is upon the earth, and every tree that has seed-bearing fruit; they shall be your food." Those first humans (let's call them, as does Soloveitchik, *Adam Rishon*, the first Adam) are told to assume command, to take charge, to rule. Soloveitchik depicts *Adam Rishon* as the warrior/conqueror, the one commanded to exert power, to strive for domination. One might color *Adam Rishon* scarlet and purple for nobility. *Adam Rishon* is created in God's image, God's majestic, cosmic, expansive image.

The second account of human creation presents a vastly different model of human moral responsibility. In it we read: "The Lord God took the man and placed him in the Garden of Eden, to till it and tend it. And the Lord

God commanded the man, saying, 'Of every tree of the garden you are free to eat; but as for the tree of knowledge of good and evil, you must not eat of it; for as soon as you eat of it, you shall die.'" No conqueror he, this human being (we will call him Second Adam, *Adam Sheni*) has been assigned to take care of a garden, to do the weeding and pruning. As for his menu, he is immediately slapped with a warning to stay away from the one tree that, we learn later, might inflate this Adam's sense of self-worth. No warrior he, *Adam Sheni* is withdrawn, humble, and modest. It is *Adam Sheni* who was made from the dust of earth; it is he who remains mindful of his proximity to the earth. Color *Adam Sheni* in pale earth tones befitting his modesty. *Adam Sheni* may also have been created in God's image, but one can only imagine it as God's immanent, nurturing, barely discernable image, the image of God in the still small voice.

Both *Adam Rishon*, the dominant warrior type, and *Adam Sheni*, the modest gardener, are models for human moral responsibility, in Soloveitchik's thinking. Each model looms in importance relative to the realities of a given issue, depending on what is needed to restore proper balance. For example, the enslaved, the poor, the disenfranchised, and the lowly usually require for themselves the model of *Adam Rishon* as they require in most cases the empowerment of the warrior; theirs is the need to assert dominion in order to gain the respect to which all have a right. Because of their impoverishment, they require the moral example of *Adam Rishon*; generally speaking, they need to assert greater mastery over their own lives.

On the other hand, with respect to environmental issues, collectively speaking, we probably require the model of *Adam Sheni*. For, as I see it, we have been ruthless and intemperate in extracting from the earth its riches and its sources of energy. We have been unrelenting in advancing the frontiers of technology, often ignoring the risks accompanying rapid advancement. We have been remiss and lacking in foresight in our pursuit of short-term convenience at the expense of long-term hazard. All in all, we have exceeded our role as masters of the forests, the lakes, the air, the fish, birds, and other living creatures. We desperately need to see ourselves as *Adam Sheni*. If we are to begin the restoration of balance in the earth's ecosystem, we must begin to see ourselves more as gardeners and less as masters of the estate.

Like many, I find solitude best when hiking in the mountains. This past Monday, the day after Rosh Hashanah, I treated myself to a hike in the Shenandoah National Park. After about three miles of hiking, I reached a rocky outcrop with a marvelous western view. As I listened to the sounds of the forest and my own breathing, as I scanned the scenic vista laid out before me, I became aware, as often I do in such settings, of my smallness. I felt not too different from the deer, the chipmunks, and the other wildlife who at that moment shared with me the bright light and gentle warmth from the sun. For a moment, it seemed that if I could retain that sense of being a small part of a very large world, that sense of being but one of many of the earth's creatures, then I might behave more respectfully than I often do toward our common habitat.

As I continued to peer out over treetops to the valley below, I thought of the sukkah, that three-walled, temporary, outdoor structure that many Jews build for the fall harvest holiday, the eight-day holiday of Sukkot. Among its functions, the sukkah serves, especially for contemporary dwellers of urbs and suburbs, as a reminder of and an actual bridge to nature. Tradition tells us to build our sukkah with porous roofs in such a way as to allow clear vision of the sky. Thus, whether one's sukkah stands on a rooftop in Jerusalem, on the balcony of a skyscraper in New York City, or on a patio or lawn in Charlottesville, when one looks up, one sees not the plaster ceiling of the house or office, or the vinyl top of one's automobile—one looks up and sees that above all enclosures, those that make our world seem small and in control, a much higher ceiling rests. When one sits in the sukkah, one becomes more aware of the largeness of the physical world and one's own relative smallness. One loses one's sense of domination and mastery. In this fashion, the sukkah becomes a metaphor for higher environmental consciousness, for a disposition in which we appreciate the natural world and our modest place within it.

There was once a dispute between two landowners with adjoining properties over a parcel of land that lay between them. Finally, unable to resolve the dispute, they appeared before the local rabbi. Unable to resolve the dispute from their stories, the rabbi asked to be brought to the land in question, whereupon he said: "Since I cannot resolve this dispute on the basis of your equivalent testimonies, I will ask the land for a verdict." The two men were amused to see the rabbi bend down and listen to the ground. When he rose he said: "The land was laughing, it has told me: 'Each man thinks he owns me. The truth is I own them, for both are dust and will return to dust.'"

We humans are dust and will return to dust. Yet while we live, we do have choices as well as the capacity to make about how to utilize it. In this regard, Jewish tradition describes an important category of *Halachah*/Jewish Law that is pertinent to the issue of human restraint and environmental responsibility. The prohibition *Ba'al Tashcheet*—Do not destroy derives from a passage in Deuteronomy, which reads:

> When in your war against a city if you have to besiege it a long time in order to capture it, you must not destroy its trees, wielding the ax against them. You may eat them, but you must not cut them down. (*Deuteronomy 20:19*)

Our tradition understands this prohibition as extending far beyond the circumstances described in the Torah. The sages understand the prohibition *Ba'al Tashcheet* to be applicable to any wanton misuse of resources under any circumstances, misuse of which poses a threat to civilization. These sages of our tradition could not have anticipated the scale to which twentieth-century humans possess the capacity to undo the earth's ecological balance and human civilization along with it. However, they consistently decline to justify questionable and risky means by even the most legitimate of ends. They certainly could have found no justification, for example, for the use of plastic rings to hold our beer cans together. Nothing wrong with the idea of convenience here, except that those plastic rings do not degrade for five hundred years and kill fish and sea mammals in the meantime. The category of *Ba'al Tashcheet* applies here and to all cases where we produce dangerous imbalances in the ecology of our earthly abode.

In practical terms, if we are to get serious about our *teshuvah*/repentance/turning in matters of environmental responsibility, it would seem that the first order of business would be to educate ourselves and each other, to identify the issues and our educational resources, to learn about local, regional, national, and global efforts, to form well-considered opinions on a public policy level, to encourage our governmental leaders to enact and enforce effective policies.

Finally, each of us can look within and ask: What can I do to be more responsible as a dweller upon this planet? Can I substitute paper products for nonbiodegradable plastic? Can I separate out and recycle newspapers, glass, and aluminum? Can I dispose of my automobile oil in recycling centers so it won't seep into the groundwater? Can I resolve to help bear the expense of sane legislative measures that will promote a return to ecological balance?

One of the more enigmatic figures of Jewish legend was Honi the Circle Maker. Honi once saw an elderly man planting a carob tree. As carob trees take many years before they bear fruit, Honi asked why the old man was so engaged. Did he expect to live so long as to enjoy the fruit of that tree? "No," replied the elderly man, "but when I was born I found a world full of fruitful trees that my grandparents and those of their generation had planted. I too wish to leave the world full of fruitful trees that my grandchildren and those yet-to-be born will enjoy." (based on *Taanit 23a*)

Before heaven and earth:

May we truly repent for our environmental abuses.

May we resolve to restore balance to the ecosystem of the earth.

And may we acquire the moral disposition of Second Adam, of those tillers in the gardens of the earth, that we might leave it healthy and full of fruitful trees.

GIVE ME YOUR HAND
Rosh Hashanah 5757/1996

In the play *Death of a Salesman*, Arthur Miller depicts the pathetic and increasingly wretched life of Willy Loman, a low man, a man who fails again and again to rise above his misery in any way that might arouse sympathy; he is a man about whom no one cares, no one except his wife. Despite his faults, failures, shortcomings, and sloppy deceptions, she maintains her love and concern for him. Thus, at a key point in the drama, she positions herself downstage center, faces the audience, and calls out:

"Willy Loman is having a breakdown. Attention must be paid!"

"Attention must be paid" is a good summary of the message of the High Holiday season of turning, returning, and repentance. Over and over again the words and images evoked by the High Holiday liturgy push us to pay attention to life when it breaks down and manifests its fragility. Over and over, the holiday prayers and the melodies concentrate our gaze so we can face our flaws of spirit, mind, and deed. Over and over, we call on God to help us do *teshuvah*, through individual deepening, interpersonal growth, through communal repair and restoration. Over and over, the language of tongue and body reminds us that attention must be paid by us and, we pray, by God to the overwhelming need for healing among us.

When I consider the community in and around Congregation Beth Israel, I usually think of our strengths: I think of our collective talent in so many fields in and out of academia; I think of our diversity, that we are young and old, retirees, baby boomers, generation X-ers, and youth; I think of our Jewish diversity: we are secular, Zionist, traditional egalitarian, Reform, Conservative, Renewal, neo-frum and f.f.b. (frum-from-birth), feminist, eco-Kosher, among others. However, viewed from another angle, the same congregational community appears as a collection of Jewish Willy Lomans. Does it not, at times, seem that collectively and as individuals, we are breaking down? We are breaking down in our bodies, in our spirits, and in our relationships, and many of us, at the same time, accompany or care for others who are breaking down.

Are there among us any who in the past year did not suffer some loss, some incapacity, some extreme stress due to an illness, your own or another's, a death, a disrupted relationship, a missed or lost opportunity? I know for a certainty that there is no one in this room who did not and does not still bear the pain suffered from the collective losses experienced when TWA Flight #800 went down, or when the buses were blown up in Jerusalem, or when Yitzhak Rabin was assassinated, or when we once again became aware that incivility and intolerance among Jews continues unabated, or when we learned about the fate of Alicia Reynolds (a woman who had been raped and murdered while commuting to Charlottesville), or heard that the schoolchildren in a small Scottish town were gunned down, or read reports of more mass graves in Bosnia and in Burundi.

These events from the year completed cause us pain but not only these. Two and three blocks from where we worship homeless people mingle with the middle class on the downtown mall. Our local public schools are threatened with white flight as teachers and administrators struggle to find ways to teach high- and low-achieving kids at the same time. Drugs and crime are everywhere. Pollution invades the water we drink and the air we breathe. As such, we are individuals in need of healing residing among others in need of healing in a community in need of healing in a world in need of healing. Lots of healing is required. Attention must be paid!

For the many kinds of ills many kinds of healing are required. Regarding the healing of individuals, we do well to learn from the wisdom of Jewish tradition. By way of such learning, one might ask: "How do we heal one another?" A beginning of a response arises from the sickbed scenarios found in the Talmudic Tractate Brachot, where we read:

> Rabbi Hiyya ben Abba fell ill and Rabbi Yochanan went to visit him. He [Rabbi Yochanan] said to him [Rabbi Hiyya]: Are your sufferings welcome to you? He [Rabbi Hiyya] replied: Neither they nor their reward. He [Rabbi Yochanan] said to him: Give me your hand. He gave him [Rabbi Yochanan] his hand and he raised [healed] him.

Altering the roles, the tractate continues:

> Rabbi Yochanan once fell ill and Rabbi Hanina went in to visit him.

> He [Rabbi Hanina] said to him: Are your sufferings welcome to you? He [Rabbi Yochanan] replied: Neither they nor their reward. He [Rabbi Hanina] said to him: Give me your hand. He gave him [Rabbi Hanina] his hand and he raised him. (*Berachot 5b*)

These two stories of *bikkur cholim*, of rabbis carrying out the mitzvah of visiting a sick friend and colleague, offer one kind of healing paradigm. Healing requires paying attention to the one who is ill. It always necessitates someone outside the self to help effect the healing. In each case, rabbis who had previously been willing to entertain the theoretical possibility of the ultimate benefits of suffering are quite ready to give up these benefits in exchange for relief from pain. One might expect that rabbis who trusted in eternal reward in the next world as a compensation for temporary suffering in this world might leap at the chance. But, no, neither the suffering nor the reward for suffering is desired or welcome by these pious rabbis, nor would they be welcome by most of us, I suspect. In each account, healing comes from attending to the patient, through physical touch, by means of a tangible expression of caring. The human caregiver acts as a divine stand-in, a godly agent of healing. And yet the healing capacity is not a gift unique to any particular individual. Nor can the caregiver heal himself by himself. The Caregiver Extraordinaire, Rabbi Yochanan, when ill, requires the hand of another before he can rise from his bed.

Can one human being really heal another? The Hasidim take it for granted that their rebbe, their leader, is a *Tzaddik*, a completely righteous man who has been granted special healing power. As to the healing powers of ordinary mortals, a story:

> Once a group of Hasidim decided to travel to their master, the holy Seer of Lublin, although they had almost no money for the journey. They set out on foot, hoping they would meet someone on the road who would offer them a ride in his coach. However, that did not happen. After a few days, their money had run out, they were exhausted, and famished.
>
> Suddenly, one of the Hasidim had an idea. One of them could pretend to be a great rebbe. When they would arrive at the next village, everyone would run out to welcome the great "rebbe" and his Hasidim, and would offer donations that would allow them to hire a wagon and horse. Although not happy about using this ruse, they justified it

by their desperate situation. After all, to save a life, many things are permitted, and they were nearly starving to death.

So they appointed one of their group as the "rebbe" (a role he accepted reluctantly and only after being pressed into it by his friends). Another took on the role of the rebbe's personal attendant while two of the Hasidim went ahead to announce the arrival of the great "rebbe."

The "rebbe's" appearance caused a great stir among the residents of the small village. One man, an innkeeper, was especially excited. He said to himself, "I will ask the rebbe to heal my infant son with his blessing." The innkeeper welcomed the Hasidim to the village and treated them all to a hearty meal. Immediately afterwards he fell down at the feet of the "rebbe" and cried out, "Rebbe, please heal my baby son." The imitation rebbe was confused and flustered. "What does he want from my life?" he thought. "Now a real rebbe could of course help this man, but I, of course, am not a real rebbe." His friends whispered to him, urging him not to worry, but just to say a blessing for the child. And, so, not having any other option, the false rebbe entered the room at the back of the inn where the child's crib was and shut the door, while his friends waited in the inn. He blessed the baby and then returned and blessed the innkeeper that his child have a complete recovery. The grateful innkeeper gave the "rebbe" and his Hasidim a generous donation, enough for them to hire a wagon and horse and food for the remainder of their trip to Lublin.

Some days later, their stay in Lublin finished, the same group of Hasidim were passing through the same village on their return home. Once again, the innkeeper came forth to greet them. He said, "Rebbe, how can I ever thank you for healing my child? As soon as you left, he asked for something to eat and is now completely healthy." This time also the innkeeper provided the "rebbe" and his Hasidim with a good meal. But as soon as they left the village, the Hasidim demanded of their friend that he tell them what he had done on their previous visit. "Since when are you doing miracles?" they asked. "We know you're not a rebbe. What's going on here?" "I didn't do anything." he replied. "Leave me alone." But they kept pestering him until he told them.

"As you well know, I am no rebbe. But I'll tell you what happened." When I went into the back room and stood by the sick baby's crib and looked down into his little face that grimaced from pain and suffering,

I realized that I had fallen into a deep pit. Then, after I blessed the baby and came out and looked at the anguished father's face and his tear-stained cheeks my heart broke within me. At that moment, a Psalm verse came to my mind:

"O God, You know my folly and my sins are not hid from You. Let not those who hope in You, O Lord of hosts, be ashamed for my sake; let not those who seek You be disappointed because of me, O God of Israel."

"Then I turned to God and prayed silently, 'This good man believes I am a rebbe, but of course I am not. I'm just a simple person with many sins to my credit. But why should he lose out because of that? He has true faith in the tzaddikim (Righteous Ones) and believes that You listen to their prayers. Why should he be disappointed because of my faults? So I beg You to heal his child because of his faith, because he thinks I'm a rebbe.' And it seems that God listened and healed this child. That's all I did and that's all that happened."

We too, of course, are not rebbes. We may not even believe in them. However, we all have the capacity to be "rebbes." We all have the capacity to look into the anguished faces of those who suffer, to give them our hands, our support, our prayers, and our blessing. And, who knows, but God may listen and, for their sake, if not for ours, may enable healing.

But does God listen? Does God heal? Does our tradition countenance prayers for healing? For some it may seem strange, to others obvious, that Judaism does indeed include as part of daily prayer a collective petition for *Refuah Shleimah L'chol Makoteinu*, complete healing for all our afflictions. It also encourages personalized petition on behalf of particular individuals. More public and perhaps, more well known these days, is the custom of offering a *Mi Shebeirach* prayer on behalf those specifically known to us who suffer.

Consider the suggestive setting for the *Mi Shebeirach*: The Torah is out and opened. Members of the congregation ascend the *bimah*, the high place in the sanctuary, from which the ancient, sacred scroll is read. As those honored with *aliyot* bless the Torah, they touch the fringe, the *tzitzit*, symbol of Jewish allegiance to the ancient covenant, to the parchment and then to their lips, they grasp the *etzim*, the tree-like posts, connecting themselves to the profound myths and teachings contained within the scroll, in symbolic affirmation. Then the entire congregation listens to words that our Jewish ancestors have listened to, lived by and died for, interpreted and rejoiced in for over two thousand years. The parchment, kissed so indirectly, delicately, and lovingly, is but a thin boundary, an organic membrane, separating heaven and earth.

The scene evokes return to the Sinai moment. We are as close to the Source of revelation as we can get; we are straining to hear, straining to understand God's words. As we pause in our active listening, we turn toward the Source and say or chant:

Mi Shebeirach Avotenu, Avraham, Yitzhak, V'Ya'acov, V'Imotenu, Sara, Rivka, Rachel, V'Leah—May You who blessed our ancestors Abraham, Isaac, and Jacob, and Sarah, Rebecca, Rachel, and Leah, bless and heal these people who are suffering whom we now name (using, if possible their Hebrew names and the names of their mothers), in the fullness of compassion, giving them strength and health. May You speedily send perfect health to them in all their limbs and sinews among all those who suffer illness. Grant them *healing of body* and *healing of spirit*. And let us say, "amen."

What's going on? Why do we do it? What do we expect? Miracles? Well, some of us probably do expect miracles. Others (I'm in this camp) reject the idea of miracles as occurrences outside of the rules of nature, but have borne witness to miraculous occurrences well within the natural. I count among these the birth of every child, the regular rising and setting of the sun, the daily renewal of the lives of each one of us, our hearts and bodies and minds, which, at times, function reasonably well, the smile of a friend, the hug of a loved one. Furthermore, I know of too many examples of miraculous recoveries from illness or despair to ever give up on the power of human will, to ever deny the curative potential of meditation and prayer, or to ever demean the capacity of the medical arts, even when the risks are high, the prognosis poor, and the chances slim.

I know that sometimes prayer actually can help effect a cure. I also know that a public prayer for healing can situate one's need for healing in the context of a community, a community, we hope, whose warmth and caring capacities will be aroused so that tangible and intangible help can be offered.

Does God respond to prayers for healing? As I see it, the gates of healing are always open, but curing will take place within the bounds of nature.

The Talmud reports a dialogue in which a Roman philosopher queries a rabbi, not about illness but about other aggravations that one might suppose God could simply eliminate: "'If your God has no desire for idolatry, why does He not abolish it?' The rabbi replies: 'If it were something of which the world has no need, He would abolish it. But since people worship the sun, the moon, stars, and planets, should He destroy the universe on account of fools?' The world pursues its natural course, and as for fools who act wrongly, they will have to render an account" (*Avodah Zarah 54a*).

"The world pursues its natural course" is the response given to another query: "Suppose a man stole a measure of wheat and went and sowed it in the ground. It would surely be right that the wheat should not grow. But the world pursues its natural course. Further, supposing a man has intercourse with his neighbor's wife, it would surely be right that she not conceive. But the world pursues its natural course" (*Avodah Zarah 54b*).

In other words, having set in motion the forces of nature, God will not contravene them. God will not perform miracles of that sort, but will be present to help us face the challenges of each moment and stage of life.

Moreover, we humans are mortal. When the possibility of physical cure diminishes to the point of negligibility, one must look to a healing of the spirit without a curing of the body. The *Mi Shebeirach* makes the important distinction between healing of body (what we usually mean by a cure) and healing of spirit (arriving at a state of inner equilibrium, tranquility, and peace that is irrespective of bodily health.) There is a distinction. Maintaining it is crucial if one is to face each stage of life with the attention demanded by our tradition, with the desire to discern the appropriate moment for struggling to overcome a dire condition and the appropriate moment for acceptance of the same.

When King David discovered that the sick child born of his relationship with Batsheva had died, he arose from the earth, washed, anointed himself, changed his clothes, came into the sanctuary and worshiped. He then returned to his own house and ordered his servants to provide him with a simple meal. Incredulous at his actions, the servants said: "'You fasted and wept while the child was alive, but now when the child is dead, you rise and eat bread.' He replied: 'While the child was yet alive, I fasted and wept, for I said, who knows whether the Lord will not be gracious to me that the child may live. But now that he is dead, wherefore should I fast? Can I bring him back again? I shall go to him, but he will not return to me'" (*II Samuel 12:21–23*).

As it was for King David, so it is for us: there is a time to pray and work for bodily health, and a time to cease working and praying for bodily health. At that point, healing involves the acceptance of events or conditions over which one has no control.

None of us welcomes illness. We think of it as a nuisance, an inconvenience, or as an evil. However, some of us have experienced how an illness, even in the absence of a cure, may trigger genuine healing of the spirit and inner growth for the patient and those close by. According to one midrash, up until our Patriarch Jacob, there was no illness. People simply lived and then suddenly died. Jacob prayed to God, requesting the gift of illness as a signal. According to the midrash, we humans require illness as an intimation of our mortality because there is work to be done at the end of one's life. Because there are accounts to be rendered, affairs to be put in order, and farewells to be made, we require notice. Illness is a wake-up call to attend to the crucial business at hand.

> At this season of beginning, on this day of reckoning, we are bidden to pay attention to what is broken in the world and in ourselves;

> We are challenged to begin a multileveled process of healing within the broad limits of the possible.

> We are called to create out of disparate households a community of caring, where hands are outstretched and blessings freely offered.

> May this be among our goals in the new year now upon us.

THE WAY WE SPEAK
Yom Kippur 5751/1990

The Prophet Isaiah directs our attention to the ethical underpinning of our Yom Kippur ritual, to the necessity of looking beyond our observance as we "afflict our souls" in the traditional manner. We are not to regard our fasting, our confessions, or our prayers as sufficient, as ends in and of themselves. They are intended rather to effect inner transformation that yields improved ethical awareness and behavior. In this regard, one notes a particular ethical concern of our tradition. That is, Jewish tradition concerns itself to a high degree with speech and its potential for abuse, "for the sin which we have committed with our words."

"For the sin which we have committed with our words" is the oft-repeated line from our Yom Kippur confessionals. It is but one of the several articulations about transgression through speech found in the full, traditional Al Cheyt confessional. Of its forty-four lines, at least one-fourth refer to transgressions through improper use of words, including: speaking perversely, corrupt speech, insincere confession (even in the midst of confession), desecrating God's name, foul speech, foolish talk, denying and lying, scoffing, slander, idle gossip, talebearing, and false promises or insincere oaths.

Thus, our Yom Kippur liturgy clearly places to the forefront the concern for our abuses of speech. To one who lives in a society that accords a high priority to freedom of speech, to unfettered, uncensored, free speech, such a concern for potentially abusive speech may seem oddly primitive or at odds with a culture that promotes its free exercise. Regarding public policy, most of us probably prefer few limitations to free speech, and for good reasons; acceptable limitations might include treasonous, libelous, or slanderous speech, or that which could incite violent or criminal acts. However, our Yom Kippur liturgy refers not to public policy but to individual responsibility. It addresses itself to the need, especially in a society that values free speech, for individuals to use that freedom with discretion and care.

At one far end of the spectrum of abusive speech, consider the "big lie." A particularly pernicious form of destructive language is that perfused with racial hatred. A fraudulent work such as the so-called *Protocols of the Elders of Zion*, for example, would be as laughable as it is ridiculous, were it not for the fact that its lies, its claims of a worldwide Jewish conspiracy, inspired Hitler and the Nazi program of genocide. Furthermore, the Nazi propaganda machine consciously disseminated blatantly false and deceptive claims, over and over again, to justify the "final solution" to the "Jewish problem." Amazingly, the big lie technique, constant repetition of overt falsehoods, works to an extraordinary degree; it works on the human tendency to be gullible. Nor did the impact of the *Protocols* themselves die with Hitler's death. The scurrilous tract resurfaces periodically throughout the world, including in this country. It is particularly favored today in Saudi Arabia and other Arab countries where it provides a rhetorical basis for anti-Israel policies.

But, of course, the examples of abuses through speech are not all so pernicious or extreme. Nor are they all so laced with evil design. Perhaps the most pervasive examples are the "little lies" of Madison Avenue and Hollywood advertising, the speech and symbolic speech that convinces our children that ill-constructed, frustrating, expensive, imported globs of colored plastic will fly, spew fire and smoke, perform magical feats, and clean up their rooms. Or the ones that imply instant success, adulation, and gratification of every kind, if only we adults will purchase the correct brand of beer or automobile.

Take a look sometime at the advertisements in any fancy magazine. Note how often sex appeal is used to sell a product. Note the implied connection between alcoholic consumption, sex, and success. And then consider the issues of teenage pregnancy, AIDS, or alcohol abuse. Even the "little lies" may have seriously negative dimensions.

However, are there not transgressions through speech that are yet closer to home? I enjoy listening to children play. I have noticed that with children, there often arises a key moment where, depending on the words spoken, the activity will either proceed constructively and happily, or will degenerate into teasing, name-calling, recriminations, or worse. At that key point, a child might say, "Kevin, let's not argue. Here, you take the ball for a while and then Becky gets it. We'll take turns." Or the scenario might ensue as follows: "You already had the ball. Let go, you idiot. I'm going to tell." "I'm not an idiot. You're a pig-face and a dumb idiot." At that stage, no one is calm enough to propose constructive resolutions.

Are we adults much different? I, for one, could benefit well from more patience in the realm of *Dibbur Peh*, oral speech, and more care. I could benefit well, and perhaps you could too, from the teachings offered by our tradition in this regard.

In general, Jewish sources consistently assign great significance to the power of an individual's words, and they warn against the adverse consequences that often result from abuse of this power.

The Hebrew term *Lashon Hara* (literally "evil speech") has the restrictive meaning of "slander" or the more general sense of any destructive language. About *Lashon Hara* the Talmud says: "There are three offenses for which one is punished in this world and forfeits his portion in the world to come: these are idolatry, incest, and murder; but Lashon Hara is equivalent to all three." A strong statement. How could our sages regard destructive speech as an offense comparable to idolatry, incest, and murder?

The beginning of an answer will emerge from an examination of the following midrashic passage dealing with the first verses of *Psalm 12*. The psalm reads:

> Help, Lord, for the Godly man ceases, for the faithful fail from among the children of men. They speak vanity every one with his neighbor. With flattering lips and a double heart they speak. . . . [They] . . . have said: "With our tongue we will prevail; our lips are our own; who is lord over us?"

The rabbis understand the psalm to mean that Lashon Hara, destructive, vain speech, demonstrates a haughty disregard for one's modest role in the universe; its usage, in effect, denies God. Employing Lashon Hara implies that we regard ourselves as free of God's ethical demands: we consider ourselves our own masters as we declare rhetorically, "Who is Lord over us?" Furthermore, once one takes this step, our sages say, then the whole building, the entire society-enhancing ethical system of Judaism, cracks, crumbles, and falls. So, we can begin to see how Jewish tradition deems Lashon Hara an evil force, as destructive of the social fabric as the sins of murder, incest, and idolatry.

Moreover, Jewish tradition specifically ascribes Lashon Hara with the power to kill. As we read in the Biblical proverb, "death and life are in the power of the tongue." Moreover, the prohibition in Leviticus against talebearing, a form of abusive speech, is followed immediately by the injunction against standing idly by the blood of one's neighbor. Several commentators interpret this juxtaposition to mean that the practice of talebearing consists of the same insensitivity as silently witnessing the extreme suffering of one's neighbor.

Not only does destructive speech involve extreme insensitivity, but, the Talmud says, Lashon Hara (figuratively or actually) kills three people: the one who utters the evil, the listener, and the one spoken about; and, curiously, the Talmud finds the listener as meriting worse punishment than the one who utters the evil.

Obviously, the one spoken about slanderously suffers from damaged reputation, loss of respect, perhaps loss of friends, loss of job, loss of self-respect, even loss of life. And, of course, most will acknowledge the guilt of the one who speaks evilly or slanderously. He, too, suffers because of the guilt and possibly because, as the bearer of rumors, he also loses respect, trust, and may end up with the same symptomology as the object of his slander. But, the listener? According to the sages, the listener need not listen. As the middleman in the process of spreading slander, he has the capacity to put a stop the process, to dampen its effect. By simply listening, he encourages the one who slanders, and in doing so, allows the destructive enterprise to unfold.

Furthermore, Jewish tradition wisely refuses to equate destructive speech with any false or unflattering speech. Maimonides offers the example of speaking in another person's favor, but in the presence of enemies of that person. This, he indicates, would prompt negative or even devastatingly harsh reaction. In other words, Judaism defines destructive speech functionally, as that language which, because of its content, or because of the context, will yield negative results. Consequently, our tradition sets before us a high standard regarding our speech: one must not only be attentive to the truthfulness of one's words, but must also be wary of the unintended effect that they may cause.

According to an oft-told tale:

> Once a man approached the Chafetz Chaim, one of the greatest rabbinic scholars, known for his careful attention to sensitive speech. "I would like to undo the results of my talebearing." The sage answered him: "Take a pail full of feathers to the top of a mountain. Then empty the feathers into the strong mountain gusts and return to me." When the man returned, the Chafetz Chaim instructed him further: "Now, you must return to the mountain and gather up every feather."

That is, one problem with destructive language about persons is that, by its nature, it is not subject to confinement. Its damaging effects spread across towns, continents, and generations. Once spoken, a word cannot be retrieved, just as the pillow feathers could no longer be gathered up. Rather, such a word gains momentum as it travels from person to person, magnifying its effect in geometric progression. Thus, as a practical matter, our sages concern themselves so much with destructive speech because, once unleashed, it cannot be unspoken.

Therefore, Jewish tradition sees in the various forms of abusive speech offenses so serious that only hyperbolic descriptions can adequately describe the severity of their destructive impact. Lashon Hara undercuts the ethical fabric of society. It can destroy the lives of those who utter it, those about whom it is uttered, and those who hear it. And once let loose, evil speech spreads uncontrollably.

The opposite of Lashon Hara is Lashon Tov, good speech. Lashon Tov can take many forms; it can come as consolation, comfort, words of peace, teaching, love, or blessing. As *bracha*, or blessing, Lashon Tov is an occasion taken to bring holiness, Kedushah, into the world.

Because Judaism concerns itself with all of life, not simply what we do when we cluster together with other Jews to worship, because it regards our human task as bringing greater harmony and holiness into the world, as joining God in a partnership to complete and perfect an—as yet—incomplete and imperfect world, for these reasons, Judaism places such great stress on what one does with every precious moment, and with how one utters every precious word.

The authors of the traditional High Holiday prayer book composed the Al Cheyt confessional in a double acrostic. That is, each pair of transgressions begins with a successive letter in the Hebrew alphabet. It is as if to say, by each letter of each word we speak, we have the ability to miss or to hit the mark, to increase destruction and chaos, or to promote holiness and peace. We have the potential to transgress and also the ability to make amends and increase blessing.

Let us look closely at how we use language. Let us examine seriously our tendencies to abuse the power of words in disparaging others, whether in their presence or in their absence, by bearing tales, whether of falsehood or of damaging truth.

As we emerge from this holiday period, renewed and cleansed, may we learn to avoid destructive language and to use speech for good and for blessing.

May all the words of our mouths and the meditations of our hearts be acceptable to You, O Lord, our Strength and our Redeemer.

ON HOMOSEXUALITY: RETHINKING LEVITICUS 18:22
Yom Kippur 5761/2000

One of the risks taken on by a rabbi serving a Reform congregation is that any ritual decision is likely to be received with at least two responses: (1) why must we become so traditional? and (2) why must we become so liberal? Roughly speaking, I hear both kinds of response in approximately equal portions after almost every liturgical innovation.

In this regard, several years ago, I decided, with the approval of our Ritual Practice Committee, to replace the Torah readings found in the Gates of Repentance for the High Holidays with those customarily read in most Conservative and all Orthodox synagogues. I wanted to restore the traditional readings, not to move us in a traditional direction per se, but because, in my view, we non-Orthodox Jews are as capable as are our more traditional coreligionists of confronting, wrestling with, and deriving meaning from the more challenging passages traditionally designated for these days. I do not argue that the substitutions offered by recent Reform *minhag*, custom, are not more uplifting, accessible, and contemporary than those presented by older *minhag*. I simply think we are capable of wrestling with the more difficult passages without wilting our Jewish identities in the process. Of course, I expected some congregants to question this decision and to argue for the restoration of the more immediately accessible and uplifting selections. In my view, such questioning, along with the ensuing discussion, contributes to the collective Torah learning, whether or not it leads to changes in practice.

Last year, a particularly respectful and thoughtfully articulated objection was voiced about the use of the traditional reading for Yom Kippur afternoon, an objection that I reformulate as follows: I have said that we can and should wrestle with the material, but, in fact, during the afternoon of Yom Kippur, the local custom has always been for us to focus primarily on the *Book of Jonah*. Thus, we really do not have a significant opportunity to wrestle with the Torah portion at all. Rather, we read the text of *Leviticus 18* and are left with the unresolved issues it raises and, in at least one case, a very objectionable impression. This situation is not dissimilar from Christian churches where the New Testament reading may contain overt anti-Jewish polemic, which, without a contextualizing commentary, simply falls unfiltered, leaving its damaging impression on the ears and in the minds of all who listen.

Thus, with your permission, I will proceed to discuss the most problematic verse of our afternoon Torah portion, *Leviticus 18:22*, in the light of this morning's Haftarah. The verse reads: "Do not lie with a male as one lies with a female; it is an abhorrence ['abomination' is often the translation for the Hebrew *to-evah*]." The verse in question occurs in the context of a list of prohibited sexual relations, including several categories of incest, adultery, and bestiality, and it is one of the two mentions in the Torah of prohibited male homosexuality. Whereas it is possible to understand the concern for holiness in our most intimate relationships as the motivation for inclusion of this portion on a day when we seek to examine in depth all of our primary relationships, this verse often strikes the contemporary ear as jarringly insensitive to a vulnerable segment of society. Thus, I want to discuss Jewish perspectives on homosexuality, in general, and, in particular, some approaches that may permit us to rethink our understanding of *Leviticus 18:22*.

Without a doubt, this verse has been used over the years, both by those who regard the Bible as sacred writ and by those who do not, as justification for opposing the granting of civil rights to homosexuals. It has lent an air of righteousness to those who would deride, demean, oppress, or harass gays and lesbians.

With regard to our congregation, I make no assumptions about the attitudes and opinions about homosexuality and rights for homosexuals; I make no assumptions about prevailing opinions on the proper Jewish communal response to the desires of homosexuals, other than this: whether one identifies as gay or straight or something in between, whether one is more or less convinced about the role of nature and nurture in forming a person's sexual orientation, whether one is personally less or more tolerant, I assume there is common agreement that the language of "abhorrence" or "abomination" to describe homosexual orientation or behavior is unacceptable, unnecessary, and hurtful. Lest we require reminders that gays and lesbians are still vulnerable and a target of hatred, the recent shootings in the gay bar in Roanoke should suffice.

On this day of serious self-reflection, we will soon hear the words of the Prophet Isaiah, who insists that our rituals, our prayers, our fasting, and all our inner piety direct us outside of ourselves and point us toward the ills of society and our responsibility to address them. The Prophet Isaiah insists that when we fast, we remind ourselves of our duty to feed the hungry, house the homeless, heal the wounded, comfort those in pain, protect the vulnerable, empower the marginalized and disenfranchised, and strive for the social change that will enable those on the periphery to move toward the center.

A pertinent aside from the world of contemporary politics: we Jews, even in America, have known and do remember the marginalization and disenfranchisement that has characterized most of our history. If Joe Lieberman's nomination as Democratic candidate for vice president means anything, I would say it powerfully symbolizes the end of Jewish marginalization in America. It answers, and I would hope once and for all, the question posed to the Jewish dignitaries of the Napoleonic Sanhedrin two centuries ago when our European ancestors first experienced the joys of emancipation: can a Jew be both actively and proudly Jewish and at the same time a loyal citizen of the nation? For two centuries, we Jews have been intellectually engaged in finding ways of saying, "Yes, we can be both Jewish and solid citizens." The nomination of Joe Lieberman bears the symbolic meaning that, at long last, a majority of non-Jews in the United States agree. It also means that we Jews must accept the responsibilities that accompany our position as members of the in-group. It means that, more than before, we must "remember that we were slaves in Egypt," we must attend to the pain of those who remain on the margins of society, we must fight for the rights of those still in the disenfranchised or disfavored minority, among them those with nonheterosexual orientations.

How is one to understand and interpret *Leviticus 18:22* in the light of Isaiah's insistence that we reach out to those who are made to suffer? How are we to interpret it in the light of contemporary sensibilities that sharply contrast with those that inform the Biblical verse? As everyone here should know, Jews do not read the Torah unmediated. Rather we read it through the thick lens of tradition. That thick lens sometimes alters or undoes the most literal understanding of verses with otherwise unsavory implications. Thus, for example, when the Torah says, "an eye for an eye, a tooth for a tooth, a life for a life," rabbinic tradition derives complex rules of compensation for personal damage. When the Torah says that one must take one's "stubborn and rebellious son" down to the town elders, where he will be stoned to death, the rabbinic tradition confines the definition of "stubborn and rebellious" in such a way as to ensure the impossibility of its occurrence. In short, the rabbinic tradition has been wonderfully elastic in its ability to interpret and pragmatically apply the difficult laws of Torah.

With the verse in question, does one find a growing tolerance or increasing openness toward homosexuality in rabbinic thought? Does *Leviticus 18:22* receive the kind of creative, interpretive treatment applied to other problematic verses? Without reviewing it in detail, the answer is, "No, not really." The few references to homosexuality in the Talmud seem to assume it rarely occurs in the Jewish community, is not known among women, and is not an orientation or disposition but simply a behavior that one may choose or avoid.

There are, however, some more recent signs, some inklings of movement toward a Jewish approach that would yield more tolerance and, even, a posture of acceptance. Let us look at the issue from several angles:

The first angle: Shmuel Boteach, the Orthodox rabbi who has recently made a name for himself as a sex expert, says, as one might expect from someone of his perspective, that homosexual acts are wrong, but—and here he departs from the standard line—not because they are aberrant or deviant. They are wrong simply because the Torah says so. Both heterosexual and homosexual love are instinctive, according to Boteach, and natural; the only reason one is called holy and the other abhorrent is that the one leads to propagation, while the other does not. Propagation is a communal responsibility. Avoiding it is objectionable.

One implication of this approach to the Biblical prohibition: although Boteach still regards homosexuality as sinful, he removes the association of deviance and, thus, also the rancorous labeling that fuels hatred and demeaning characterizations. At worst, homosexuals violate a Torah prohibition just as others violate other Torah prohibitions. No one is perfectly righteous, after all. And we do not demean those who violate other Torah-based prohibitions. In fact, we remind ourselves, especially on Yom Kippur, that we must include all Jews in the prayer quorum and in the community, saints and sinners, no matter the level of righteousness. And this is a good thing, for otherwise, our synagogues would be very empty. What I mean is that even if one regards a homosexual's behavior as sinful, one should no more exclude such a person from the community than one would exclude a Shabbat violator, or someone who fails to eat kosher food, or another who wears clothes that have not been checked for *shatnez*, the Biblically unwarranted mixture of wool and flax.

A second implication of Boteach's approach: since he relates the "sin" of homosexual love to propagation, one might see a window of even greater tolerance and welcome in that more and more gay or lesbian couples have chosen to adopt or otherwise raise children. And, as we all know, some raise children that one of the partners has fathered or mothered. I do not know of scientific studies of these kinds of families, but the few I have observed seem to me as stable and as loving and as nurturing as the best of the more conventional family units I have known.

A second angle: A few years ago, Rabbi Robert Kirschner wrote about a legal precedent for a more lenient view by analogy to the treatment of the deaf as witnesses in Jewish law. ("Halakhah and Homosexuality") For hundreds of years, the deaf were not regarded as proper witnesses in cases that came before Jewish courts of law. Why? It was assumed that deaf people possessed insufficient intellectual faculties to serve as reliable witnesses. As medical science began to demonstrate the absence of a correlation between deafness and intelligence, Jewish Law altered its view on the admissibility of a hearing-impaired person as a legal witness.

Kirschner draws the analogy between the scientifically altered views of the hearing-impaired and the scientifically altered views of homosexuality. Kirschner posits that the notion of homosexuality as abomination rests on the assumption that sexual orientation is chosen. By way of overcoming such an assumption, he refers to studies that demonstrate that sexual orientation is determined by a complex interaction of biological and social factors. It is no more chosen than the color of our hair or our predisposition for chocolate. Of course, one might alter one's hair color or suppress one's predisposition. However, it could be argued, in the case of a disposition as integral to a person's identity as sexual orientation, if no harm to others transpires as a result of its expression, why should one deny or repress this part of oneself? If one accepts as valid Kirschner's reasoning, then one might admit another window of possibility for a more progressive approach toward homosexuality within Jewish Law.

A third angle: I would return to the verse itself. I would point out that *Leviticus 18:22* speaks of behavior, not orientation. It prohibits a man from "lying with a man"; it does not condemn the orientation or predisposition of a man to "lie with a man." The difference is significant. I would argue that because the Torah speaks only about behavior and seems to have no knowledge about sexual orientation, the verse has nothing to say to those who would make policies or form attitudes about homosexuality, about the orientation. Moreover, the opening verse of *Leviticus 18* indicates that the underlying reason for the entire list of prohibited relations is to avoid behaving like the Canaanites and the Egyptians, from whose ways of thinking and acting we wish to distance ourselves. If so, then it is worth noting with regard to all injunctions pertaining to our perpetual war with the Canaanite nations, it has been acknowledged by rabbinic commentators long ago that these nations no longer exist; the people who currently occupy those lands are not the same people about whom the Torah spoke; therefore there are no nations (other than Amalek) with whom we should see ourselves as perpetually at war. If so, then, there are no nations from whose ways we must perpetually distance ourselves, either. To put it quite bluntly, my brief commentary on the verse might read: the Torah here forbids male homosexual acts because such acts mimic the ways of certain ancient idolatrous nations. The verse does not speak about homosexual behavior that arises as a result of sexual orientation. Nor does it address homosexual behavior that arises as a result of influences from contemporary culture.

One final angle: No issue of social importance should be decided without seeing the faces of those whom such decisions affect. When we consider the complex subject of human sexuality and the formation of the policies and principles that will inform attitudes, we must have human faces before us. The gay and lesbian individuals and couples I have known seem to me no more or less upright than heterosexuals; they seem no more or less modest in their public displays of affection, no more or less suitable to administer programs, teach, hold elected office, police our streets, practice law or medicine, parent children, or anything else. They seem no more or less capable of abusing power, including through sexual encounters. They are, however, more likely to be marginalized and victimized, as, regrettably and shamefully, the Roanoke shootings remind us.

Thus, I am proud to be part of a Jewish denomination that for three decades has consistently supported the civil rights of gays and lesbians and in recent years has moved toward greater and greater accommodation of the Jewish needs and desires of Jewish gays and lesbians. I am proud to be part of a movement whose rabbinic body this past March overwhelmingly passed a resolution declaring that the relationship of a Jewish, same-gender couple is worthy of affirmation through appropriate Jewish rituals of union. Most of all, I am proud to be part of a religious tradition that encourages multivocality, insisting that we struggle with the uncomfortable and objectionable texts that have a claim on us in the light of other texts that also have a claim on us, and in light of contemporary wisdom that claims us as well. I am proud that our tradition allows itself to respond to changed perceptions of what is true and wise in ways that yield yet greater truth and still more profound wisdom.

May it always be so.

TZEDAKAH: THE FINAL MOVEMENT IN THE JEWISH SYMPHONY
Yom Kippur 5755/1994

The rhythms of the Ten Days of Awe carry us through distinct stages of varying intensity, changed focus, and altered themes. Like the movements in a classical symphony, each stage may recall motifs of the others even as it introduces new themes and variations. One central conceptual rubric for the notion of rhythmic movement is the three-part motif from the *Unetaneh Tokef* prayer: "*Teshuvah, Tefillah, U'Tzedakah Ma-avirin et Ro-ah Ha-gezerah*—Repentance, prayer, and righteous deeds avert the severe decree."

Note the flow of themes in terms of the kind of attention and energy required for their fulfillment. *Teshuvah:* We begin Rosh Hashanah intent on accomplishing *teshuvah*, turning, returning to a path that brings us closer to our ideals. *Teshuvah* is about getting on track, about becoming the kind of people we know we can be. Primarily, a process of *teshuvah* requires us to turn inward, to direct our energies at self-reflection, to undergo an examination of our inner, spiritual life and its implications for our habits of behavior.

Tefillah: Praying is what we do a lot of during the Days of Awe, especially on Yom Kippur. Often, our prayers take the form of rational expressions in words of ancient or more recent composition. Or they may arise from the stirrings of our hearts, sometimes taking on verbal form and sometimes dissolving into simple, mere breath. Our prayers also include the shrill notes emitting from the primitive shofar. Like our words of prayer, the wide end of the shofar points upward toward the heavens. In verbal and nonverbal prayer, we primarily direct our energies upward in aspiration of transcendence.

In *teshuvah*, we turn inward. With *tefillah*, we peer upward, so to speak. With *tzedakah*, we primarily direct our attention outward, to those around us, those sitting near, family and friends, and then to all those who comprise our community, and, finally, to all with whom we share, for a brief span, this planet. According to the three-part motif, once we redesign our interior selves and after we refocus our gaze to the Master of all worlds, we then regard our fellows and recognize our obligations to them. Only then, after passing through these three directional movements, inward, upward, and outward, has one fully and properly engaged in the Days of Awe.

Tzedakah is the third movement, whose fullest liturgical expression occurs in the morning of Yom Kippur, with its rousing Haftarah. In it, the Prophet Isaiah implores us, belittles us, and demeans us, throws the book at us, lest we, even for a moment, feel satisfied that by our ritual acts of abstinence from food and drink, by our intonation of lengthy prayers, by donning the garb of piety for an entire day, that by all these symbolic gestures we somehow fulfill our obligations to our Maker. "Forget it," bellows Isaiah, in effect. "Your pious rituals count for nothing, less than nothing, if they do not produce deeds of caring toward those most in need, acts of kindness toward those most devoid of kindness, efforts toward empowerment and systemic change for those most disenfranchised."

Back in the challenging and dangerous days of May 1948, immediately after the brand-new State of Israel had just been declared, many new responsibilities fell to Prime Minister David Ben Gurion, among them the necessity of appointing foreign ambassadors. While the armies of nine Arab countries attacked, while boatloads of destitute refugees from the DP camps of Europe began to arrive, Israel had joined the family of nations, and so ambassadors had to be selected. Fortunately, as a nation of immigrants, Israel abounded in native speakers of most of the world's languages.

One of them was Reuven Rubin, the painter, and the designer of the Israeli flag, who was from Romania. Ben Gurion summoned him and asked him to serve as ambassador to Romania. The prospect of a diplomatic position was so far from anything that Rubin the painter had ever considered that it boggled his mind. I imagine the dialogue went something like this:

"Ambassador to Romania? Why, Mr. Prime Minister, what do I know from being an ambassador?"

"My dear friend," responded Ben Gurion. "What do I know from being a prime minister? But, you see, there aren't so many of us here. So it's up to us."

"It's up to us" well restates Isaiah's ringing message and the essence of the concept of *tzedakah*. It's up to us. There is no one else to rely on if we wish to improve our congregation, our community, our society, our nation, and our world. It really is up to us. Though simple, undeniably clear, and irrefutable, how often do we heed the injunction? In the same vein, a folk tale:

> There was once a king who had an only daughter. And when it came time for her to marry, he announced to the entire kingdom that everyone was to be invited to her wedding. But no one was to bring a gift—they were only to bring a bottle of wine from their own vineyards.
>
> That's all, just one bottle of wine from their own vineyards. And everybody would line up and empty the bottles into a huge vat in the royal gardens. At the appropriate time, the king would step forward and draw the wine from the communal vat to make a *L'chayim*, to toast the bride and groom.
>
> Well, one of the local vintners, Shmulik by name, thought to himself: "Why should I bring my good, precious wine that I have worked so hard to produce? I'll bring a bottle of water. No one will know the difference. It will go unnoticed in the thousands of bottles of wine."
>
> So early on the morning of the wedding, everyone in the kingdom lined up, ready, holding their bottles of wine and then emptying them into the enormous vat. At the appointed moment, the King turned the spigot and drew the first glass of wine from the combined wine of the entire kingdom. But, alas, what poured out was clear water. It seems that not only Shmulik but everyone had had the same idea. If I bring water, no one will know the difference.

Yes, there is a very real human propensity, to which no one is immune, to let others take care of the common good and say, "I'll do little and no one will know the difference." "No," declares Isaiah. "Your failure will be noted, if not by your friends and neighbors, than surely by the One who notes and records all things."

In my years in Charlottesville, I have often marveled at how so many in our Jewish community seem to heed Ben Gurion's "there aren't so many of us here, so it's up to us" and who refrain from taking the path of Shmulik. This attitude has made our tiny Jewish community more vibrant than it otherwise would be, more of a community than it otherwise would be. Thus, it concerns me that as we grow in size that it will become more easy to slip into the way of Shmulik.

Specifically, I worry that because some have taken on voluntary positions of leadership in our congregation and performed their tasks with dedication and skill, that others will feel that they are not needed, that their noninvolvement does not matter or is not noticed. The truth is that there is so much more we could and should be doing, especially in the realm of *tzedakah*.

We are so much less involved than we should and could be in joining others in addressing the most dire of community ills: poverty, drug use, violence, teen pregnancy, and the spillover of all these into the public school system and the courts and the jails. It's up to us.

Moreover, we could be much more engaged in issues affecting public policy, locally, regionally, and nationally, issues for which a religious institution rooted in a rich tradition of ethical wisdom is well suited. It's up to us.

Furthermore, we could engage more vibrantly in the unfolding discussions of the many critical issues of global significance: issues pertaining to the environment, human rights, population, women's rights, utilization of natural resources, hunger, and others. It's up to us to at least engage in the discussion.

Regarding the Jewish homeland, I hope and pray that peace and cooperation increasingly replace war and violence in Israel and between Israel and her neighbors, but I worry. I worry that we American Jews will disengage, that we will fail to perceive and monitor the dangers still lurking for our brothers and sisters in Israel. And I worry that we will fail to recognize and address the exciting and unprecedented challenge of incorporating the reality of a thriving Jewish state into our Jewish gestalt. In other words, I worry that the noble experiment that is Israel—the creation of a Jewish political entity and a reborn Jewish persona—will cease to interest us. We Jews of the Diaspora have an unprecedented opportunity to engage in the transformative Jewish phenomenon of Israel. It is surely up to us to do so.

And let me add, because it is so immediate: I worry that, as we plan a building project leading to a facility that will adequately house the wide array of activities desired by future generations of Jewish residents, just as did the Leterman, Kaufman, and Walter families back in 1881, that the generosity of some will cause the rest to slip into the mode of Shmulik. I worry that some will think to themselves: "No one will notice my bottle of water among all the wine. No one will notice my meager contribution among the many generous contributions." Here, too, it truly is up to each and every one of us—or it just will not happen and we will have failed to provide for ourselves, for our own children, for our neighbors, as well as for those who will follow us, seeking to act out their Jewish identities in this blessed region.

In short, at this stage of the High Holiday symphony, Isaiah comes to implore us to begin to direct our energy outward, to transform our inward searching into other-directed service, to lower our gaze from the heavens to the human beings with whom we dwell, to translate our pious words into righteous deeds.

Rabbi Israel Salanter once posed the question: why was the human created with two eyes? One is to look at the soul within, to reflect and examine, to critique and assess, to take care of our inner selves. The other is to look outwards, to see the physical, material requirements of our fellow human beings, especially those who are least well off, that we might help one another to live better lives.

As Ambassador Rubin was about to depart for his new post in Romania, he suddenly realized that he probably ought to have a flag of Israel. However, though he himself had designed the flag, stores did not carry them. Israel had no flag factory. So the wife of the ambassador, Esther Rubin, spent the night before their departure snipping and sewing a flag of Israel out of two of her children's pajama shirts. May we all come to the realization as fully as did the Rubins: there aren't so many of us here. It is up to us.

INWARD, UPWARD, AND OUTWARD
Yom Kippur 5753/1992

"On Rosh Hashanah it is written and on Yom Kippur it is sealed: How many shall pass on and how many shall come to be; who shall live and who shall die.... But Teshuvah, Tefillah, and Tzedakah, repentance, prayer, and righteous deeds temper judgment's severe decree."

These words from the prayer *Unetaneh Tokef* stand at the core of the High Holiday liturgy; they challenge each and every worshipper with three tasks: repentance, prayer, and righteous deeds, each of which entails movement in a distinct direction, inward, upward, and outward, each of which implies a particular kind of faith.

Teshuvah/repentance moves one inward; it pertains to faith in the self, the faith necessary before one can conduct any project of inner renewal. *Tefillah*/prayer moves one upward; it pertains to faith in the Almighty, a personal relationship with the Source of all being. *Tzedakah* moves one outward: it pertains to our fellow humans, the people with whom we share the space upon which we walk, the air from which we draw breath, the resources from which we derive our sustenance.

We do well to contemplate each of the three tasks and their distinct directional associations.

Once there was a poor, single parent, a woman who scrimped and saved and took extra jobs cleaning house so that her daughter could attend college, which she did. When the daughter returned home after the first marking period, she excitedly told her mother, "Mom, I'm doing real well. I'm second in my class." "Second, you say. You think I scrimped and saved and worked myself to the bone so that you could be second?" So the daughter went back to college and applied herself with great diligence, and, sure enough, on the next visit home, she told her mother, "Mom, I did it. I'm now first in my class." "First, you say. I guess it can't be much of a college."

Many of us have voices inside us like the mother of that girl, telling us not only that we have failed, but that we are essentially failures, not only that we have fallen short, but that we are essentially inadequate. True, these Days of Awe bid us to acknowledge our faults, our slip-ups, our goofs, serious and not-so-serious flaws, to confess our sins of omission and commission, but never are we to regard ourselves as fundamentally sinful. Rather, even as we admit our failings at this season, we must never forget the very first teaching of the first chapter of the Torah that the ancestor of every human being, Adam, was fashioned *B'tzelem Elohim*, in God's image. We must, therefore, never lose faith in ourselves, never lose sight of our essential worth. When our tradition teaches that the Gates of Repentance are always open, it means that, no matter what, we can never stray irrevocably out of reach, impossibly far from a better path.

As I look at the list of Al Cheyts, the sins for which we confess, I am struck by how fitting a list it is, at how many really do apply to me. If one is missing, though, perhaps it is the sin of holding ourselves in too low a regard, in failing to possess self-esteem high enough for one made in the image of the Almighty.

Moreover, it seems to me that popular culture conspires to lower our self-esteem, to rob us of faith in ourselves. The media bombards us with images of success, prowess, and beauty, sublime concoctions of Hollywood, entirely unattainable by real people who work for a living, struggle for their achievements, and who age with the passage of time.

A single example of how the media conspires: in the television coverage of the Olympics, the underlying assumption seems to be that the typical viewer cares only about American performers, mainly those who have gold-medal potential, and is only interested in results. I happen to enjoy track and field. I would like to see every event, even those with no Americans, even the preliminary races where no one wins anything, and not just the last laps of a long race, but every lap. I enjoy watching the effort expended, the strategy of the entire event, and the competitors who never make it to the final heats. For me, but not for the networks, there is more to the events than simply winning.

And, have you noticed, if a potential gold medalist earns only a silver, for a certainty, some TV interviewer will ask how it feels to have fallen short, to have disappointed, to have failed. Can it be a failure to earn a silver medal in the Olympics, competing with the best athletes in the world?

Most of us will never compete in the Olympics. Nor will we play basketball like Michael Jordan or violin like Isaac Stern. Should we therefore not engage in sports or in music? For a few, perhaps, the reasonable goal might be to play like Michael Jordan. For most of us, the enjoyment of the activity or playing our best constitutes the reasonable goal.

Abraham, the first Jew, was called by God with the words "*Lech Lecha*—Get yourself going." One commentary notes that the words literally mean "go to yourself." That is, in order for Abraham to leave his homeland, to set out on the adventure that was to become his destiny, he had first to turn inward, to know himself, to appreciate himself, to have faith in himself. That is the first task of these days.

Each of us is bidden, at this season, to turn inward, to cast off false, superficial, and unreasonable goals, to recognize his or her essential worth, to nurture self-esteem, to cultivate faith in self, all as a prerequisite for becoming, not Moses, not Michael Jordan, not Michael Jackson, probably not the winner of an Olympic medal, but the person she or he is uniquely capable of becoming, the one made in God's image.

For many of us, the second task, the prayer directed upward toward God, is the most problematic. Many of us have ambivalence about God: we want to believe, but we're just not sure. Or we do believe in a God who created the universe, who started the show, but we don't think S/He stops by much anymore. We doubt God's continued concern for us. Some of us actively disbelieve. We do not see the evidence for belief, or, if we do, we find it more than outweighed by evidence to the contrary.

Evidence to the contrary abounds. Every generation and age has its extremes of suffering and misery. Where is God in the misery and in the suffering? Where is God in the tragic death of the twenty-year-old UVA student Sharon Spitalny, *aleha ha-shalom*, may peace be upon her, who succumbed to a blood disease on the day after the Rosh Hashanah just passed? Where is God for the parents, brother, sister, and friends of that bright-eyed, cheerful, good-hearted girl who will never have the opportunities one expects of a full life? Evidence to the contrary abounds. I would be the last to deny it.

And yet, in time, God willing, those who knew Sharon best, will emerge from the depths of grief, comforted—partially, healed—at least enough to get on with living, perhaps even enriched, not that the cost justifies the gain, but with an enhanced ability to feel compassion. Maybe that is where God is, in the resilient and triumphant response to loss and to suffering. And in all the deeds of decency or nobility, the heroic achievements, the anonymous kindnesses, the acts of compassion that cannot be repaid, the help rendered, for which thanks cannot be returned—that too is where God is.

That second task of these days involves prayer, not just faith. But how can one pray to a God dimly or inconsistently perceived? Does faith precede prayer, or can it be the other way around? How can one pray with shaky faith? I once heard Rabbi Samuel Dresner offer this insight, commenting on the words of the Shema:

> "Set these words which I command you *upon* your heart." Why doesn't it say "*in* your heart?"
>
> Because most of the time, the heart of man is tightly closed and the words of God are unable to enter. But, every so often, there is a rare, precious moment, a moment of joy or awe or insight when the heart of man opens a little bit, and if we pray regularly, then when the heart opens, the words are there and they can enter.
>
> But if we never pray, then when that rare moment comes and the heart opens, there are no words available to express what we feel.

On the value of routinized prayer, Rabbi Abraham Joshua Heschel, *Zichrono L'vracha*, may his memory be a blessing, tells this parable:

> There was a small Jewish town, far off the main roads of the land. It had all the necessary municipal institutions: a bathhouse, a cemetery, a hospital and law courts and all sorts of craftsmen—tailors, shoemakers, carpenters, masons. One trade however was lacking: there was no watchmaker. In the course of years many of the clocks became inaccurate and their owners decided to just let them run down and ignore them altogether, since there was no one available to fix them. There were others, however, who maintained that as long as the clocks ran, they should not be abandoned. So they wound their clocks day after day, even though they knew they were not accurate.
>
> One day the news spread throughout the town that a watchmaker had arrived. Everyone rushed to him with their clocks. But the only ones he could repair were those that had been kept running—the abandoned clocks had grown too rusty! (*Man's Quest for God*, p. 27)

And this is why we pray regularly—so that the words may be *on* the heart, lubricated, available, if and when the heart ever opens.

Not only are we bidden to turn inward, to perform *teshuvah*, not only are we bidden to direct our prayers upward to God, allowing the words to be *on* the heart, but we are bidden to the third task of these days, to cast our attention outward, toward our fellows in a posture of *tzedakah*.

It goes without saying that our tradition teaches that religious ritual disconnected from righteous behavior is bogus. The Prophet Isaiah alerts us every Yom Kippur morning, in the midst of our fast, that our self-imposed affliction is worthless without the specific righteous deeds to which it must direct us. And that is why it is so fitting to give charity at this season, to join lofty words with concrete deeds on behalf of Jew and non-Jew alike. That is why it has become a tradition to place a *pushka*, a box for charity, next to the candles that are lighted on holidays and every Shabbat, so that charitable giving becomes as much a ritual as candle lighting. That is why it is so fitting that we bring food to the synagogue for the Emergency Food Bank and dollars for Disaster Relief on behalf of those suffering due to the destructive forces of nature. That is why we ought to be particularly mindful at this season about how we might help our brothers and sisters in Israel and around the world.

All of these righteous deeds and others ought to occupy us at this season, but the outward movement to which we are called ideally begins very close to home. A prose poem, by way of illustration, from the Russian author Ivan Turgenev:

> I was once walking in the street when a beggar stopped me. He was a frail old man, with inflamed eyes, blue chapped lips, filthy rough rags and disgusting sores. Oh how poverty had disfigured this repulsive creature!
>
> He stretched out his red, swollen, filthy hand and whispered for alms. I had reached into my pocket, but no wallet, no coins, no money did I find. I had left them all at home.
>
> The beggar waited, and his outstretched hand twitched and trembled slightly. Embarrassed and confused, I seized his hand and pressed it and I said: "Brother, don't be angry with me. I am sorry but I have nothing to give you. I left my wallet at home, brother."
>
> The beggar raised his bloodshot eyes to mine. His blue lips smiled and he returned the pressure of my fingers. "Never mind," he stammered. "Thank you, thank you for this, for this too was a gift. No one ever called me brother before." ("The Beggar Man")

Sometimes the righteous deed to which one is called is not a matter of the checkbook or the wallet, but rather a matter of affirming the humanity of the one before you.

A second story:

The rabbi officiated at a funeral and when the service was over, the mourner would not leave the grave. The rabbi tried to lead the man away but he would not go. The rabbi said: "The service is over now, you have to leave." But the man shook him off, and said: "You don't understand. I loved my wife." The rabbi said: "I'm sure you did, but the service is over now. You have to leave." The man shook him off again and said: "You don't understand. I loved my wife." The rabbi said: "I'm sure that you did but still, the service is over. You have to leave." The man shook him off again and said: "But you don't understand. I loved my wife—and once I almost told her."

The outward movement to which we are bidden on these days is movement out of our selves, out of our shells, out of our silences; it is a call for relationship, for combating loneliness, a call for sharing our friendship and our love while we have the means to do so.

A final illustration of the call to turn outward, a story from medieval Hebrew literature:

Once there was a king who was trying to impress a woman. He says to her: "Do you know how rich I am?"

She is not impressed.

He tries again. He says to her, "Do you know how many servants I have?"

She is not impressed.

He tries again. He says, "Do you know how much land I possess and how many people in the world envy me?"

She is not impressed.

And then he says: "Do you know that I have a headache, and that my feet hurt, and that I have had a hard day, and that I have some very difficult decisions that I must make tomorrow and I don't know what to do?"

And when he says that, she leans over and takes his hand and says: "I am so sorry. Can I be your friend?"

Not only are we called on to move toward our fellow humans; we ought also to allow them to move toward us. We need to trust one another, to have faith in each other. In spite of everything, we need to admit our mutual interdependence and allow the other to regard us with all our imperfections, sore feet, headaches, and all.

And so, on this most solemn day, this day upon which we are called to repentance, prayer, and righteous deeds,

May we turn inward, renewing our faith in ourselves.

May we turn upwards, renewing our faith in the God of compassion.

And may we turn outward, renewing our faith in the human capacity for goodness, for sharing, and for love.

ISRAEL AND HOPE
Rosh Hashanah 5768/2007

Jewish tradition regards Abraham as the first Jew, the one who established that identity by a series of actions, central among them making *aliyah* to *Eretz Yisrael*, emigrating to the land promised to his progeny through Isaac. That promise has been under repeated threat in real, historical time, including during the period of the Prophet Jeremiah. Jeremiah witnessed Jerusalem undergoing destruction, her citizens forced into exile. In the Haftarah designated for the second day of Rosh Hashanah, Jeremiah depicts the mountain of Abraham's fateful binding of his son as a location of yearning, promise, and hope, as we read: "Hear the words of the Lord, O nations, and tell it to the isles far off: the One who scattered Israel will gather them in, and watch over them as a shepherd the flock ... they shall come with shouts of joy to Zion's heights."

As Jews the world over begin to celebrate her sixtieth birthday, I want to share some reflections on the significance of the State of Israel to Jewish identity, even for Jews who live elsewhere. As we undertake the annual task of spiritual self-examination, seeking purposeful ways to incorporate prayer, study, and deeds of social justice into the fabric of our lives, as we notice where and how we fall short as Jews challenged by our tradition to aspire to holiness, I would suggest that we direct some of that attention to the way the State of Israel calls us and the way we respond.

In his satirical novel *Operation Shylock*, Philip Roth appears as a character who discovers another man who disconcertingly also goes by the name Philip Roth. The false Philip Roth has attracted publicity by promoting two interrelated programs, one an implausible scheme he calls Diasporaism, which seeks to return Israeli Jews to the countries of their birth, and the other the organization Anti-Semites Anonymous, a twelve-step group for self-acknowledging anti-Semites. Cleverly, Roth's pairing provides a mirror opposite to real history: Zionism, in its various forms, gained momentum in the late nineteenth and early twentieth centuries when more and more Jews began to sense that the stubborn persistence of anti-Semitism in

Christian Europe would always prevent the great national movements for the liberation of peoples and nations from extending their freedoms to Jews. Thus, Jews who seek liberation for Jews would have to take matters into our own hands and create a movement of "auto-emancipation," to use the language of Leo Pinsker, one of the early Zionist thinkers. Zionism, then, is a movement whereby we Jews have sought to end nearly two thousand years as a wandering, stateless people and return once again to the land of our historical origins. Roth's satire, then, reminds us of the core assumptions of Zionism while at the same time challenging us to enter the conversation about the place of Israel in our Jewish identities. To wit: to what extent does each of us have both an ego and an alter ego, Philip Roth and Philip Roth, one who loves Israel and one who wishes it would go away?

The Jewish return to sovereignty is regarded by some as a miracle of Biblical proportions. If so, it is a very messy miracle. It is one thing to maintain a high moral stature without military power, as tolerated or victimized visitors on foreign soil. It is quite another to maintain that stature with a strong army on one's own soil surrounded by sworn enemies while hosting others as potential resident victims of one's own moral failings.

My friend David Forman, Reform rabbi and an Israeli since the 1970s, is most known for founding Rabbis for Human Rights. That is, David is a lifelong Zionist with solidly left-leaning credentials. In recounting his experiences as a soldier in the first war in Lebanon in 1982, he recalls being told that the enemy combatants would use women as shields behind which they would fire mortars. A decision needed to be made about whether the Israeli soldiers would shoot the unarmed women to remove the human shield or not. They decided to refrain from shooting them. Two of Rabbi Forman's close friends were killed by those mortars. Would their lives have been saved if the unit had decided differently? Possibly. The only certainty is that sovereignty assures the impossibility of easy moral choices. The miracle of Israel is indeed a messy one, but one to which we Jews of the Diaspora dare not lose our sense of connection, one in whose profundity and greater purpose we dare not lose hope.

About some of the contours of the hope we require as Jews connected to the messy miracle of Israel, I want to share two stories I heard recently from Rabbi Michael Marmur, the dean of Hebrew Union College in Jerusalem. The first involves the late Hugo Gryn, who was a prominent Reform rabbi who had spent most of his career in Britain. In a memoir, Rabbi Gryn describes his days as a child along with his father in Auschwitz. He writes:

That year the festival of Chanukah was early—the first week of December. The Jewish prisoners in our barracks—Block 4—decided that we would celebrate by lighting a menorah every night. Bits of wood and metal were collected and shaped into light holders and everyone agreed to save the week's meager ration of margarine that would be used for fuel. It was my job to take apart an abandoned prison cap and fashion wicks from its threads.

Finally, the first night of Chanukah arrived. Most of Block 4 gathered around the menorah—including some Roman Catholic Poles, several Protestant Norwegians and . . . a German count who was implicated in the attempt on Hitler's life but somehow had his life spared. Two portions of margarine were melted down—my wicks in place—but as we chanted the blessing, praising God who "performed miracles for our ancestors in those days and at this time," and as the youngest person there, I tried to light the wick, there was only a bit of spluttering and no flame whatsoever.

What the "scientists" in our midst failed to point out was that margarine does not burn!

And as we dispersed and made our way to the bunk beds I turned not so much to my father, but on him, upset at the fiasco and bemoaning this waste of precious calories. Patiently, he taught me one of the most lasting lessons of my life and I believe that he made my survival possible.

"Don't be so angry," he said to me, "you know that this festival celebrates the victory of the spirit over tyranny and might. You and I have had to go once for over a week without proper food and another time almost three days without water, but you cannot live for three minutes without hope!" (*Chasing Shadows: Memories of a Vanished World*, pp. 236–237)

When folks hear that I have recently made two trips to Israel, one to participate in a five-day bicycle ride to attract attention and funds for Progressive Judaism in Israel and one to celebrate the *simcha* of my niece's wedding and to study Torah, they frequently ask: "So how are things in Israel? What is the mood there?" Although I claim no special insight from these or other visits, I do have some strong impressions, including two that contradict each other. They relate to hope and the lack thereof.

First, if the subject is political—Israel's political leadership, the outlook for a strong and effective prime minster, governmental ethics, efficiency or progress in electoral reform, the ability of the military to continue to solve every security problem after the demoralizing war with Hezbollah, the chaos in Gaza following the unilateral pullout, the weakness and disarray among the Palestinian leadership, continued demonization of Israel among most nations in the Middle East, increasing attempts by some academic institutions and religious bodies in the West to isolate Israel, not to mention the looming threat of a nuclear Iran—then I reply: feelings of despair are dominant. Never before have so many Israelis among my friends expressed the intention not to vote in the next elections. Such a disposition reflects an unprecedented and disturbing level of political hopelessness. That is, if one seeks evidence of some grand vision of hope of the kind articulated by Rabbi Gryn's father, hope in dramatic or miraculously sweeping changes for the better, I see little evidence.

The second story, though, one that I heard from Rabbi Marmur, presents a different vision of hope:

> At the height of his power, when it appeared that all of Europe was at his feet, Napoleon ordered three soldiers to be brought to him: a Russian, a Pole, and a Jew. To each he said that they could ask anything of him, and he would see to it that their wish was fulfilled. The Russian asked that the Czar be deposed. The Pole called for the creation of a free and independent Poland. The Jew asked for some schmaltz herring.
>
> Napoleon agreed to the requests of all three, so the Russian and the Pole left the encounter enthralled by the prospect of having brought salvation to their nations. Napoleon's chief of staff was given the job of finding some schmaltz herring to give to the Jew, who was allowed to return to his village.
>
> When the story of the meeting with Napoleon came out, members of the community came to the Jew and asked him why he had not made better use of the opportunity. Why didn't he ask for a homeland for the Jews or for guarantees of security? The Jewish soldier answered thus: "Do you think Napoleon will really topple the Czar or free Poland? I, on the other hand, at least got some good schmaltz herring."

Some hope has grand dimensions. Other kinds have more limited scope. Both strike me as Jewish and necessary and suggestive of the complexity of the spiritual language we require as we integrate the reality of the messy miracle that is Israel into our Jewish consciousness.

For, whereas I cannot report much in the way of grand visions of hope, no Yitzhak Rabin riding in on a white steed, I do find quite bit of "schmaltz herring" in the limited and modest efforts to improve the Israeli social fabric, to resist cynicism, to provide the disadvantaged with economic opportunities, and numerous efforts to heal and feed and clothe those who cannot do so without help. The list of these efforts by Israelis to apply the highest of Jewish values to bring tangible improvement to some corner of Israeli society is impressively long. The lengthiness of the list reflects the wide chasm between the prophetic ideal and the messy reality of Israeli society and at the same time the widespread refusal to retreat from the challenge of engaging that messiness or using it as an excuse for complacency.

A random and short sample of the kinds of efforts that constitute some good schmaltz herring:

Under the rubric of Otzma, a program sponsored by the United Jewish Communities, young American men and women come to Israel to learn Hebrew, to study Israeli society, and, most of all, to volunteer in various programs of community service. One of the settings in which my son, Benjamin, served as an Otzma volunteer last year was Peace Players International, an organization that has operations in several conflict-ridden places in the world. Peace Players International endeavors to begin bridging the gap in understanding by organizing basketball for teenagers from both sides of the conflict. In Israel, for example, Arab teens from Tul-karem play Jewish kids from Tel Aviv. During the year, a new league was organized for girls. The organizers were unsure whether Arab parents would support such an activity for their daughters, so they modestly strove to fill eighteen places for the Arab girls. Eighty showed up at the first tryout. No one thinks Peace Players International will bring an end to the conflict between Israelis and Palestinians. It will be enough if it succeeds on its own limited terms of increasing the number of Israeli and Palestinian teens who see each other as more similar than different, as fellow athletes with complexion problems and hormonally driven appetites, rather than as implacable enemies.

A second item: as I walked the streets of the German Colony and downtown Jerusalem this past summer, I noticed new symbols in the windows of some of the restaurants. These round, blue-and-white stamps bear the words *Tav Chevrati Ki Echpat Li*—A Social Seal Because I Care. I learned that the establishments displaying these blue emblems have been certified by a group of caring Jerusalemites to comply with a certain standard vis-à-vis employees' rights and accessibility for people with physical disabilities. Patrons can obtain business-type cards to leave at such establishments to indicate that the extra costs borne by compliance with these standards are appreciated. Surely the *Tav Chevrati* seal will not by itself transform Israel into a prophetic beacon of moral light for the world. However, I do know that the effort to raise public awareness about and support for some concrete issues of great concern for an often-ignored social segment will strengthen the muscles of humane practice.

A third item: early in the summer I became aware of a new synagogue in Tel Aviv. It has no denominational affiliation and has as its primary target secular Israelis who would not normally be found in any synagogue. The organizers assume that among secular Israelis are those who hunger for a spiritual life and who could find a spiritual home in Judaism, but who have well-developed (and I might say well-founded) allergic reactions to religious orthodoxy and have not yet experienced the possibilities inherent in nonorthodox approaches to Jewish spirituality. This synagogue, *Beit HaTefilah*, The House of Prayer, recently commissioned popular Israeli musicians to compose music for liturgical settings with the goal of creating a distinctly Israeli liturgical mode that might appeal to secular Israeli tastes. I will admit that the melodies I have heard from the project do not appeal to me. However, I applaud this effort to reclaim Jewish tradition, to restore the Jewish soul of Israel, and to resist the sad tendency to cede Judaism to ultra-Orthodox extremists. I cannot predict the trajectory of *Beit Tefillah*'s growth, if it will inspire similar efforts elsewhere in Israel, or if these efforts will join together with those already under way in the Conservative and Reform movements, which together are entering a second generation of contribution to a richer, more diverse, and healthy religious climate in the Jewish state. I do know that the effort already under way comes from a place of optimism and has already opened up new spiritual possibilities for a group of Israelis potentially lost to their heritage. And that is something deeply hopeful.

On the long list of modestly hopeful efforts, I could also mention the PACT program supported by our local United Jewish Fund for Charlottesville, a program that makes a huge difference in providing learning environments for Ethiopian youngsters who have the potential to obtain a decent college education. I could mention the Shalom Hartman Institute in Jerusalem, which by offering a vision of Jewish pluralism in its programs for rabbis, Jewish educators, and others, serves as a rare model for interdenominational respect among those who seriously engage Judaism but do so from differing points of view. I could mention a long list of efforts by the Movement for Progressive Judaism in Israel in the realms of education, social justice, and environmental awareness, in establishing worshiping communities and meaningful life cycle options, and more. The list of tangible but modest examples of the hopeful, schmaltz herring variety goes on.

We Jews must not despair even when we fail to see signs of grand hope, when not ready to declare as fulfilled Jeremiah's vision of "the One who scattered Israel [having] gather[ed] them in, [as] . . . they . . . come with shouts of joy to Zion's heights." Yet we must not allow the absence of such grand visions to blunt our appreciation for the many limited but truly marvelous and sometimes heroic efforts undertaken by those who have not given up their ideals.

May we turn and return in seriousness to the messy miracle of Jewish sovereignty, finding in it ever new, tangible, and meaningful ways to connect our personal Jewish stories to those springing from the Jewish homeland, taking encouragement from the many expressions of optimism and hope there, ever open to the new and grand hope that might emerge from the Source of all hope.

ON THE ETHICS OF JEWISH EATING
Yom Kippur 5770/2009

The Magid of Dubno used to tell this story:

> A man from a village once came to the big city where he lodged at an inn overnight. Awakened in the middle of the night by loud beating of drums, he inquired drowsily, "What's all this about?" Informed that a fire had broken out and that the drum beating was the city's fire alarm, he turned over and went back to sleep.
>
> When he returned to his village, he reported the incident: "They have a wonderful system in the big city. When a fire breaks out, people beat drums and before long the fire is put out." Excited, the villagers ordered a supply of drums and distributed them to the population. Several weeks later, when a fire broke out in the village, there was a deafening explosion of drum beating, and while the people waited expectantly for the flames to subside, their homes burned to the ground.
>
> A passing visitor remarked: "Idiots! Do you think that a fire can be put out by beating drums? The drums are no more than an alarm for people to wake up and extinguish the fire themselves." (modified from *Kol Haneshamah*, p. 9)

In a similar fashion, *Chapter 53 of the Book of Isaiah* instructs us about the rituals we perform, which, like beating drums, are meant to arouse us to higher consciousness and to the performance of deeds. The rituals, as Isaiah instructs, are as useful as a fire alarm in rousing us to action and just as worthless if sounded absent those actions.

We might epitomize Isaiah's message as follows: "Your rituals and your ethics must align! Do not suppose for a moment that rituals devoid of the ethical awareness they are designed to arouse accrue to your merit. They do not. Rather, the rituals and the awareness and the deeds of social conscience that follow must be woven together into a single fabric of a religious life. If one of these strands is missing, the fabric unravels, worthless."

One could apply Isaiah's challenge that we align rituals and ethics to a host of arenas. One is the arena of dietary discipline known as *kashrut*. As a point of reference, let me share my particular story as it pertains to *kashrut*: when I was in my early twenties I began a journey of rediscovery that led me from a state of disillusion with Judaism to one of engagement with it. At the same time and as a child of what we called back then the counterculture, I became aware of the expanding ethical concerns related to the environmental impact of large-scale industry. Among these concerns were those related to food. Thus, along with treasured paperback volumes I've kept from those days, the pages now brown and brittle, by the likes of Abraham Joshua Heschel and Martin Buber, stands an even browner and more brittle volume by Francis Moore Lappe called *Diet for a Small Planet*. Essentially a recipe book, *Diet for a Small Planet* promoted an ecologically driven philosophy of eating lower on the food chain as a more rational, less wasteful, less damaging, and more healthy use of the earth's energy. These volumes represented dual tracks in my spiritual formation, one Jewish and one general, tracks that sometimes intersected and sometimes seemed to exist apart.

I grew up in a home where a kosher Empire chicken appeared only when my grandma or my "Orthodox" relatives from Connecticut visited. At all other times, every manner of *traifa*/non-kosher fare comprised our cuisine. Thus, my reengagement in Judaism as a young adult included what for me were new discoveries about *kashrut*, the Jewish dietary laws, and some of the ways in which they may be understood.

I learned, for example, that the medieval Jewish philosopher Saadya Gaon divided all 613 categories of mitzvot into two broad categories, laws that have rational explanations (like don't take things that belong to others, a good, rational rule for those who prefer a civil society) and those that do not lend themselves to rational explanation. Among these, Saadya presents *kashrut* as a prime example. Moreover, the fact that no rational basis exists, in Saadya's view, for an adherence to *kashrut* implies that by adhering to its rules, one demonstrates faithfulness. In other words, the only reason to follow a rule that has no rational basis would be one's trust in its source. It reminds me of the way Jack Bauer, on the TV show *24*, routinely implores a colleague to comply with some extreme and incomprehensible deviation from protocol, saying, "You've got to trust me on this." Those who do comply with his odd and extreme requests clearly do trust him. In the same way, those who observe traditions that make no rational sense demonstrate trust in their divine source.

However, I also learned that not everyone agrees that the laws of *kashrut* have no basis in reason or are devoid of meaning except as an opportunity to demonstrate faith. One of my early mentors once explained that to him *kashrut* was about reminding us that the food we eat (and he meant meat especially) does not come originally as we find it in the grocery store, in plastic-wrapped packages, that the entire process by which food becomes kosher was meant to instill in us a deliberate and mindful disposition, especially when the food involved taking the life of a sentient being.

I learned that some thoughtful commentators over the years, notably Rabbi Abraham Isaac Kuk, the first Chief Ashkenazic rabbi of pre-state Palestine, find in the core of *kashrut* a vegetarian ideal. They notice that the menu of permitted foods given to the first humans in the idyllic Garden of Eden was purely vegetarian, that only after great disappointment with humanity in the period after Noah's flood did God relent, striking a compromise with the human lust for animal flesh. Only then did the menu of permitted food expand to include meat, permitted, that is, only when all the blood was drained, only when the process of slaughter would instill maximum awareness about the life that was being taken for the sake of human craving.

Gradually, I came to acquire a blended (and admittedly inconsistent and changing) personal approach to *kashrut*. In a general way, simply having it in mind as a standard makes me more conscious and more appreciative than I otherwise would be of the food that sustains me. And even when adherence to the disciplines of *kashrut* fails to perform its intended consciousness-raising function, they do provide me with a Jewish way to discipline my eating. Thus, the prosaic act of eating, especially if a bit of inconvenience is involved, becomes an opportunity to reinforce Jewish identity.

Fast-forward to 2006 when articles published in the *Jewish Forward* began to expose the labor practices of Agriprocessor, at the time then the largest producer of kosher meat in the United States. These practices included poor working conditions that most would consider unethical and some of which have been subsequently identified as violations of state and/or federal labor laws, which in 2008 led to a well-publicized raid on Agriprocessor's plant by federal immigration officers. This past summer, the Rubashkins, the prominent Lubavitcher family who owned and managed Agriprocessor, sold the company's plant in Postville, Iowa.

Although the legal case is unresolved, the publicity has been embarrassing, to say the least, to any Jew who feels, as I do, bound up with both the noble and ignoble deeds of those of our tribe. Even before the raid, the negative publicity had already stirred debate among some Jews about the extent to which kosher standards should encompass ethical treatment of workers. It is by no means obvious to all concerned that the two should have anything to do with one another. In fact, within the world of Jewish Orthodoxy, where one finds most of the consumers of kosher products, there has been little support for pressing a linkage between rules of *kashrut* and the ethical treatment of laborers or other matters of ethical awareness, such as those pertaining to the environment.

In my view, the apparently unethical practices of the Agriprocessor company constitute an egregious and embarrassing example of the failure to heed Isaiah's clear message to align ritual and ethical principle. In one fell swoop, Agriprocessor has supplanted in the public mind the whimsically positive stereotype that had equated *kashrut* with quality and integrity (recall the Hebrew National commercial: "We answer to a Higher Authority"?) with a more sinister association between Jewish ritual and an arrogant disregard for human rights. Not only does this transformation constitute ready grist for any lurking anti-Semites, but it raises the old canard about Jews as those who care about the letter of law but disregard its spirit. Agriprocessor has also caused rabbis like me a special kind of grief in making it that much more challenging to invite and encourage those Jews who, in the absence of such negative associations, might have considered taking on aspects of Jewish dietary discipline as enhancements to their sense of Jewish identity and as paths toward an awakened spirituality associated with eating.

Yet I will continue to invite and encourage nonetheless, lest I allow the Rubashkin family to define the boundaries of my Jewish world. Rabbi David Hartman often says that Israel is far too important to be left to the Israelis. By this he means that Jewish identity, even for Jews who live in the Diaspora, cannot properly be separated from the noble Jewish experiment of our day, the extraordinarily difficult and surprising entry into history of a Jewish state. Therefore, all Jews have a claim on that state and have a responsibility to exercise that claim with their support and their criticism. In the same way, I would argue, Jewish ritual, *kashrut* included, is far too important to be left to the Orthodox or the ultra-Orthodox. That is to say, Jewish identity for serious Jews of all stripes must include an encounter with the traditions, the values, the meaning-making frameworks that come to us as part of the heritage of all Jews. We too are charged to learn about, wrestle with, and incorporate into our spiritual journeys these rituals in ways that make sense to us. And we are charged to do it in the manner taught by Isaiah, with the fabric whose strands, ethics and ritual—and the mindful awareness of both—are woven together in tight alignment.

One year, in the early 1800s, Rabbi Israel Salanter was asked to certify the *kashrut* of the matzah being made at a certain factory for the coming Pesach holiday. Upon inspection, he found that the process by which the matzah was made met all the standard criteria for *kashrut* for Pesach. However, he also learned that the workers in the matzah factory had enumerated a list of grievances with regard to their working conditions. Rabbi Salanter subsequently ruled that the *kashrut* of the matzah was dependent not only on adherence to the rules pertaining to Pesach but also on the business laws pertaining to the treatment of workers.

In this regard, we may take heart from the loudest voice insisting on the linkage between ritual and ethics that has emerged from the Rubashkin scandal, a commission called *Hekhsher Tzedek* (Certification of Ethical Practice), a group of mostly Conservative rabbis led by Morris Allen of Minneapolis. After some two years of study, *Hekhsher Tzedek* issued guidelines for those who would receive its Seal of Ethical Practice. In the preamble to those guidelines, the group declares its mission:

> To bring the Jewish commitment to ethics and social justice directly into the marketplace and the home. The Commission's seal of approval, the Magen Tzedek, will help assure consumers that kosher food products were produced in keeping with the highest possible Jewish ethical standards, values and ideals for social justice in the areas of labor concerns, animal welfare, environmental impact, consumer issues and corporate integrity. The Magen Tzedek, the world's first Jewish ethical certification seal, synthesizes the aspirations of a burgeoning international movement of sustainable, responsible consumption and promotes increased sensitivity to the vast and complex web of global relationships that bring food to our tables.

Of course, the devil is in the details, or rather one might say, God is in the details. No one yet knows exactly how *Hekhsher Tzedek* will apply broad ethical principles to the complex details of kosher food production in the real world. No one knows which understandings of the five areas of concern will hold sway or what compromises might be acceptable. No one yet knows exactly how *Hekhsher Tzedek* might respond, say, to a company that complies with one set of concerns, maybe those pertaining to labor practices, but ignores important environmental issues. It also must be noted that no one knows if the idea of a Jewish seal of high ethical standards will have real traction, if enough consumers will care enough to insist that companies bring their practices into compliance with the standards required to obtain the seal or if companies on their own will seek compliance, either for altruistic or for business reasons.

Nonetheless, I am encouraged by the effort. Whereas the highly public misdeeds of fellow Jews embarrass me as a Jew, the serious attempt to bring an important area of ritual observance into alignment with Jewish ethical values inspires me.

Echoing Isaiah, Rabbi Abraham Joshua Heschel once said:

> The teaching of Judaism is the *theology of the common deed.* The Bible insists that God is concerned with the everydayness, with the trivialities of life . . . in how we manage the commonplace. The prophet's field of vision is not the mysteries of heaven . . . but the blights of society, the affairs of the marketplace. He addresses himself to those who trample upon the needy, who increase the price of grain, use dishonest scales and sell the refuse of corn. The predominant feature of the biblical pattern of life is unassuming, unheroic, inconspicuous piety. (*Insecurity of Freedom*, pp. 102–103)

Isaiah did not rail against ritual, only against ritual that failed to align with ethical awareness and ethical behavior in everyday circumstances. We do well when we find ways to grow spiritually, to explore ever-new avenues to allow rituals to enliven our souls, to consider among the menu of options even the rituals like *kashrut* once considered reserved for Orthodox. We do well when we rededicate ourselves to ever-deeper alignments between our inner lives and outer practices, between our ritual performance and our ethical behavior.

THE CHALLENGE OF YIGAL AMIR
Rosh Hashanah 5757/1996

It is often said that the proper role of a clergy person is to comfort the afflicted and to afflict the comfortable. With the latter in mind, we consider the tragic assassination of Yitzhak Rabin.

How shall we tell the story of that event? How shall we place it in the larger narrative of our people? How will its telling affect our lives? Responses to questions such as these will no doubt vary as much as does one's relation to the tradition, people, land, and state of Israel. But all of us, Jews alive today, must speak of the tragedy in all its sadness and must confront its challenging dimensions, for only when we confront the significant events of the past can we move securely into the future. In my view, much is at stake in how we tell the story of the murder of Rabin. To quote David Elcott and Irwin Kula:

> The meaning of the story, the way this narrative will be told and retold is unclear. The images are before us, but they are inchoate: Is this a culmination or a beginning, a replay from our biblical past or an unprecedented event? Is this the harbinger of a civil war or the first stage of a reconciliation among Jews? ("Renewing the Covenant in the Face of Unbearable Pain")

Much is at stake. Thus, we ought to come to terms with this most tragic event so that we can do our part to transform a profound tragedy into a redemptive triumph, lest the tragedy send our people on a downward spiral of strife and dissolution. We must engage in this review of the dysfunction in our Jewish family, lest it spread, exerting a power far more lethal than any external military threat, far more insidious than the impact of assimilation, apathy, or alienation.

The tragedy of Rabin's death had multiple dimensions, among them the sadness of the sudden and unexpected demise of a human being: a man, a husband, a father, a grandfather, and a friend. At the funeral, Rabin's granddaughter, Noa ben Ami, spoke poignantly of the human qualities of her saba—gentleness, humor, warmth—qualities that might have endeared him to a larger public. The Jewish nation was robbed of its head of state, and with it, much confidence and perhaps some innocence. We suddenly felt bereft, confused, angry, disoriented. It triggered paths of emotion that had been dormant since the assassination of JFK. In Rabin's death, most Jews and many non-Jews as well lost a symbol of peace that seemed more attainable than at any previous time, more, it is likely, than with any previous Israeli leader.

However, for many Jews, the most disturbing dimension of the tragedy consisted in the nature of the assassin: a Jew, a young idealist with an enviable education in both Jewish and secular studies.

Yigal Amir's act sent shockwaves through the ground of Jewish religious tradition. I still feel the tremors. They shook some of the most basic premises upon which our faith rests. They rattled the foundations of the building in which the Jewish people live. As the shockwaves subside, we Jews must begin to address three areas of concern in the most serious fashion, if we are to redeem our faith, our people, and our ancestral home.

We direct our attention first to the issue of Jewish community itself. In the wake of Yigal Amir, the question posed by *Psalm 15* becomes distinctly nonrhetorical: "*Adonai, Mi Yagur B'Oholach; Mi Yishkon B'har Kodshecha?*— Lord, who will live in Your tent, who will reside on Your holy mountain?" That is, who counts as within the community of the righteous or the potentially righteous? Only Jews? Only certain Jews? Whom do we regard as part of our community? And who regards us as part of or excludes us from theirs?

Who counts as part of the Jewish family? Within the larger Jewish world, who is authentically in and who is not and who gets to decide? For a long time, it has been clear to me that the old UJA slogan, "We are one," does not describe reality. Okay, so we Jews are diverse in beliefs and in modes of living. Yet now the question looms: when I or someone else says, "we Jews," who is included and who is excluded by the term? If some Jews could consider Yitzhak Rabin, a Zionist hero to many, as an outsider to the community that counts, as one of the enemy, as a legitimate target for extermination, then no one is safely in the fold.

Perhaps the remarks delivered by the Sephardic Chief Rabbi Bakshi Daron this past summer on Shabbat Pinchas should not surprise us. On that Shabbat we read the Torah's account of a plague besetting the Israelites and of a certain Zimri, an Israelite who has sexual relations with a Midianite woman. The zealous Pinchas ends the plague by killing Zimri. In his Shabbat homily, Rabbi Bakshi Daron likened Zimri to the Reform movement and added: sometimes it is necessary to take extreme action. The chief rabbi seemed to be justifying the murder of Reform Jews! Does it not cause amazement that someone so high in the Orthodox rabbinic establishment of Israel would employ such words of incitement less than a year after similarly violent and provocative words had translated so clearly into such a violent and diabolical deed?

Of course, the ideal of Klal Yisrael, of Jews somehow comprising part of one community no matter what our differences, suffers attacks on many fronts. In Jerusalem, as I imagine you have read, ultra-Orthodox and ultrasecular Jews have clashed, at times violently, over the issue of whether Bar Illan Street shall remain open or closed to traffic on Shabbat. More than the nature of a Jerusalem neighborhood on Shabbat is at stake here; underlying the dispute is the question: by what measures and by whom shall the quality of life in Jerusalem be determined?

The division between secular and ultra-Orthodox runs very deep. I could not help but notice how, at the funeral of his father, Rabin's son stumbled badly over the Aramaic lines of the Mourner's Kaddish while he read the Hebrew quite smoothly. Of course, Hebrew is his native language, so he read it like he would have read a newspaper, but the Mourner's Kaddish as a prayer was completely unfamiliar to him! What a sad commentary on Jewish education in Israel! What a frightening vision of two segments of the Israeli population having grown so distant!

Moreover, whereas for years, Orthodox spokespeople have tried to delegitimize the non-Orthodox, especially the Reform, both in and outside Israel, some non-Orthodox spokespeople have begun to fight back, using similarly strident name-calling.

Furthermore, there is a deeper dilemma that often goes unmentioned, one that warrants airing. There is an underlying philosophical dilemma created by the very existence of the sovereign Jewish State of Israel. The scholar Avi Ravitsky points out that we Jews think of modern Israel as both *home land* and *holy land* without full awareness of the essential contradiction inherent in a land that one regards as both. (oral presentation) Consider: in a holy place one exhibits awe and wonder. Moses removed his shoes at the burning bush. Jacob built an altar at Beit El. But at home, one relaxes, puts one's feet up, untucks one's shirt, and cracks open a six-pack.

Ravitsky explains by analogy: a man in prison misses his wife. However, if his prison term is long, two processes ensue: first, he may come to find replacements for the wife, perhaps other interests or objects of desire.

Second, in all likelihood, as the years pass by, the mental image of his wife will become less real and more dreamlike. In time, the dream image will become the ideal, the object of his longing rather than the actual woman.

But what if the prison term suddenly ends and reunion takes place? Will the ideal wife of the man's dreams allow for his real wife? The clash between real and imagined could be quite traumatic.

In a similar way, when our ancestors no longer lived in Jerusalem, replacements were found: Pumpeditha, Toledo, Bari, Prague, Vilna—all were likened to Jerusalem. At the same time, Jerusalem became a sublime concept, an object of poetry and dreams. Exile yields this contradiction between the sublime ideal and the dusty reality, between holy and home.

To elaborate just a bit more: according to some midrashim, when our ancestors went into exile, the Shechina, God's Indwelling Presence, went along, leaving its holy haunt of Zion. Subsequently, if one were to return to the ancestral homeland, which one would think of as desirable, one could be accused of abandoning the Shechina. Historically, over the many generations of our exile, most rabbinic scholars saw it as meritorious to make *aliyah*, to return to the land of Israel, if only because many of the mitzvot, the religious obligations, can be performed there alone. Using this rationale, three hundred well-known rabbinic scholars made *aliyah* in 1210 so they could live more pious lives.

Yet, on the other hand, there were rabbis who warned of the dangers of making *aliyah*: true, they agreed, more mitzvot can be performed, but that means one has more obligations. After all, we do not always do so well with the ones we already have. More mitzvot create more opportunities to slip up or fall into sin. Of course, *aliyah* in the abstract is good, but perhaps not quite yet. Perhaps the time is not right. Or perhaps the stakes are too high and we are not quite ready. In other words, even though we long for an ideal holy land, we have reasons to fear a real one; we may not be ready for such a challenge.

I can relate to this notion of fearing the holy, of sensing the contradiction inherent in a land that is both holy and home. Certainly, before my first visit in 1970, I had some lofty and ideal notions of Israel; I expected to experience a sudden sense of Klal Yisrael, of the oneness of Jews from everywhere, and a feeling of history compressed and quickened at the western wall; I expected a Jerusalem of gold. Now, after dozens of visits, including two one-year stints, although I actually retain a powerful and abiding sense of the holiness of Israel, I hold onto this notion with difficulty, over against the realities of traffic congestion, bus fumes, rude clerks, teenagers spitting sunflower seeds, and ubiquitous cellular phones.

One might say that Yigal Amir has raised to the point of urgency the inherent contradiction of a land that one regards as both home and holy. Perhaps the time is not right. Perhaps we are not ready. And yet, we cannot turn back the clock. So how can we Jews redeem the place that both draws and repels us?

A third major challenge posed by Yigal Amir can be illustrated by a widely reported phenomenon. Following the assassination, many sons and daughters of modern Orthodox Israelis came home from their universities of religious high schools and announced: "Abba and Ema, I think I don't want to be religious." While their impulse to separate themselves from the assassin's world view speaks well of these sensitive young Israelis and reminds us that not all Orthodox Jews are fanatics, it directs us to a hard fact: the Torah, as a sacred text among many, is dangerous. And by "Torah," I mean the entire canon of sacred Jewish literature, both Biblical and post-Biblical.

Perhaps when Baruch Goldstein committed his heinous deed, killing nineteen Muslim worshippers one Purim, we should then have realized it and not been so ready to dismiss Goldstein as crazed. Surely, now, none of us should fail to realize that Amir was sane and sober, that he drew support and justification for his evil deed from sacred Jewish literature and from some rabbis who taught it. As he learned it, the Torah categorized Rabin as a *rodef*, a pursuer with intent to kill, and as a *moser*, a traitor to the Jewish people. The Torah permits the slaying of a *rodef*; it countenances the killing of a *moser*, even requires it, out of the need for communal preservation. Of course, it is one thing to learn an ancient text in a classroom and quite another to apply it to real life, with all its complexities. And there are many ways to understand a difficult text besides taking it at its face value. Tragically, Amir and his rabbis failed to probe beyond the surface.

The Biblical account instructs; it recounts the story of the Babylonian siege of Jerusalem some 2,580 years ago. It was a time when Jew fought against Jew, when prophets were imprisoned, kings were dethroned, priests murdered, and ritual sacrifice, the only means enjoined in the Torah for worship of God, ceased. As a final act of brutality, a Jewish extremist murdered the last Jewish governor of Jerusalem as a traitor. In remembrance of the murder of that governor, Gedalyah, Jews have fasted from dawn to dusk every year on the anniversary of his death. That day of fasting, for a Jew murdered by a fellow Jew, takes on renewed meaning for those of us who would remember both our ancient and recent past while striving to reconstruct a Judaism that will take us into the future. Though I never did so before, I intend to observe Tzom Gedalyah this year in memory of Yitzhak Rabin and as an act of resistance against human brutality and extremism.

Following the death of Gedalyah, our ancestors trudged into exile, full of guilt and sadness, anxious over the loss of home and homeland, but with an abiding faith that the covenant could not be broken. Two generations later, our ancestors reemerged under the leadership of Ezra and Nehemiah with a reconstructed religion based on a Torah that was to be read and studied, not in the rebuilt Temple but in the marketplaces.

Centuries later, under Roman rule, following similarly catastrophic upheaval and destruction, the rabbis reconstituted covenantal religion once again. Again, in a milieu marked by zealotry, internal battles, and the murder of Jewish leaders who spoke of peace, the rabbis envisioned a faith that blamed gratuitous hatred among Jews, *Sinat Chinam*, more than Rome, for our own suffering. They reconstructed Judaism as a complex fabric woven from these strands: Torah study, ritual practice, and the performance of deeds of kindness and love. Their goal: gratuitous love should replace gratuitous hatred.

As we begin a new year, we Jews have arrived once again at a momentous era, one calling for radical innovation that looks both to the past and to the future. The murder of Yitzhak Rabin has demonstrated to us that in an age when we Jews have entered the realm of political self-determination, never again willing to assume the status of victim, the "old-time religion" does not prove entirely adequate; it must undergo transformation. And how must that transformation take place? As in the past, we will continue the necessary process of consolation, we will construct a compelling reading of Torah, and we will redeem our Jewish future, by looking to the past and by recovering the key meta-principles that will undergird our recreated religion.

The meta-principles are there for us to recover. They include:

(1) *Tzelem Elohim/To be in the image of God:* The first meta-teaching in the Torah is that every human is fashioned in the image of God, *B'tzelem Elohim*. This concept ought to place the brakes on any notion of superiority toward which one might tend. It ought to thwart any interpretation of Torah that would have one devalue the humanity of another.

(2) *Brit/Unconditional, Covenantal love:* "Ma Tovu Ohalecha Yaacov— How goodly are your tents O Jacob"—are the words of blessing with

which we often begin our worship. Not "tent" but "tents." There have always been and will always be many tents within the Jewish camp. We must maintain our ability to live with one another as a family even in disagreement, even when the view of the other prevails. We must learn to mimic the Almighty, who, in defeat against the rabbis over a matter of ritual practice, as the rabbis tell it, could smile and say, "My children have defeated me. My children have defeated me." Members of a covenantal community must be willing to give in to one another, even in matters of serious concern, and continue to set up their tents in the same camp.

(3) *Mipnei Darkei Shalom/We must walk paths of peace:* The Torah begins not with an account of the Jewish people but with the creation of humanity. Our membership in the human race precedes our membership in the Jewish people. Thus, we begin the Jewish year in universal celebration of the birthdays of the world and of the human race. As such, we must never become so self-absorbed as Jews that we ignore the suffering of non-Jews. When we do, among other transgressions, we bring shame upon our people and upon God. Among other things, the death of Yitzhak Rabin at the hand of a Torah-observant Jew undermined the image of the Torah as a force for good. It is my greatest hope that we who worship in this community will take on the responsibility to engage in a process of restoring luster to the image of Torah through words and deeds by which we bring credit to God and the Jewish people.

(4) Finally, we ought to raise to prominence the meta-principle of *theological humility*, a concept taught with most vigor by Rabbi Harold Schulweis. The Prophet Micah teaches that God expects us to walk humbly. If we are to walk, act, and think in humility, then surely we shall realize that no one spiritual path will suffice for all, not in the world at large and not even in the smaller Jewish world. There are many paths that lead one up the mountain. We may choose one of the Jewish ways, and it will get us up that mountain in fine fashion. But our theological humility ought to inhibit us from pronouncing other paths inferior.

Several weeks ago, on a sunny afternoon, I stood in the cemetery on Mount Herzl, by the grave of Yitzhak Rabin. While there, I offered this prayer:

> Let us not give in to the vision of Torah, of the Jewish people, or of the Jewish homeland that drove Yigal Amir to take the life of this man. Rather, let us be among those who seek to renew, restore, and redeem the Jewish enterprise for the sake of our children and for the sake of the Almighty. *Im Yirtze Hashem.* With the help of God, may it be so.

ACKNOWLEDGEMENTS

Many people have taught and inspired me over the years. I would be remiss not to offer appreciation to the following among them.

The rabbi of my childhood, Rabbi Jack Stern of blessed memory, did much of his teaching through the masterful telling of stories and by exuding personal kindness and warmth. Rodney Sheratsky of blessed memory taught English at Northern Valley Regional High School in Demarest, New Jersey. Had it not been for his insistence on clarity in written expression, I might never have known the joy and challenge of the sermonic form. Rabbi Steven Shaw, as assistant director of Rutgers Hillel, opened up Jewish tradition for me as a viable alternative to the ways of Eastern religion. As director of UCLA Hillel, Rabbi Richard Levy introduced the possibility of joining my personal spiritual searching to a career path when he fatefully asked, "Have you ever thought of going to rabbinic school?"

I owe much to the scholars with whom I studied at Hebrew Union College and to the many friends and colleagues with whom I have learned then and since. Over the years, I have gained many powerful insights from the teachers at the summer Rabbinic Torah Seminars of the Shalom Hartman Institute in Jerusalem, not the least from its founder, Rabbi David Hartman himself. Back in 1974, as a first-year rabbinic student in Jerusalem, I enrolled in Philosophical Implications of Rabbinic Thought, a class Rabbi Hartman taught at Hebrew University. In many ways, the issues Rabbi Hartman posed for his students back then continue to animate my spiritual explorations to this day.

Back in my early days as a Hillel director in the 1980s, I was generously invited into a most extraordinary community consisting of the dynamic and creative colleagues who directed Hillel Foundations throughout North America. As a group, they modeled a dynamically inclusive brand of Jewish community that transcends denomination, encourages open discovery among the spiritual riches of Judaism, and promotes social responsibility.

Since the early 1990s, for about a week each August I have joined a group of rabbis and spouses in the hills of North Carolina for the Summer Kallah of the Greater Carolinas Association of Rabbis. This group engages in a relaxed pattern of serious study, prayer, and informal conversation out of which has often arisen the sweet light of inspiration, not to mention a dependable community of rabbinic friends. In somewhat more concentrated bursts, I derived much from the teachers at the Wesley Theological Seminary in Washington, DC, from whom I received a Doctor of Ministry degree in 2002. Similarly, I have gained significantly from my involvement in the Morei Derekh Program in Jewish Spiritual Direction (and from its faculty, including Amy Eilberg, Alan Morinis, and Linda Thal), from the Mussar Institute (under the leadership of Alan Morinis), and from the Rabbinic Leadership Program of the Institute for Jewish Spirituality (and its faculty, including Rachel Cowan, Nancy Flam, Myriam Klotz, Sheila Peltz-Weinberg, and Jonathan Slater).

The community in and around Congregation Beth Israel in Charlottesville have been extraordinarily encouraging of the spiritual explorations of this rabbi and have expressed unfailing eagerness to receive the reports of those explorations, to react to them, and to engage in the conversations they would trigger. Even the highly accomplished academics in the congregation have routinely been generous in their expressions of approval for the manner of my sharing. My appreciation for these frequent, confidence-building expressions cannot be overstated.

Without the generous backing of two specific members of Congregation Beth Israel, Yacov and Sonia Haimes, this collection would not have come to be. I am indebted to them for their support and encouragement. Even more, I am grateful for their friendship over the years. It is because of the friendship of such fine exemplars of Jewish values as Yacov and Sonia that I have always felt my rabbinic career to be one of privilege.

Anne Sussman used her keen editorial eye to provide many improvements to the sermon drafts. She deserves credit for these improvements but no blame for the faults and shortcomings that remain. For these I alone bear responsibility.

I dedicate this collection to these six: to my father, Michael Alexander; my mother, Goldie Alexander of blessed memory, who gave me life; to my sister, Judi Siegel of blessed memory; to our children, Talia and Benjamin; and to my dear partner in life for forty years, my wife, Dela Alexander.

My father has always served as my best model for living a balanced life. I suspect my mother would have preferred a different career than that of rabbi for her older son, but her unconditional support remains my solid foundation even in her death. My sister Judi may have been the kindest person I have ever known. Although she died twenty-five years ago, her passing still leaves a painful hole in my life even as it empowers me often to take worthwhile risks I would otherwise avoid. Talia and Benjamin have transformed themselves into delightful, menschlich adults. Their generously offered reactions matter greatly. Dela did not know she was marrying a future rabbi when we wed in 1973. I also did not know it. Nonetheless, she has shared the journey of marriage and school and raising children and losing loved ones and more school and working to make a Jewish home and engaging in the work of building Jewish community and much more. Without her support, friendship, love, and critique, I would not have had ground upon which to stand, much less wings for flight.

To all of the above and to the Holy Source of all blessing, I express my gratitude upon reaching this delicious moment.

BIBLIOGRAPHY OF SECONDARY SOURCES

Adler, Morris. "Death Can Enlarge the Domain of Our Life." In *Lights from Jewish Lamps*, edited by Sidney Greenberg, 312–313. Northvale, NJ: Jason Aronson, 1986.

Alter, Robert M., with Jane Alter. *How Long Till My Soul Gets It Right? 100 Doorways on the Journey to Happiness*. New York: Regan Books, 2001.

Amichai, Yehuda. *Open Closed Open*. New York: Harcourt, 2000.

Anderson, Walter. *Reality Isn't What It Used to Be*. New York: HarperCollins, 1990.

Bialik, Hayim Nahman, and Yehoshua Hana Ravnitzky. *The Book of Legends: Legends from the Talmud and Midrash*. New York: Schocken Books, 1992.

Biema, David van. "Mother Teresa's Crisis of Faith." *Time*. August 23, 2007. http://www.time.com/time/magazine/article/0,9171,1655720,00.html

Borowitz, Eugene. "Tzimtzum: A Mystical Model for Contemporary Leadership." *Religious Education* 69 (no. 6, 1974): 320-331.

Borowitz, Eugene, and Francine Schwartz. *The Jewish Moral Virtues*. Philadelphia: Jewish Publication Society, 1999.

Brin, Ruth. *Harvest: Collected Poems and Prayers*. Wyncote, PA: Reconstructionist Press, 1986.

Buber, Martin. *Hasidic Tales: Later Masters*. New York: Schocken Books, 1948.

Bulka, Reuven P. "Forgiveness." In *Three Times Chai: 54 Rabbis Tell Their Favorite Stories*, edited by Laney Katz Becker. Springfield, NJ: Behrman House, 2007.

Chico, Laura Shipler. "The Person I Want to Bring into This World." *This I Believe*. NPR. August 27, 2007. http://thisibelieve.org/essay/27267/

Cohen, Treasure. "Between Parent and Child," In *Lifecycles: Jewish Women on Life Passages and Personal Milestones, Volume I*, edited by Debra Ornstein, 262-268. Woodstock, VT: Jewish Lights.

Elkins, Dov Peretz. *Yom Kippur Readings: Inspiration, Information, Contemplation*. Woodstock, VT: Jewish Lights, 2005.

Feinstein, Edward M. "Almost Perfect." http://www.vbs.org/page.cfm?p=470

Feinstein, Edward M. *Capturing the Moon: Classic and Modern Jewish Tales*. Springfield, NJ: Behrman House, 2008.

Fine, Alvin, "Birth Is a Beginning." *In Gates of Repentance*, edited by Chaim Stern, 283–284. New York: Central Conference of American Rabbis, 1978.

Fulghum, Robert. *From Beginning to End: The Rituals of Our Lives*. New York: Villard Books, 1995.

Gellman, Marc. *Does God Have a Big Toe? Stories about Stories in the Bible*. New York: Harper and Row, 1989.

Gillman, Neil. *The Way into Encountering God in Judaism*. Woodstock, VT: Jewish Lights, 2004.

Goldstein, Niles. "Let's Get Over Ourselves," *World Jewish Digest*, September, 2007.

Gladwell, Malcolm. *The Tipping Point: How Little Things Can Make a Big Difference*. New York: Little, Brown, 2000.

Green, Arthur. *The Language of Truth: The Torah Commentary of the Sefat Emet, Rabbi Yehudah Leib Alter of Ger*. Philadelphia: Jewish Publication Society, 1998.

Green, Arthur. *Seek My Face, Speak My Name*. Northvale, NJ: Jason Aronson, 1992.

Greenberg, Aharon Ya-acov, ed. *Torah Gems*. Tel Aviv: Yavneh, 1992.

Gryn, Hugo. *Chasing Shadows: Memories of a Vanished World*. London: Viking, 2000.

Heschel, Abraham J. *The Insecurity of Freedom: Essays on Human Existence*. New York: Farrar, Straus, and Giroux, 1959.

Heschel, Abraham J. *Man's Quest for God*. New York: Charles Scribner's Sons, 1954.

Heschel, Abraham J. *The Sabbath: It's Meaning for Modern Man*. New York: Farrar, Straus, and Giroux, 1951.

Jabes, Edmond. "The Key." In *Midrash and Literature*, edited by Geoffrey H. Hartman and Sanford Buddick, 349--360. New Haven: Yale University Press, 1985.

Jaffe, Hirshel. *Why Me? Why Anyone?* New York: St. Martin's Press, 1986.

King, Bernie. "Making Music with Whatever Is Left." *The American Rabbi* 29 (Spring, 1997): 13–19.

Kaplan, Aryeh, translator. *The Seven Beggars and Other Kabbalistic Tales of Rebbe Nachman of Breslov*. Woodstock, VT: Jewish Lights, 2005.

Kirschner, Robert. "Halakhah and Homosexuality: A Reappraisal." In *Homosexuality, the Rabbinate, and Liberal Judaism: Papers prepared for the Ad-Hoc Committee on Homosexuality and the Rabbinate*, Selig Salkowitz, Chair. New York: Central Conference of American Rabbis, 1989.

Kula, Irwin and David Elcott. "Renewing the Covenant in the Face of Unbearable Pain." New York: CLAL, 1995.

Kushner, Harold. *Who Needs God*. New York: Summit Books, 1989.

Kushner, Lawrence. "Death without Dying." In *Who by Fire, Who by Water: Unetaneh Tokef*, edited by Lawrence A. Hoffman, 109–112. Woodstock, VT: Jewish Lights, 2010.

Lamott, Anne. *Traveling Mercies: Some Thoughts on Faith*. New York: Anchor Books, 2000.

Lappe, Francis Moore. *Diet for a Small Planet*. New York: Ballantine Books, 1971.

Ledbetter, Angie. "HeroicStories #178: A Child's Gift." HeroicStories. http://www.heroicstories.org/ (story since removed from site).

Leibowitz, Nehama. *Studies in the Book of Genesis*. Jerusalem: World Zionist Organization, 1972.

Levenson, Jon D. *The Death and Resurrection of the Beloved Son: The Transformation of Child Sacrifice in Judaism and Christianity*. New Haven: Yale University Press, 1993.

Levy, Richard, ed. *On Wings of Awe*. Washington, DC: B'nai B'rith Hillel Foundations, 1985.

Lieber, David L., senior ed. *Etz Hayyim: Torah and Commentary*. New York: Rabbinical Assembly, 2001.

Lifton, Robert Jay. *The Broken Connection*. New York: Simon and Schuster, 1979.

Luzzatto, Moses Chaim. *The Path of the Upright*. Philadelphia: Jewish Publication Society, 1996.

Morinis, Alan. *Climbing Jacob's Ladder*. Boston: Trumpeter Books, 2002.

Morinis, Alan. *Everyday Holiness: The Jewish Spiritual Path of Mussar*. Boston: Trumpeter Books, 2007.

Musser, Fred. "The Tabernacle." In *Illustrations Unlimited*, edited by James S. Hewett, 244. Wheaton: Tyndale House Publishers, 1988.

Ochs, Vanessa. "Keeping Faith Without Faith," *Jewish World Digest*, September, 2007.

Pearl, Judea, and Ruth Pearl, eds. *I Am Jewish: Personal Reflections Inspired by the Last Words of Daniel Pearl*. Woodstock, VT: Jewish Lights, 2004.

Putnam, Robert. *Bowling Alone: The Collapse and Revival of American Community*. New York: Simon and Schuster, 2000.

Remen, Rachel Naomi. *My Grandfather's Blessings*. New York: Riverhead Books, 2000.

Rolheiser, Ronald. *The Holy Longing: The Search for a Christian Spirituality*. New York: Doubleday, 1999.

Rose, Elaine. "Praying What We Mean." *The American Rabbi* 29 (Summer, 1997): 62-63.

Sanford, Matthew. *Waking: A Memoir of Trauma and Transcendence*. Emmaus, PA: Rodale Books, 2008.

Sardello, Robert. *Facing the World with Soul*. New York: Lindisfarne Books, 2004.

Schulweis, Harold M. *In God's Mirror: Reflections and Essays*. Hoboken, NJ: Ktav Publishing House, 1990.

Shenker, Israel. "E. B. White: Notes and Comment by the Author." *New York Times*, July 11, 1969.

Steinberg, Milton. "To Hold with Open Arms." In *A Treasury of Favorite Sermons by Leading American Rabbis*, edited by Sidney Greenberg. 275-280. Northvale, NJ: Jason Aronson, 1999.

Stevenson, Mary. "Footprints in the Sand." http://www.footprints-inthe-sand.com/index.php?page=Poem/Poem.php

Sullivan, Deirdre. "Always Go to the Funeral." *This I Believe*. NPR. August 8, 2005. http://www.npr.org/templates/story/story.php?storyId=4785079

Telushkin, Joseph. *The Book of Jewish Values: A Day-by-Day Guide to Ethical Jewish Living*. New York: Harmony Books, 2000.

Teutsch, David A., editor in chief. *Kol Haneshamah*. Wyncote, PA: The Reconstructionist Press, 1989.

Zion, Noam, and David Dishon. *A Different Night*. Jerusalem: Shalom Hartman Institute, 1997.